THE CONSTITUTION OF FINLAND

Finland is a small modern Nordic country with a politically stable welfare system and a constitutional history dating back to the 1700s. The constitutional system contains features retained from the years of Swedish and Russian rule, was reconstituted by the arrival of independence in 1917, and was reformed by the Constitution Act (Perustuslaki) in 2000. The system, which is formally rigid but actually flexible, is characterised by unique tensions, including parliamentarism versus presidentialism and a high level of constitutionalism versus the virtual absence of judicial review.

This book offers an introduction to the history and current content of the Finnish constitution, including chapters on the constitutional background, democratic institutions and their functions, judicial institutions and their role in securing the rule of law, fundamental rights and future directions and challenges. The constitutional effect of the European Union and the European Convention on Human Rights are discussed, and where appropriate a comparative dimension is offered, providing a clearer view of the strengths and weaknesses of the Finnish system.

The book is contextual and critical, providing students and teachers of constitutional law and politics with a reliable and concise resource which will facilitate understanding of the living constitution and the debates surrounding it. It is written in an uncomplicated manner, with an emphasis on clarity, and includes lists of further reading and relevant websites at the end of each chapter.

Constitutional Systems of the World
General Editors: Peter Leyland and Andrew Harding
Associate Editors: Benjamin L Berger and Alexander Fischer

In the era of globalisation, issues of constitutional law and good governance are being seen increasingly as vital issues in all types of society. Since the end of the Cold War, there have been dramatic developments in democratic and legal reform, and post-conflict societies are also in the throes of reconstructing their governance systems. Even societies already firmly based on constitutional governance and the rule of law have undergone constitutional change and experimentation with new forms of governance; and their constitutional systems are increasingly subjected to comparative analysis and transplantation. Constitutional texts for practically every country in the world are now easily available on the internet. However, texts which enable one to understand the true context, purposes, interpretation and incidents of a constitutional system are much harder to locate, and are often extremely detailed and descriptive. This series seeks to provide scholars and students with accessible introductions to the constitutional systems of the world, supplying both a road map for the novice and, at the same time, a deeper understanding of the key historical, political and legal events which have shaped the constitutional landscape of each country. Each book in this series deals with a single country, and each author is an expert in their field.

Published volumes

The Constitution of the United Kingdom
The Constitution of the United States
The Constitution of Vietnam
The Constitution of South Africa
The Constitution of Germany
The Constitution of Japan
The Constitution of Australia

Forthcoming titles in this series

The Constitution of France
Sophie Boyron

The Constitution of Ireland
Colm O'Cinneide

The Constitution of the Russian Federation
Jane Henderson

Link to series website
http://www.hartpub.co.uk/series/csw

The Constitution of Finland

A Contextual Analysis

Jaakko Husa

·HART·
PUBLISHING

OXFORD AND PORTLAND, OREGON

2011

Published in the United Kingdom by Hart Publishing Ltd
16C Worcester Place, Oxford, OX1 2JW
Telephone: +44 (0)1865 517530
Fax: +44 (0)1865 510710
E-mail: mail@hartpub.co.uk
Website: http://www.hartpub.co.uk

Published in North America (US and Canada) by
Hart Publishing
c/o International Specialized Book Services
920 NE 58th Avenue, Suite 300
Portland, OR 97213-3786
USA
Tel: +1 503 287 3093 or toll-free: (1) 800 944 6190
Fax: +1 503 280 8832
E-mail: orders@isbs.com
Website: http://www.isbs.com

British Library Cataloguing in Publication Data
Data Available

ISBN: 978-1-84113-854-1

Typeset by Hope Services (Abingdon) Ltd
Printed and bound in Great Britain by
TJ International Ltd, Padstow, Cornwall

Acknowledgements

I have many people to thank for their help and support while writing this book. The Finnish Lawyer's Association was kind enough to help me with a grant which was used for language correction purposes. When it comes to constitutional law in general and the Finnish Constitution specifically, I am greatly indebted to Professor Emeritus Antero Jyränki; not only due to his books and articles but also to our lasting friendship which does not recognise boundaries of age. Moreover, he also read the manuscript and offered helpful comments and suggestions. I also wish to acknowledge university teacher Maija Pitkänen who helped me with the manuscript by pointing out inconsistencies. Nick Kirkwood must be thanked for his help in correcting my English. I would also like to acknowledge the editors of the series for accepting this book for the series and their help in finalising the manuscript. However, all mistakes, blunders and errors are my own.

Jaakko Husa

Contents

Table of Cases

Other cases

European Court of Justice

European Court of Human Rights

Conseil constitutionnel (France)

Bundesverfassungsgerichthof (Germany)

United Kingdom

USA (Federal Supreme Court)

Table of Statutes

Finnish statute law

'It is merely empty words if legal writers insist on upholding a rule as "valid law", admitting that practice "wrongly" follows a different rule.'

Alf Ross
On Law and Justice (University of California Press, 1958) 50.

1

Constitution in General Context

———»•‹«———

Introduction – Constitution in Finland – Constitutional Field – History of Constitutional Law – Sources of Constitutional Law – International and European Borderlines – Conclusion

INTRODUCTION

This book about the Finnish Constitution is intended to be a resource for international students and teachers of constitutional law and government. Accordingly, certain groups of readers with a public law background may regard this book as different or at least non-mainstream. The author has relied heavily on his experience in comparative law while struggling to create a volume which is easily accessible to those who know nothing or only very little about the Finnish system. This has to do with the international and comparative tenor of the book. In accordance, national doctrinal experts may feel that some of the stresses here are not fully in concert with national doctrinal constitutional law. Yet, this is something that cannot be avoided in a book that is intended for an international audience and not for national doctrinal purposes.

The writing style and emphasis in this book has drawn theoretical inspiration from a great Scandinavian legal realist Alf Ross (1899–1979), instead of from a nationally based doctrinal study of constitutional law. Ross understood the concept of valid law more broadly than is normal in the doctrinal study of law. While this author is not perhaps a devoted follower of all the ideas of legal realism, he has certainly drawn inspiration from some of Ross's ideas. For the most part, realism is considered to be the tendency to stress the actual workings of the system instead of the written rules. Besides touching on realism, constitutional culture (or mentality) is stressed throughout this book. Constitutional culture refers here to the cognitive long-term social or mental structure which makes it possible for politicians, civil servants, judges and lawyers to grasp the constitutional environment in which they exist.

The choice to follow a modestly realist and culture-oriented path has been made in the spirit of the series entitled 'Constitutional Systems of the World' and seeks to offer a realistic and critical overview of the Finnish constitutional system while also discussing fundamental questions about the very nature of constitution and constitutionalism. The text of the Finnish Constitution can be easily downloaded these days from the internet by anyone interested, but the text of the Constitution Act is just a part of the whole system.[1] The real trick is to understand law in context. These choices distinguish this book from the one published in the series entitled 'International Encyclopaedia of Laws': this book does not follow any set format, but rather a contextual and critical approach is adopted.[2]

This opening chapter examines the Finnish definition of the field, main features of constitutional history, sources of constitutional law, and finally international and especially European dimensions from the Finnish point of view. The function of this first chapter is to provide a base for later discussions concerning constitutional institutions, rule of law, fundamental rights, constitutional change, and the challenges of the future. This book provides a critical outline of the main principles and doctrines which make up the living Finnish Constitution. The approach entertained covers historical context, institutions, processes, main sources and key principles of valid constitutional law. The focus is on the main characteristics of the system, but nonetheless some important and internationally interesting features are specifically introduced and discussed in order to highlight some of the critical issues of constitutional law in action. First of all we will consider the scope of 'constitution' and 'constitutional law'.

WHAT IS THE CONSTITUTION IN FINLAND?

If we start not from black-letter law but from the constitutional mentality we may say that 'As to its central parts constitutional law is perfectly well

---

[1] www.om.fi/21910.htm.

[2] I Saraviita, *Finland—Constitutional Law: International Encyclopedia of Laws* (Kluwer, Alphen, 2009).

political.'[3] This quote comes from the most influential Finnish constitutional lawyer and professor during the twentieth century, Paavo Kastari (1907–91). Many of his ideas are still present through his disciples and through his numerous influential writings. The above quoted sentence starts his extensive book's preface concerning the Finnish constitutional system and it reflects his general thinking about constitutional law as a whole. His idea encapsulates much of the Finnish manner of conceiving constitutional law as profoundly connected with the political system, yet at the same time highly regarded even in the sense of a binding set of normative rules and principles. This is why this quote serves as an excellent point of departure for this book which analyses and describes the Finnish constitutional system as a living constitution and not merely as a set of written rules or rigid normative principles. Accordingly, instead of detailed description of formal constitutional documents, the text here seeks to outline the context of the Constitution and concentrates on its practical working and interpretations. This book is—and let this be once more underlined—written for an international audience, not for national doctrinal purposes. Consequently, there is not much doctrinal material concerning the proper interpretation and application (ie what *ought* to be the content of the Constitution) of Finland's foundational laws. However, due to the legal nature of constitutional law the normative element is not missing even though its role is not crucial to this book.

The hard core of Finnish constitutional thinking is easy to detect, at least, if one simplifies it a great deal. In Finland the Constitution is conceived as a sort of a cornerstone of all legislation and exercise of public power. It is regarded as being important by lawyers and politicians as well as citizens and other private parties. In short, the Constitution matters. It contains basic rules and principles on the organisation of the State, checks and balances between government branches and fundamental rights. From the point of view of constitutional comparison and history, the Finnish Constitution Act is a fresh one, which entered into force on 1 March 2000. Even though the written constitutional document is this recent it does not include all of the relevant constitutional rules or principles. Doctrines and practices (even customs) play a considerable role in defining the scope and content of the Constitution.

---

[3] P Kastari, *Finnish Constitution* ['*Suomen valtiosääntö*'] (Suomalainen lakimiesyhdistys, Helsinki, 1977) v.

From a purely formal point of view the Constitution is mainly rigid, but in practice it has proved to be somewhat flexible, allowing for different interpretations and practices. Our discussion begins by defining the field, ie what the Constitution means in Finland and what its typical characteristics are, as well as how the Finnish manner differs from other ways of understanding it. However, before discussing the Finnish Constitution it is important to be familiar with the legal system in general, as within the Finnish legal system constitutional law occupies systematically defined place.

Private Law and Public Law

As is well known, continental European law in the Roman-Germanic legal culture (or so-called civil law) is heavily influenced by the distinction between private law and public law. Often this distinction is said to be based on the Roman law tradition and especially the *ius commune* tradition which appeared in the Middle Ages and used Roman law as an intellectual and sometimes even substantive point of departure. Basically, in civil law culture private law is regarded as being different from and opposed to public law. The traditional common law attitude has normally resisted this kind of categorical approach to law.[4]

At the rudimentary level private law deals with matters that are private (eg marriage, heritance, contract, tort, etc) whereas public law deals with the use of public power. In Finland constitutional law, administrative law, tax law, penal law and criminal procedure law are all public law in the strict sense: they deal with the relations between private parties and public power. In practice the term public law normally tends to refer only to administrative and constitutional law. These two areas of law are intertwined in several ways and often it is difficult to draw a clear line between them. Demarcations are shady: for example, environmental law is a mixture of public law and private law but also a mixture of national and international law.

So, in general, Finland belongs to the 'civil law' culture, as do all the Nordic systems; but the division into public law and private law is not regarded nearly as fundamental as is the case in the heartlands of

---

[4] See JWF Allison, *A Continental Distinction in the Common Law* (Oxford University Press, Oxford, 1996).

civil law, ie Germany, France, Italy, Netherlands and Spain.[5] Private law (*yksityisoikeus*) in Finland is very much similar to other civil law countries when it comes down to the substance: private rights tend to be defensive protecting mainly private ownership and in general property rights. Public law (*julkisoikeus*) is traditionally regarded as a barrier protecting private rights against intrusion from public power. Generally speaking, Finnish public law deals primarily with the State itself. This traditional picture has, nevertheless, changed during the last decades: administrative law and public power have experienced privatisation and the ideology of so-called 'New Public Management' has brought public procedures closer to those of private corporations. Yet, Finnish public power is still very much governed by the rules of public law.

However, the mere distinction into public law and private law has lost some of its earlier significance; sometimes fundamental rights and general rules of administrative law may also have an effect on private organisations (if public duties are privatised). During the last 15 years constitutional law has extended its reach to various branches of law. These developments have been coined as constitutionalisation of the legal system. However, how are the Constitution and constitutional law conceived in Finland?

DEFINING THE FIELD

To start, we may claim that constitutions are generally collections of normative-type rules and principles which lay out the fundamental and superior law of a state. So, if one seeks to analyse or even to describe in a reliable manner a constitutional system one must normally start from the concept of the State.[6] This is simply due to the modern state and constitution being closely knitted together, especially in German-Nordic legal culture; and without the State it would prove to be very difficult to grasp the idea of constitution itself.[7] This is so because constitutions derive their life-force and legitimacy from certain political communities: they do not live or succeed without a defined political community within which they function. Put simply, a constitution regulates the

---

[5] The expression 'Nordic' refers to the Nordic countries which are Denmark, Finland, Norway, Sweden and Iceland.

[6] See eg, F Venter, *Constitutional Comparison* (Juta/Kluwer, Lansdowne, 2000) 8–9.

[7] See H Kelsen, *Reine Rechtslehre* (Verlag Österreich, Wien, 1960/2000) 283 *ff*.

actions and form of this public political community. Ancient Greeks called this *politeia* (πολιτεία) and they regarded it to be a kind of a soul of the polis (πόλης).[8] The reasons for this are obvious. A constitution is accepted by and for this same community, and to a large extent it deals with self-regulation of a polity or community, ie the State. This feature does not depend on legal-technical matters, ie is the constitutional document written or unwritten, codified or un-codified, or are there many constitutional documents or just one, etc? We may perhaps claim that in the world of international public law the concept of state seems to be somewhat clear, ie at least there are certain basic ingredients that are normally conceived as being integral elements of a state as a legal entity. Unfortunately, the same does not apply to the concept of constitution.

German and Swedish Conceptual Ingredients

In Finnish law, as in many other legal and political systems, the concept of constitution (or constitutional law for that matter) is difficult to define in a precise manner. One of the main problems is conceptual and is caused by the constitutional history of Finland. The Finnish concept means literally 'rule of the state' or 'state-order' (*valtiosääntö*); it originates from the Swedish *statsförfattning* of which the Finnish concept is a direct translation. Both the Finnish concept and its Swedish mother-concept have their background in the German concept of *Staatsverfassung*. Accordingly, the Finnish 'rule of the state', ie constitution means pretty much the same thing as the word constitution in other European countries belonging to Roman-German legal culture. However, Nordic systems have certain differences with other Roman-German legal-cultural constitutions. Importantly, the expression 'constitution' does not mean the same as the more narrow and formal concept of basic law (*perustuslaki*), which also stems from the German-Swedish conceptual heritage of *Grundgesetz/grundlag*.[9]

In the Finnish system there is one separate written enacted constitutional document having the formal hierarchical *Grundnorm* status. *Grundnorm* (*perusnormi*) here refers broadly to the idea of Basic Norm

---

[8] By far, the most famous of these discussions is the one by Aristotle, *Politics*, Book III (Ἀριστοτέλης, Πολιτικά, βιβλίο Γ') (Nomiki Bibliothike, Athens, 1993).

[9] But see B Auffermann and S Laakso, 'Gesetzgebung im politischen System Finnlands' in W Ismayr (ed), *Gesetzgebung in Westeuropa—EU-staaten und Europäische Union* (VS Verlag, Wiesbaden, 2008) 65–97, 65.

which is a legal rule or rather collection of legal key norms that form the underlying basis for the whole legal system. There is no single Basic Norm in the Finnish constitutional system, unlike Hans Kelsen's (1881–1973) assumption in his legal theory, but mutatis mutandis the written constitutional rules have superiority over other legal norms. The legal-linguistic problem is that this 'Basic Law' describes itself as the Constitution of Finland in its section 1, even though it does not cover all that is understood to be material constitutional law. Paradoxically, the document which regards itself as the Constitution of Finland is actually only 'the Basic Law of Finland'.[10] Importantly, the official Swedish translation is *Finlands grundlag* which translates literarily as 'Basic law of Finland'.[11] Due to these reasons, it would be inaccurate to call this constitutional document the Constitution of Finland, even though this seems to be the translation which Finnish constitutional experts commonly use. Nonetheless, this translation is functionally not accurate.

For the benefit of present purposes and to minimise unnecessary conceptual traps, 'Basic Law' is henceforth called the Finnish Constitution Act or in short the Constitution Act (abbreviated sometimes as CA). Importantly, the Constitution Act refers to a certain statutory Act and not to the whole Constitution which is clearly a broader concept. Constitutional law, accordingly, is the body of law which governs all such things which are constitutional in a substantive sense.

Constitution Act of Finland

The Finnish Constitution Act (2000) covers the codified core material regulating the use of public political power and consists of provisions on key organs of the State, how these key organs are appointed, what their main functions are, competences and interconnected

---

[10] Kelsen separated material constitution (*materielle Verfassung*) and formal constitution (*formelle Verfassung*). In his theory of law he states that the first one was partly written and partly unwritten (*teils aus Normen geschriebenen . . . teils aus Normen ungeschriebenen*), whereas the latter was purely a written constitutional document (*geschriebene Verfassung*), Kelsen, *Reine Rechtslehre* (1960/2000) 228–29.

[11] Constitution Act stipulates that all Acts must be promulgated both in the Finnish and the Swedish language (section 79.4). Accordingly, both language-versions are authentic versions. For Finnish and Swedish as legal languages in Finland, see H Mattila, *Comparative Legal Linguistics* (Ashgate, Aldershot, 2006) 55–58.

relations.[12] It also deals, although in a broader and more abstract manner, with the organisation of the machinery of public power in general, and the basic principles concerning the structure and usage of its competences. Administrative law deals with similar questions but in more detail. Moreover, the Constitution Act also deals with the constitutional rights and freedoms, setting out the rights and duties of individuals (see chapter four for more detailed definitions). From a theoretical point of view the Act contains norms (altogether 131 sections, in Finnish called '*pykälä*', ie paragraph) regulating organisation, behaviour of state, competences and rights. It is divided into 13 chapters as follows: (1) fundamental rules, (2) constitutional rights and liberties, (3–4) the Parliament and its activities, (5) the President and the Government, (6) legislating, (7) state finances, (8) international relations, (9) judicial functions, (10) supervision of legality, (11) general outline of public administration, (12) national defence, (13) and final provisions of a legal-technical nature.

For an outsider struggling to comprehend the Finnish constitutional system and its peculiarities, the Constitution Act is a reasonably good starting point: it is easy to pinpoint since it calls itself the Constitution Act; it is hierarchically superior in its relation to other Acts and regulations; and it can be changed, amended or repealed only using the same qualified procedure which is required while enacting the Constitution Act itself, ie it must be approved by two parliamentary sessions in between which elections are held, and in the final decision-making the proposal must receive the support of two-thirds of the votes cast in the Parliament. Nonetheless, it must be repeatedly stressed that the Constitution Act covers the Finnish Constitution only partially.[13] The Constitution Act is a single piece of legislation which is easy to recognise on a formal basis, whereas the Constitution of Finland is a larger totality which can be recognised only on a substantive basis. In a word, the Finnish Constitution Act is very much a typical, codified, and modern-day constitutional act.[14]

---

[12] *Suomen Perustuslaki* 731/1999 [the numerical identification refers to *Suomen säädöskokoelma* (The Statutes of Finland) which is the official collection of enactments and ordinances, and here it indicates that this Act was passed by the Parliament as Act number 731 in the year 1999. However, it came into force on 1 March 2000].

[13] According to section 1.2, 'The Constitution of Finland is established in this Constitutional Act'.

[14] For a brief overlook see RL Maddox, *Constitutions of the World* (Routledge, London, 1996) 79–82.

For the purpose of the Finnish doctrinal study (*'oikeusdogmatiikka'* as in German *Rechtsdogmatik*) of constitutional law it might be enough, although not according to all writers, to narrow the concept of Constitution merely to the legal-positivistic Constitution Act. Broader sense covers not only the formal Constitution Act but also all those (hierarchically below the Constitution Act) legal regulations that deal with the form and organisation and competencies of the State and fundamental rights and freedoms of individuals in their relation to public power. Basically, it encompasses everything that concerns the Constitution in a material sense. Further, this broad material sense of Constitution also covers rules, principles and doctrines created by constitutional practice. These are customary-law-type norms that are conceived as a part of the legally binding Constitution of Finland. The problem with the customary type of rules is that they are difficult to place in the hierarchy of norms; mostly they fill gaps which the codified system leaves empty (see chapter eight).

In the Finnish doctrinal writing on constitutional law there have traditionally been differing opinions about the nature and even the very existence of customary constitutional law.[15] Partially, this reflects an even more fundamental distinction within constitutional law: the demarcation of law and politics. Some have acknowledged customary rules while others have been more critical towards the concept of binding customary constitutional law. According to Professor Emeritus Antero Jyränki, who was once a disciple of Kastari and today is the leading expert on Finnish constitutional law: 'The distinction between legal and political Constitution is a sliding one.'[16] Debate over customary elements clearly proves this.

Be that as it may, the constitutional system itself has been relying and relies to this day partially on certain unwritten and informal rules and principles—this cannot be denied by anyone who cares to really look at how the system actually works and functions, many times in concert but sometimes even in opposition to the text of the Constitution Act (see chapter eight). This fact comes certainly as no surprise to non-positivistic comparative constitutional research, or as KC Wheare once said: 'what the Constitution says is one thing, and what actually happens in practice may be quite another'.[17] As chapter five will reveal, the

---

[15] See S Matsui, *The Constitution of Japan* (forthcoming).
[16] A Jyränki, *Power and Freedom* [*'Valta ja vapaus'*] (Talentum, Helsinki, 2003) 223.
[17] KC Wheare, *Modern Constitutions* (Oxford University Press, Oxford, 1980) 4.

Finnish Constitution has been de facto quite flexible due to the doctrine of exceptive Act (*poikkeuslaki*), enabling material changes to the Constitution without altering the formal texts of constitutional Acts. Today this channel for altering constitutional texts indirectly has become a rarity. Even though constitutional culture has transformed the legacy of exceptive Acts it is still present, as we will later see in more detail: this legacy may be regarded as a constitutional ruin, but all the same very much a living ruin (see chapter eight).

Constitutional Culture

How can the Finnish system be characterised from a broader comparative point of view? The Finnish constitutional system may be usefully seen in parallel with other Nordic systems. Comparatively speaking, the Finnish constitutional system belongs to Nordic systems which are based on political and constitutional consensus in which there are typically long-established constitutions combined with legally binding interpretation, added together with some lesser binding customary law features. None of the parliamentary Nordic unitary state constitutions are as difficult to amend or to change as is the constitutional system of the United States, where the written Constitution (1789) is often merely a starting point for constitutional interpretation by judicial organs. What separates the Nordic constitutions from the German and continental European constitutional culture is the fact that there are no separate constitutional courts in any of the Nordic countries. In addition, the Nordic approach differs—perhaps with the exception of Norway—sharply from the American Constitution in the sense that the substance of constitutional law is not mainly based on the decisions of the courts which decide on concrete cases dealing with relations between the public and private sphere.

However, even within the Nordic constitutional sphere, Finland's system seems to be a bit peculiar since instead of a constitutional monarchy it is a republic with a President possessing some significant constitutional competences. Against this backdrop, it may be stressed that the Finnish constitutional system also has certain features that are unusual in today's constitutional world, as we will see later.

In sum, Finland belongs to the sphere of Nordic unitary state constitutions in which the main bulk of the constitutional law is written, but which also gives room and partially recognises the binding force of doctrines and some customary constitutional law. Even though Finland has a formal Constitution Act, some important elements of the formally rigid, yet partially flexible Constitution are based on un-codified constitutional rules, principles and some practices having a customary character. Academic study of constitutional law also plays a role, but not to the same degree as in German constitutional culture. Finally, there is no separate constitutional court for interpreting constitutional law in a judicially authoritative manner. In fact, the question of constitutional judicial review of parliamentary legislation has always been a very delicate question in the Finnish system. By and large, a weak form of presidentialism and parliamentary concentrated control of constitutionality of legislation are culturally fundamental characters of the system. Notwithstanding, some of the key features of constitutional culture are facing growing internal criticism; European Union membership and European human rights have stirred much domestic doctrinal discussion and debate.

SHORT HISTORY OF FINNISH CONSTITUTIONAL LAW

Today, the Republic of Finland (*Suomen tasavalta*) has a population of about 5.4 million people; of these 80 per cent belong to the Evangelical Lutheran Church. Finland is an economically prosperous and a politically stable unitary state with a multiparty system. This has not always been the case. Due to the fact that constitutions are intertwined so closely with states means that the history of a state or a nation is of importance while trying to understand a constitutional system. This is also true with the Finnish constitutional system. In spite of this, even though the present Constitution Act entered into effect as recently as 1 March 2000, some parts of the present Act itself may be properly conceived only if constitutional and political history are taken pertinently into account. In short, substantive continuity was all but broken in 2000.

Some would say that there is something special in constitutional law in general, whereas for areas of law such as contract law or criminal law the relevance of history is not so crucial. Broadly speaking, we may claim that 'institutions of government with which public law is concerned develop in very specific ways'.[18] This fact forms an obstacle for

---

[18] J Bell, 'Public Law in Europe' in M Van Hoecke (ed), *Methodology and Epistemology of Comparative Law* (Hart, Oxford, 2004) 259–69, 267.

comprehending foreign constitutional systems without difficulties. Yet, sensitivity toward historical and social contexts is of considerable help while trying to obtain this kind of comprehension.

Further, one may even claim that the importance of history within the field of constitutional law is of the utmost importance. Simply put, to understand foreign peculiarities demands knowledge of history, ie knowledge of the contexts of a constitution.[19] Without this context the picture of a constitutional system would be too restricted to the mere wording of a formal Constitution Act. How things came into being is an important piece of information in any analysis which claims to be contextual. As famous legal historian RG van Caenegem put it, 'Today's constitutional debate would be shallow without knowledge of the historical antecedents.'[20]

This book is based on the idea according to which constitutional history is of too much importance to be left alone in the scholarly ivory tower; it should be seen as a crucial element if one wishes to understand the different layers of a constitution. In this sense, constitutions are like icebergs of which only the tips are easily seen. The Finnish system, specifically, contains layers from the Swedish rule, Russian rule, period of independence, and the present EU Member State-driven phase. A perfect example is the Code of Procedure (*Oikeudenkäymiskaari*) which was originally enacted as a part of the Swedish Code of 1734. During the Russian period the Code of Procedure stayed in force and it continued to do so after Finland gained her independence. In fact, this Code is still in force today although in a much different form than originally. However, we may take another example which is closer to the constitutional system: the Constitution Act's section 125.1 concerns the general qualifications for public office which are 'skill, ability and proven merit' (*kyky, taito ja koeteltu kansalaiskunto*). These qualifications have remained basically the same since they were first introduced in the Form of Government 1772.

The layers are dealt with here in chronological order but also in a thematic manner. These layers are intended to set the scene for the discussion in subsequent chapters, not to provide a full historical account.

---

[19] *cf* F Venter, *Constitutional Comparison* (Juta/Kluwer, Lansdowne, 2000) 44.
[20] RG van Caenegem, *An Historical Introduction to Western Constitutional Law* (Cambridge University Press, Cambridge, 1995) ix.

Swedish Rule (ca 1200–1809)

Before 1809 Finnish constitutional and political history was common with that of Sweden's and, moreover, long after that there was significant interaction within different fields of law and to an extent also in constitutional law. Furthermore, the story of Nordic cooperation in the late 1900s in the legislative field is well known. But, how far back in history should we go for the present purpose? In practice, the knowledge concerning the law of ancient Finns is scarcely known, in accord, actually the constitutional history as we understand it today begins in the Middle Ages. It should be borne in mind that Finland was governed in accordance with Swedish traditions for more than 600 years. Finland was not merely occupied or ruled by Sweden; it was genuinely part of the Swedish realm. This fact carries many significant explanations for anyone trying to understand the Finnish system and its contextual background. For example, constitutional language rights and the legal status of the Swedish speaking part of the population would be impossible to understand without knowledge of the common Finnish-Swedish history.

Early Phases

Talking about early phases is difficult not only due to the obvious chronological reasons but also due to the terminology; in the modern sense the oldest rules were constitutional in a material sense. Otherwise the old rules would not be regarded as genuinely constitutional in the modern sense as they were temporary and there was no legal hierarchy.

Finland became a part of the Swedish State in around the thirteenth century. Constitutional rules, if there were any, were limited to changing customs of personal rule. From the fourteenth century there were different 'laws of the land' (*maanlaki*) or sort of general laws and Royal Codes (*kuninkaankaari*) in force which all contained various legal rules; some of these were of a constitutional nature regulating the appointing of the Monarch and use of the Crown's power. The King normally gave, while taking the throne, the King's Oath or King's Affirmation (*kuninkaanvala*) in which certain temporary rules were agreed upon on concerning the reign of the Monarch in question. One may say that these oaths and affirmations were, in their nature, forms of agreement with the Monarch and estates concerning the share and use of power. Their constitutional significance was diminished due to their ad hoc nature. Free

Finnish commoners gained the right to take part in electing the Swedish king in 1362. Yet, these rights were not constitutional in the modern sense, but were like medieval privileges of the estates as corporate bodies.

When a new Monarch took the throne, new oaths were taken and agreed upon. In fact, monarchs ruled with the help of the powerful nobility. In other words, rules of governance changed depending on the Monarch in power. The relationship between the ruler and the ruled was pre-constitutional in the sense that it was of a personal nature. In 1544 Sweden was organised permanently in a form of hereditary monarchy by strong-man Gustavus Vasa (ruled 1523–1560). Later, in 1611, the Estates got the King to recognise the partial competency of the Estates to take part in the legislative function in a form of irregularly convening Diet of the Estates (*säätyvaltiopäivät*). Then, a quasi-constitutional document was enacted in 1617 when a specific Parliament Act (*valtiopäiväjärjestys*) was formally adapted and entered into force.

Looking back, we may claim that the first genuine constitutional document appeared in 1634 when the Estates of the State declared a specific legal document to confirm how the Government must be organised and how it must function when the Monarch is under-aged or outside the country. The real importance for the later development of the constitutional system was, however, in the 1634 document's rules which laid out the structure of the central government in assisting the Monarch in ruling the State. Constitutionally, the period 1680–1718 has been called the Age of the Sovereign Rule (*itsevaltiuden aika*). This is the period when Finland's constitutional history properly started.

Nevertheless, no matter what the semi-constitutional documents declared, the State was ruled in a rather autocratic manner from 1693–1719. However, during 1719–23 the first modern constitutional documents came into force and the system was profoundly changed. These constitutional documents were the two Forms of Government (*Hallitusmuoto*) and novel Parliament Act. This phase really embodied a true separation from the old tradition which contained personal constitutional agreements between the estates and the Monarch. The most important change was made in the 1719 Form of Government which required the Monarch to always comply with the common decision of the Diet of the Estates. This meant, in practice, that the highest political power shifted from the Monarch to the Royal Council and to the estates themselves. Comparatively speaking, these documents and the system that they brought about were rather novel in Europe even though they contained the medieval structure of estates.

From the point of view of constitutional history, the period 1718–72 has been called the Age of Freedom (*vapauden aika*). From today's perspective we may discern certain weak features of the parliamentary system taking place, which explains why any monarch had difficulties in accepting it. However, the right to take part in using the public power was in fact in the hands of the clergy and nobility; it was by and large their freedom, not the freedom of the peasants. This system was nevertheless completely overturned in 1772 when Gustavus III's (ruled 1771–92) constitutional revolution in effect dragged the Swedish-Finnish Constitution from the frontier-line of constitutional modernisation back to the autocratic past. Constitutional continuity was clearly broken in both letter and spirit.

Constitutional Step Back

The Form of Government of 1772 practically placed the Monarch in the position of estates and, also, at the apex of the State's power. In a sense this was a coup d'état in which the Monarch took power away from the Diet of Estates; this was truly the end of the Age of Freedom. The King threatened the estates with the blunt use of military force and several people were arrested as a preventive measure.

This backward constitutional development was further strengthened in 1789 when the Deed of Association and Security (*yhdistys- ja vakuuskirja*) entered into force. The document of 1789 placed hardly any meaningful constitutional restrictions on the competences of the Sovereign. In 1789 Sweden was placed in the constitutional periphery; the rights of the estates were defined according to the borders of the estates. Small glimpses of well hidden enlightment philosophy shown by Gustavus III were not reflected in any questions of great constitutional significance. However, the consent of the Diet was required for new legislation and the imposition of new taxes. This was the constitutional sovereign-friendly landscape when 20 years later Finland was separated from Sweden and annexed to the Russian Empire. The period 1772–1809 has been called the Gustavian period (*kustavilainen aika*), although in Finland it lingered all the way up until 1919.

There are even today some visible traces of this period in the present Constitution Act and in the constitutional culture: bilingualism, control of constitutionality and, most importantly, the specific manner for conceiving constitutionalism in general. Obviously, it would be too grand to claim any direct historical line from the 1700s to the 2000s and yet some kind of legal-mental continuity cannot be denied. However, in order to understand how the grip of the Gustavian period came to be exceptionally resilient, a look into the Russian period is needed.

Russian Rule—Autonomy (1809–1917)

Due to the harsh actions by Gustavus III, Finland's constitutional documents and the system they brought about lagged behind constitutional developments elsewhere in Europe. Revolutionary ideas were a far cry from the Finnish perspective. After the war, the Russian Emperor Alexander I called the representatives of Finnish estates to the city of Porvoo (Diet of Porvoo, *Porvoon valtiopäivät*) in which the estates acknowledged the change in highest public power and took an oath in which they promised loyalty to the Emperor, the Russian Czsar. In turn, the Emperor declared to the estates that he would leave in force the traditional (Swedish) constitutional and legal system. In a constitutional sense, this was originally an anachronism: a kind of medieval treaty in which the ruler and the estates agreed on the constitutional basic arrangements in a manner which was completely alien to post-grand-revolutionary constitutional thinking elsewhere in Europe.[21] This, too, was the constitutional clock going backwards.

Nevertheless, no matter how constitutionally outdated the Act of Porvoo was, later it did have a great amount of significance. Thus, the Grand Duchy of Finland (*Suomen suuriruhtinaskunta*), being an autonomous part of imperial Russia under the throne of the Emperor, came into being. In Porvoo, Finland for the first time was established as a united political entity which can be called a nation (*kansakunta*), if not in the strictest legal sense. Constitutionally, this idea of becoming a nation was fundamental: 'a nation has a right to establish a Constitution' as Thomas Paine once wrote.[22] Perhaps surprisingly, it was during the era

---

[21] O Brunner (*Land und Herrschaft* 5. Auflage. Rudolf M. Rohrer Verlag, Wien, 1965) spoke of dominion (*Herrschaft*), accordingly, saying that this sort of pact between the ruler and the estates is not a modern constitutional document but a 'dominion-pact', ie *Herrschaftsvertrag*.

[22] T Payne, *Rights of Man* (Wordsworth, Hertfordshire, 1996/originally published in 1791) 153.

of the Grand Duchy when the development towards the liberal model of constitutional government actually began. However, it was not only the constitutional documents that changed: the political environment brought change into the constitutional sphere also.

Constitutionally, the most relevant factor was that the Emperor was understood—at least by the somewhat legalistically and nationalistically oriented Finns—to promise to govern Finland according to its existing constitutional laws. There was a touch of genuine national luck in this: if the constitutional laws had not been so lenient to the very strong position of the Sovereign, the Emperor would most likely not have been so willing to confirm the old constitutional order publicly in Porvoo and in a written form. Finns had now, so it was later largely assumed at least, a kind of Form of Government of their own and thus, for some, even their own Constitution. If this was a kind of constitutional revolution, it was a peculiarly silent one: nothing seemed to happen; no internal political violence broke out even though the 600-year-old connection with Sweden was severed.

Constitutional Continuity and Innovations

The small relevance of legal and cultural change is a striking feature here. Little was changed when Finland moved under the rule of the Russian Emperor after more than 600 years of union with Sweden. To take an example, the age-old privileges of the Estates were not only preserved as they were but were even extended. However, Finland was spared from Feudalism and land slavery being profound social features of imperial Russia. Instead, in Finland, one of the crucial and striking elements was the factual *constitutional continuity* and the simple fact was that the large majority of the high public officials remained in their posts. Today, we may realise the bitter irony of a situation in which the Swedish-Finnish troops still fought and died in the North when the elite wowed its loyalty to the new Russian ruler hoping to ensure good positions. This, if anything in Finnish constitutional history, reveals one core-feature of constitutional mentality; a pragmatic approach combined with formal legal points of view and the difference between the elite and the people (ie peasants actually wanted to be loyal to the Swedish Crown).

Of course, some organisational changes took place concerning the high level governance. The Czar ruled as the Grand Duke and he was represented in Finland by the Governor-General who acted through the agency of the Senate.[23] The highest domestic governmental organ during this period was the Senate which consisted of two departments: judicial (ie supreme court) and economic (ie ministry). This quintessential structure is even today part of the Finnish constitutional design.

From the constitutional point of view, the situation was challenging to say the least. As a result, some innovations were also crafted alongside the continuity. As the Form of Government (1772) and the Deed of Association and Security (1789) were originally engineered for Sweden-Finland, they could be applied only partially. Many of the holes in the system were patched with the help of the Emperor's Decrees. Nevertheless, Finns later started, during the 1800s, to assume that when Finland was annexed to Russia in 1809, an autonomous state took birth. So, this state of a sort was conceived as an internally sovereign unit, but all foreign policy-related matters belonged under the direct Russian rule. In accordance, Finns thought that the nation's constitutional Acts could be changed, amended or repealed by the Emperor but *only* with the express consent of the Finnish Diet of the Estates. This was the old Swedish constitutional tradition, a remnant from the Age of Freedom.

In fact, old Swedish ideas were tightened up: Professor Johan Jakob Nordström (1801–74) argued already in 1838 that the constitutional documents of 1772 and 1789 could be touched only with the consent of all four estates. However, the Diet was not called to assembly for a session until the 1860s. Clearly, in the space of 50 years, constitutional pressures were sure to mount even in the silent Grand Duchy. Especially after the 1860s many fundamental features of Finnish constitutional law took birth under Russian pressure, on the basis of Swedish constitutional heritage combined with a slowly growing political consciousness of an awakening nation. However, it must be underlined that all this was possible due to Russian remaining largely a foreign language in Finland and the number of Russians dwelling in Finland remaining low throughout this period. Culturally, the country remained pretty much as it had been during the Swedish period, with the exception that Finnish as an official language started to gain a foothold in a manner which would not probably have been possible under the Swedish Crown.

---

[23] The Governor-General was in fact rather close to the British Monarch's personal representative in a country, ie Lord Lieutenant. Actually, in historical comparison we may see a certain parallel between the Governor General of Finland and Lord Lieutenant of Ireland.

Constitutional Ideology in the Making

The Russian period was not always tranquil and constitutionally there were always tensions, although they were not constantly clearly visible. In the constitutional struggle—which was of course fought with political weapons—against the Russian views, professors of public law also gained a new heightened status because they could provide legal arguments backing Finnish interpretations. During those times within what was known as the period of Autonomy, many high profile professors stood against all forms of so-called Russification (ie forced means for making the Finnish system adapt to Russian rules and procedures), this fight started to take on more serious dimensions only in the 1900s. In this legal struggle, learned constitutional arguments were displayed constantly so that, as a by-product, the general Finnish constitutional consciousness also grew remarkably.[24] A constitutionally, politically, and historically important milestone was the booklet by Leo Mechelin (1839–1914) entitled, *Précis du droit public du Grande-Duché de Finlande* (1886) which shaped the understanding of the late 1800s and early 1900s concerning the nature of Finnish constitutional arrangements.

During this period, the academic study of constitutional law took it first steps, as a part of the struggle over the existence of a nation. For the later constitutional law doctrine and its academic development, Professor Robert Fredrik Hermanson (1846–1928) was of great importance: he brought many of the central ideas and theories of German public law and 1800s legal positivism to Finland. Hermanson's actual point was to operate with the concept of state (*valtio*) and to perceive the Gustavian constitutional documents from the point of view of something which did not actually exist, ie the State of Finland. This creative constitutional engineering by doctrinal experts slowly paved the way to an idea of an independent State.

For anyone looking outside the Finnish constitutional system, it is of importance to conceive that some of these autonomy-period originating features have, even today, some role in the constitutional system and more importantly in the constitutional culture; we may speak about the deep roots of Finnish constitutional thinking. The most important of these was the idea that constitutional documents bound the actions of the legislator (ie the Diet and the Grand Duke) and the constitutionality control of

---

[24] See HT Klami, 'A History of Finnish Legal Science' in *Oikeustiede-Jurisprudentia* XIX (Suomalainen lakimiesyhdistys, Helsinki, 1986) 125–276, especially 179–234.

bills started to take place before the Acts came into force, ensuring that Russian-nominated courts could not interfere with this crucial control-function. This constitutionality control was taken care of by one of the special committees of the Diet which is still the case today. Finally, an alternative doctrine was crafted to deal with the question of how to resolve a normative conflict between an ordinary Act and constitutional documents without changing written constitutional documents (see chapter eight). Moreover, the weight of constitutional argumentation in general and constitutional attitudes upheld by Finnish political culture originates from the Russian period; later Russification attempts were always countered by legalistically oriented arguments derived from the constitutional documents and the following constitutional doctrine. Finnish constitutional ideology which took shape in the 1800s was later put in use in the 1900s when open and active Russification actually started.

Against Amounting Russian Pressure

History taught that it would be better to fight political battles through constitutional argumentation. This differs from Sweden where the weight and significance of constitutional law is traditionally generally regarded as something of lesser importance in its relation to democratic institutions and especially the national Parliament (ie *Riksdag*). The Finnish experience is different from the Swedish.

So, even though there was now a constitutional basis the political system was helplessly lagging far behind the European developments of the late nineteenth and early twentieth century. The main problems were the autocratic governance of the Emperor and the scarcely democratic, corporate, basis of suffrage. In 1905, the massive General Strike led to the Manifesto of November 4 (drafted by Mechelin in the capacity of a leading Finnish constitutionalist) by the Emperor who had been weakened internally by the defeat in the Russo-Japanese War of 1904–1905. The Manifesto led to Finnish constitutional reform. The Emperor was not politically strong enough to resist the constitutional pressure at that time. The Manifesto led to the abolition of the Diet of Finland of the four Estates and to the creation of the modern Parliament. Importantly, this also resulted in a temporary halt to the Russification policy. The Manifesto promised and preceded the extensive parliamentary reform of 1906. In this important and far-reaching reform included a unicameral Parliament, guarantees for the political rights of the citizens with universal suffrage, freedom of association and assembly, and freedom of speech and press. These were not so much a genuine sign of liberal constitutional modernism but rather an attempt to create by constitutional means a unified Finnish political front to oppose the Russian pressure.

In practice, however, the new freedoms could not be fully exercised due to a lack of final consent from the Emperor. Nevertheless, the establishment of a unicameral Parliament which was elected on the basis of universal suffrage was a huge leap towards a modern political and constitutional system. Later, when the Imperial Government of Russia became paralysed due to the social and political turmoil of 1917, Finns faced a completely novel situation. When the Emperor fell in 1917 the political situation in Finland was in a parallel state of severe crisis: independence was declared on 6 December 1917 and recognised by the Russian Government on 31 December, but the ensuing tragic maelstrom with strong constitutional ingredients simply exploded out of control and bloody internal armed hostilities took place. The birth of the first truly national constitutional document was facilitated by bitter hatred, severe hostilities and a great loss of life.

When the new Russia started to transform itself into the Soviet Union, Finland was at the start of its journey to an independent state. The liberation from Russia had occurred in a peaceful manner; however, a violent internal conflict could not be avoided. A bitter Civil War, also known as the War of Independence or Rebellion between the 'Whites' and the 'Reds', took place in the early months of 1918. In general, the years 1917–19 were a time of grave confusion of all sorts, political and constitutional included.[25] To begin with, nobody really knew whether or not the old Swedish constitutional documents were in force fully, partially or not at all. The period of constitutional uncertainty ended after the bloody Civil War; but the dividing lines between the political right (Whites, who won the war) and political left (Reds) persisted long after the war and resembled later happenings in Spain and Greece. Accordingly, even today some features in the Finnish constitutional system may be fully understood only against this historical backdrop. In practice, the Form of Government (*Hallitusmuoto*) of 1919 ended the constitutional crisis during the infancy of independency.[26]

---

[25] Obviously, the Civil War was not separate from the general European political, military, social, and national turmoil in 1914–1918. More concretely, the Reds received assistance from the Russians and the Whites from the Germans.

[26] The Form of Government (*Hallitusmuoto*) 1919/94.

Independent State with a Constitution (1919–)

The constitutional compromise of 1919 accurately reflects the sort of middle-way which later made it possible to face the challenge from extreme right-wing and left-wing radicalism. Unlike in Spain and Greece, authoritarian rule was avoided: some sort of constitutionalism, rather slim in many regards, triumphed. From the point of view of later constitutional history, a crucial test for the system was when Finland managed to deflect a coup attempt of the extreme right movement (so-called *Lapuan liike*) in 1930; legalism and parliamentary democracy were the victors. This was the time when Finland, like many other states after the First World War, was facing a conflict between liberal democracy and the threat of political dictatorship. In Finland the threat of far-right dictatorship was met successfully; legalism prevailed with a partially limited democracy until 1944. This success greatly facilitated the legal-cultural justification of the 1919 Form of Government and evolving constitutionalism. Once again, legal arguments were used instead of weapons.

This important constitutional document of 1919 had two central features: first, it constructed a kind of a compromise between presidential and parliamentary models in a manner which was not really familiar elsewhere.[27] Second, it reconnected the nation with the continental European constitutional traditions followed by other Nordic countries, and such countries as Belgium, Prussia, and France. Many of the features of the 1919 Form of Government are still present in the contemporary Finnish Constitution, even though in many places the roots reach much earlier than 1919. For example, the President of the Republic enjoys even today relatively extensive competences inherited directly from the Grand Duke, ie the Emperor of Russia which, in turn, were inherited from Gustavus III's 1772 Form of Government.

System Takes Shape

The most relevant constitutional differences with the constitutional past were obviously the national sovereignty and republican principle. Even though the 1919 Form of Government included a sharing of executive power between the President and the Council of State (*Valtioneuvosto,*

---

[27] Yet, there are similar types of arrangements containing similar ingredients as, eg the Greek Constitution (1975) according to which Greece is a 'presidential parliamentary democracy' ('Προεδρευόμενη Κοινοβουλευτική Δημοκρατία').

ie Government in a narrow sense), the Act also contained a parliamentary system: government ministers were made politically responsible to the Parliament. Thus, the Finnish model mixed two markedly different sets of constitutional principles: Montesquieu's model of separation of powers and the parliamentary model. Accordingly, the system may be characterised as a genuinely mixed form of government. This created a lasting inborn constitutional tension within the institutional design of the system, which is partially still present today (see also chapters two and four).

The 1920s was a period of constitutional reform and three other constitutional documents having the formal *Grundgesetz* position were enacted. These were the Parliament Act of 1928, the Act on the High Court of Impeachment of 1922, and the Ministerial Responsibility Act of 1922.[28] To put it concisely, the general constitutional mentality that all of these documents embody is that of the formal principle of the rule of law (*laillisuusperiaate*), a feature still evidently present in the constitutional culture.[29] Each of these four documents was in force as constitutional Acts up until 2000.

The tradition of multiple-constitutional-documents was ended by the Constitution Act of 2000 when Finland departed from the Swedish tradition of many hierarchically superior formal constitutional Acts. During their lifespan, these constitutional documents were changed and amended many times, but their basic characteristics remained largely intact until 1995 when the total reform of the system of constitutional rights entered into force, completely changing the Form of Government's list (one whole chapter of the Act) of constitutional rights and freedoms. Undoubtedly, this transformed the general constitutional atmosphere so that the concept of rights moved much closer to the mainstream hardcore of constitutional law (see chapter seven).

However, it would be a great mistake to argue that nothing of interest took place during the period 1920–2000. Actually, in many cases, the Constitution was first interpreted in practice; and later a number of the changes that took place in the living constitutional system were

---

[28] Parliament Act (*Valtiopäiväjärjestys* 1928/7), Act on the High Court of Impeachment (*Laki valtakunnanoikeudesta* 1922/273) and Ministerial Responsibility Act (*Ministerivastuulaki* 1922/274). [The last mentioned Act is referred here under its short title.]

[29] A prime example of this is section 2.2 in the present Constitution Act which says that 'In all public activity, the law shall be strictly observed.'

also codified into the texts of constitutional documents as formal text amendments. Characteristically, the first steps were taken in practice and only after this in the written form. However, some limited elements remained mainly on the basis of constitutional practice and some traces of customary law emerged even throughout this period dealing with control of constitutionality and powers of the President. It should be underlined that customary law dimensions stemming from the past are not that numerous or practically significant.

One may claim that it is a typical Finnish feature to gradually adopt piecemeal changes through consensual political practices and then only later transform these practices into part of a written formal constitutional document. This may be coined 'constitutional pragmatism', aided by a certain degree of a somewhat conservative attitude towards formally changing constitutional documents, ie touching the letter of an Act. Nevertheless, when Finland entered the 1990s it was clear that the road of small gradual changes following state practice was beginning to end; not least because of its fragmented nature lacking internal coherence. However, it was Europeanisation that truly triggered the developments which were to come next.

Towards Eurostate and Constitutional Reform (1992–)

After the fall of the Soviet Union, Finland had more political freedom than in previous decades. Political freedom in this context refers almost exclusively to the freedom to manoeuvre with regard foreign policy. In 1995, Finland acceded to the European Union together with Sweden and Austria. Nevertheless, the transformation into a 'Eurostate' actually started in 1989 when Finland joined the Council of Europe. For a Nordic country, this step was taken relatively late. It was facilitated by the evaporation of fear of negative Soviet reactions after the Soviet Union grew weaker in the years before its demise. In the following year, 1990, Finland formally joined the rest of Europe in the fields of basic rights and liberties. Since 1990, the use of the European Convention on Human Rights (ECHR) and referrals to the case law of the European Court of Human Rights (ECtHR) have gradually grown from being a rarity to almost normal judicial business. A few years after the accession to the Council of Europe, Finland joined the European Economic Area in 1994 and only a year later the European Union. Both of these integrative movements increased pressure toward constitutional reform. Although, it may also be noted, that many of the pressures concerning the Constitution were to a large extent domestic as to their nature. The internationalisation merely provided proper impetus for the domestic pressures to dissolute.

As a matter of fact, reform on the Constitution was under consideration long before the Euro-phase took place. Originally the serious work started at the beginning of the 1970s, when the Council of State established an ad hoc Commission of the Constitution (*Valtiosääntökomitea* 1970). The task was to prepare a draft for the full reform of the Constitution. Even a second ad hoc commission (1974) was appointed for the same task, but harsh political disagreements between left and right wings concerning the role of Government, President and Parliament caused the full reform to fail completely in 1975. Moreover, the President of the Republic withdrew, downright cynically, his earlier backing for the reform, as he feared losing powers, which was a killer blow for the whole reformation process. After this grand failure, preparation of partial reforms was then started and after a long process certain changes were made during the 1980s and more importantly in the1990s. All of the institutional changes were designed to slowly strengthen the parliamentary dimensions and, simultaneously, to gradually weaken the power of the President. However, the basic structure of the constitutional system was left unchanged, reflecting a certain constitutional conservatism while dealing with the essentials of the system.

Interestingly, the Finnish system resembled in some of its main characteristics the ideas which the French Constitution of the Fifth Republic also embodies: semi-presidentialism combined with a parliamentary system and a certain innate reluctance to grant power of constitutional judicial review to the courts of law. The period of strong President Urho Kekkonen (in office 1956–81), especially, has been compared with the France of De Gaulle. Today, it is generally accepted in Finland that Kekkonen's unnaturally long term in office and his personal style of using influential official and unofficial power are the main reasons why the Constitution has been consciously developed in a more parliamentary direction. However, when dealing with the period of Kekkonen one must be careful to avoid too much hindsight. As a matter of fact Kekkonen was not a tyrant: he enjoyed great popularity among the Finnish voters and also among (then) Soviet leaders; it must be said, however, that there were no real alternatives. He had democratic backing of the voters even though his actions sometimes seemed to bend or go around constitutional rules.

Undoubtedly, the most significant reform during the 1990s was the full reform of constitutional rights. This reform meant remodelling the list of constitutional rights in accordance with the ECHR. Whereas to the position of the President it became clear that the Constitution had become outdated because it centralised—according to the prevailing interpretation—the exercise of power in the field of foreign affairs in the President. So, the delegation of power, which would have followed because of the accession to the European Union, would have ripped power from the Parliament and placed it in the hands of the President. To avoid this, some amendments were enacted to the Form of Government ensuring that parliamentary cooperation in matters concerning the European Union was secured. Nevertheless, this was short of meeting the requirements of true constitutional reform. The strategy of small sequential changes to the written constitutional documents had finally come to an end.

Reform was also facilitated due to the fact that the President in office at the time, Martti Ahtisaari (in office 1994–2000), was de facto weak when it came to his capability to bar the parliamentary-favouring constitutional reform in making: his sharp protests were mostly ignored as he was an outsider to the political elite and lacked the necessary connections and means. Yet, Ahtisaari was able to leave his imprint on the present Constitution Act's section 93 which still seems to secure the key role for the President in questions concerning traditional foreign policy.

Towards Total Reform

All of a sudden things started to move with unexpected speed. In 1996 a parliamentary commission (The Constitution 2000 Commission) was appointed to prepare a proposal for a full constitutional reform at very short notice.[30] This work was preceded by the paper of the working group of experts and officials (The Constitution 2000 Working Group), preparing and pinpointing the focal points for the later reform. Among these were the deconstitutionalisation of regulation concerning the

---

[30] Committee Report 1997:13 (*Komiteamietintö*). [This large report is a detailed paper which concerns the total revision of codified constitutional Act. The number 1997:13 indicates that it is report no 13 in 1997 belonging to the series of Official Printings.]

internal organisation and activities of the Parliament, a reassessment of the relationship between the highest organs of Government, whether or not Finland's accession to the European Union should be incorporated in written constitutional law, and how the control of constitutionality of Acts should be arranged. The moment was even surprisingly good for the reform and in fact many of those involved were amazed at the speed and fluidity of the process: attitudes of major political parties were open toward constitutional reform. There were hardly any political differences at all, in sharp contrast with the 1970s. However, this was far from being a miracle: what was attempted was clearly not as ambitious as it had been in the 1970s.

The Government Bill (*hallituksen esitys*) for a new Form of Government was introduced to the Parliament at the beginning of 1998.[31] During the procedure the name was changed according to the will of the Parliament into 'The Constitution of Finland' (*Suomen perustuslaki*) and also some minor changes were made to the original text-version of the Bill. The Constitution Act entered into force on 1 March 2000. According to the Act itself, the 'constitution of Finland is established in this constitutional act' (section 1). Notwithstanding this, the Act contains only part, even if perhaps the main bulk, of the Constitution of Finland, which also has some other elements to it. To be sure, not all sources of constitutional law are included in the text of the Constitution Act. To give an example, the parliamentary system developed from a President-led version to a normal majority parliamentary system partially without the formal, key constitutional sections being changed, and, this happened *before* the total reform in 2000. In a characteristically Finnish pragmatic manner, changes took place in the form of actually following constitutional practices. Thus, the new Constitution Act did not alter fundamental constitutional principles already assumed in the political culture. Importantly, when looking at the overall institutional balance, we may claim the following: 'Parliamentary government did not triumph completely.'[32] The long shadow of the Civil War, motivating constitutional engineering covertly, still existed.

---

[31] Government Bill 1998/1. [The Bill submitted to the Parliament on the revision of the Constitutional Act. Numbers indicate that it is no 1 governmental bill in 1998, belonging to the series of parliamentary documents.]

[32] A Jyränki, 'Finland: Foreign Affairs as the Last Stronghold of the Presidency' (2007) 3 *European Constitutional Law Review* 297.

SOURCES OF CONSTITUTIONAL LAW

It has been stated that a constitution is by definition 'a primary source of State law. If it were to lose that essential characteristic it would cease to be a Constitution'.[33] This is also true with Finland, even though it does not really answer the question of what the sources of constitutional law are. The Finnish Constitution and the accompanying body of law were defined earlier in this chapter. In Finnish law, the courts of law are normally the interpreters of law and the sources of law (*oikeuslähteet*) are those which courts (and public officials) turn to in order to judge what the content of law actually is. However, within the constitutional field there are also other important actors, such as the legislator and the executive branch. Unsurprisingly, Finnish general doctrine on the (internal) sources of law is not exactly the same in constitutional law as, generally speaking, in other areas of law. Thus, Finnish law allows for a certain degree of polycentrism concerning different areas of law and the accompanying doctrine on sources of law.

Constitutional law in Finland, as in other Nordic countries, has always carried a certain hallmark of constitutional realism in the sense that it has been recognised 'that not all law is positive in the sense of "formally established"', as Alf Ross has pointed out in his general theory of law.[34] Finnish general doctrine divides the sources of law into three kinds: authoritative strongly binding sources, semi-authoritative weakly binding sources and permitted sources of law that can be used. This same doctrine on sources of law is also used in Sweden and its most famous representation was built by Swedish and Finnish legal theorists Professors Aleksander Peczenik and Aulis Aarnio. We may utilise this division while describing constitutional sources in the following text. However, readers should be notified that this doctrine fits constitutional law only partially. Yet, it is useful especially to foreign readers with scarce knowledge about the Finnish system.

---

[33] F Delpérée, 'Complementary Sources to Old Constitutional Texts' in E Smith (ed), *Constitutional Justice Under Old Constitutions* (Kluwer, The Hague, 1995) 253–66, 253.

[34] A Ross, *On Law and Justice* (University of California Press, Berkeley, 1958) 101.

Classification of Sources

The first constitutionally important group of authoritative sources contains formal Acts of Parliament (concerning Parliament, government, the President, judicial organs or fundamental rights) and at the apex there is the Constitution Act which is hierarchically higher than an ordinary parliamentary Act (*laki*): to enact or to change the Constitution Act requires a two to three parliamentary majority. In a strict legal sense the Constitution Act is the highest internal source of law that holds formal constitutional primacy. Ordinary Acts are ordinary statutes which are passed by the Parliament and are based almost always on the Government's bill. There are also lower regulations which are also statutes in a material sense, ie this form of legislation also has generally binding legal force, although the issuing authority is not the Parliament. This kind of lower decree-law or in short decree (*asetus*) is issued by the Government (ie the Cabinet), President of the Republic or ministry. Power to issue decrees is specifically based on direct stipulation in the Constitution Act itself or Parliamentary Act (CA section 80.1). However, if this kind of piece of legislation concerns rights and obligations of private individuals or some other matter which belongs to the scope of parliamentary Acts by virtue of Constitution, then decrees cannot be used.

The second group of semi-authoritative sources contains institutionalised sources that actually complement the first group; here there are preparatory works of legislation (*lainsäädännön esityöt*) and key decisions of the Supreme Court and Supreme Administrative Court. Preparatory works consist of Government bills and Reports of the Parliamentary Committees. Statements by the powerful Constitutional Law Committee of Parliament have a special role as a source of law and especially as a source of the Constitution; namely, these statements are formally only weakly binding sources of law, but in practice they have a much stronger position as de facto authoritative sources for constitutional law interpretation (see chapter three). Generally speaking the role of *travaux* is crucial to the courts: it is a source which helps to find the actual intention of the legislator. Concerning the Constitution, the Government Bill 1/1998 and Committee Report (*Komiteanmietintö*) 1997:13 are the most relevant *travaux préparatoires*.

The third group of permitted sources normally consists of the general principles of law, legal doctrine, morality, and comparative arguments. However, in the field of constitutional law these have, generally speaking, a rather weak position. Instead, the state organ practice and different convention-type rules and principles created by the constitutional actors (government, president, prime minister, and parliament) themselves have a position as permitted sources of constitutional law. These kinds of sources have de facto validity in decision-making because of the material weight of the practical constitutional argument they contain, even though they do not constitute such a distinct and clearly recognised source as constitutional conventions in the United Kingdom.[35]

However, there have been some changes of importance in the doctrine and in practice. Actually, the ECHR and European Union have created an atmosphere where the legitimacy of the rules and principles seems to be derived more from international and supranational arrangements than from a domestic constitutional system. It is only from an overtly positivistic point of view that the national Constitution Act may be regarded as clearly superior in its relation to ECHR and EC law: formal legislative hierarchy does not reveal the true state of affairs. Besides, there are also some internal factors that have caused and are causing pressure on the system. There are gradual but relevant signs of slow change in national constitutional culture: many speak of the Europeanisation of Finnish law.

Transformations Brought about by Europeanisation

Together with the shift brought about by the ECHR and European Union, the tendency to regard questions of constitutional judicial review with greater seriousness than before have sharpened the willingness of the judiciary to rely on arguments of the *lex superior* type.[36] This, in turn, has meant extra momentum for the use of case law in the form of constitutional arguments being used as interpretation devices in 'normal cases' with no apparent connection to constitutional rights. Especially after the reform of 2000 one may detect slight indications of constitutionalisation of judicial functions in legal interpretation. This sort of interpretation method may, perhaps, mean a sort of persuasive authority of domestic supreme courts' case law in which the rulings

---

[35] See P Leyland, *The Constitution of the United Kingdom* (Hart, Oxford, 2007) 24 *ff*.

[36] For further discussion see V-P Hautamäki, 'Judicial Activism in Nordic Public Law' (2005) 21 *Rechtstheorie* 141. ('Although in the Nordic countries the role of judge has not traditionally been active, there are many factors that could change this role into more activist direction' at 152.)

contain constitutional rights related *ratio decidendi* in the very broad sense of the word. The expression 'case law' in this book refers to key cases with constitutional relevance by the Supreme Court, and the Supreme Administrative Court. The number of these cases is relatively small and they all concern constitutional rights without any connection to questions which concern separation of powers or the competences of the highest state organs. However, 'case law' by precedents is also constitutionally important because it means that the highest courts are not only applying legal norms but also to an extent actually create these rules in practice.

Moreover, Finnish academic constitutional doctrine has developed a deep interest in constitutional rights since the reform of 1995. One of the most challenging ideas of the academic constitutional rights movement has been the effort to reformulate the formal and traditional doctrine of sources of law and to develop new general doctrines of law. One of the outcomes of this effort is to regard courts and 'constitutionally-friendly' interpreted law in general as having a more important position than what it had earlier in Finland. The influence of modern German constitutional doctrine (*Verfassungskonforme Auslegung*) can be seen here: constitutional values and principles are seen as penetrating all spheres of law and provisions in other areas of law which, in turn, ought to be compatible especially with the constitutional/fundamental rights.[37] Even though it has not been an explicit goal, one of the ramifications of this movement's thinking is to see precedents playing a much more important role than what they were before. The movement has managed to create pressure towards a kind of legal culture in which courts and judiciary would be de facto in a more significant position than before. As a result, the movement's way of thinking about law in general seems to be advocating for an ever- greater role for constitutional law related rulings of supreme courts specifically in the area of constitutional rights. On the other hand, courts have very little if anything to say about the institutional relationships between key state-organs: rights oriented case law is virtually mute when it comes to the institutional design of the Constitution.

To summarise, the main sources of constitutional law are the written sections of the Constitution Act itself; other formal Acts and decrees dealing with constitutional matters; written statements by the

---

[37] In Germany this doctrine was created by *Bundesverfassungsgerichthof* in the famous *Lüth*-decision (BVerfGE 7, 198) in 1958.

Constitutional Law Committee of the Parliament; preparatory works of the Constitution Act, ie most importantly the Government bill 1/1998; constitutional law related, constitutional rights driven, precedent-type decisions by supreme courts; customary constitutional law forming a weakly binding 'conventional' constitutional law concerning the competences and relationships between the highest state organs; and finally academic constitutional doctrine. The last mentioned is not actually a clear source itself; instead it is something that penetrates most of the other areas in various forms by experts (mainly public law professors) taking part in law drafting, giving written opinions to the Constitutional Law Committee and writing academic publications concerning constitutional law and especially constitutional law related precedent-type case law. Apart from this it is clear that there has never been such a prominent single figure in Finnish constitutional academia as AV Dicey has been in the United Kingdom. There are no 'books of authority' in the true sense of this expression.

Altogether, it has become more difficult to define the material limits of constitution. Internationalisation and Europeanisation, in particularly, have had an important role in this non-state centred body of constitutional law. Lines of demarcation between national and non-national constitutional law have become more difficult to uphold. However, it would be too much to argue that these limits would have totally disappeared.

INTERNATIONAL AND EUROPEAN BORDERLINES

Modern states are built on an idea of national sovereignty which is accompanied with a polity, ie geographical area populated by politically organised people. Finland is typically such an area which has a border with other states. Territorially, Finland's land-borders are with Sweden (Treaty of Hamina 1809), Norway (Treaties between Russia and Sweden in 1751 and 1826), and with Russia/Soviet Union (Treaties of 1617 and 1948). With Sweden and Norway, there are international agreements that concern the common administration of border-rivers. This is one side of the question, but it does not answer the question how international obligations become legally binding in Finland.

Now, when the State of Finland undertakes an international obligation, this obligation formally binds the highest organs of the State (Parliament, Council of State, President) only; that is, if it is not followed by an explicit Finnish legal enactment making the international treaty in question a part of the Finnish legal system. In this sense the Finnish Constitution follows, at least formally, a *dualist approach* when it comes to the question of the relationship between Finnish and international law. The Constitution Act lacks such a monist rule that would automatically incorporate international treaty provisions as an enforceable part of the national legal system.[38] Finland has ratified and domestically enacted a great number of international obligations. Of these obligations, international human rights especially are of significant constitutional importance. The most central ones are those of the United Nations and ECHR (internally in force in 1990) which were attached to the Finnish system with ordinary legislative Acts without changing the constitutional Acts.[39] This, however, does not diminish the actual constitutional status of the central human rights treaties. Actually, section 1 of the Constitution Act seems to have certain weight here because it states that, 'Finland participates in international co-operation for the protection of peace and human rights'.

In the material sense, these human rights treaties are part of Finnish constitutional law and they affect the use of public power in Finland by setting restrictions and putting demands on legislative power, governmental power and judicial power. The Finnish Constitution is of course formally separate from this kind of international human rights law, but in practice these spheres of law interact and co-exist. For example, the full revision of constitutional rights in 1995 (which was incorporated as such to the Constitution Act of 2000) was prepared and carried out according to the very lines that UN human rights treaties and especially the ECHR required. So, these parts of the Constitution are in fact stemming not from national constitutional documents but from the area of international public law.

---

[38] For example, in the monist Dutch Constitution Act (*Grondwet*), there is an article (92) which makes it possible to confer legislative, judicial or executive powers to international organisations by or pursuant to a treaty. The Greek Constitution Act (1975) also provides a typical example of the monist approach; according to its article 28.1, international law is part of Greek law ('μέρος του εσωτερικού ελληνικού νόμου') and in case of norm-conflict, international law presides over all other provisions ('υπερισχύουν από κάθε άλλη αντίθετη διάταξη νόμου').

[39] The most important UN related human rights instruments in Finland are the International Covenant on Civil and Political Rights (nationally in force in 1976) and the International Covenant on Economic, Social and Cultural Rights (nationally in force in 1976).

Europeanisation

Obviously, this sort of proliferation of non-national substantive constitutional norms is well known in other EU Member States too. Besides, the Finnish constitutional rights system has always derived from foreign models and ideas (for example Belgian models in the beginning of the 1900s) as a source of inspiration, so the system has never been genuinely purely national in the material sense. Accordingly, today's formal Constitution Act actually contains only one clear restriction concerning international law obligations; namely, these obligations are not allowed to compromise the 'democratic foundations' of the Finnish constitutional system (CA section 94.3). However, the exact normative meaning of this provision is all but clear, because there is no state practice and legal writing concerning interpretation of this stipulation is divided.

As a Member State of the European Union, Finland is also subjected, not only to her own laws, but to several European treaties and also to secondary legislation of the European Commission and the Council of Europe. Finland became a member of the European Union on 1 January 1995. This was preceded by a non-constitutionally binding advisory referendum on 16 October 1994 in which 56.9 per cent of those who voted were for accession. In the material sense, many restrictions and terms that the Treaty on the Union of Europe poses are regarded as a material part of the Constitution. From the point of view of national sovereignty, the accession to Union restricts sovereignty more than any other international obligation. It is largely understood in Finland that membership in the European Union does indeed possess a substantial practical impact on the Constitution.

In comparison to Danish constitutional culture, Finnish mentality has proved to be more flexible and remarkably less nationally oriented. For example, the idea of an EU directive having a direct effect in Finnish law has been accepted without judicial resistance.[40] Most likely this, once again, seems to demonstrate the flexible Finnish understanding of constitutional law. Importantly, this does not equal non-constitutionalism but rather it tells about the living interactive relation between the constitutional rules and unavoidable need to apply those rules under changing circumstances. So, constitutional rules are not overridden but rather

---

[40] See eg, case KHO 2002:28 (in which Finnish law was deemed to be in contradiction with EU directive).

required solutions are crafted in a manner which takes into account constitutional requirements.

Growing Constitutional Pluralism

Europeanisation has undeniable constitutional ramifications. Many of the fundamental national principles are affected: domestic separation of powers and the doctrine on legislative and judicial sovereignty have gone through significant transformation since the early 1990s. Most decisive of these effects is undoubtedly the largely accepted idea of the primacy of EU law over national law, Constitution Act included.[41] Finnish legal opinion generally accepts that EU law prevails in cases of norm-conflict between national statute and EU statute.[42] Further, even the doctrine on interpretative effect of EU law on national law has been quietly accepted.[43]

However, we would be led astray if we would try to find this constitutional effect from the constitutional document itself: precedence of EU law is factual and not evidently pronounced positivistically in the rules of the Constitution Act. This expresses the constant mediation between written rules and political realities bearing constitutional relevance. Further, this silent pragmatism suggests that the Finnish approach to sovereignty seems to be a constitutional reference; a kind of a nod of the head toward the old-time doctrine which today tells so little about the actual legal freedom of movement of the State. Authoritative change in Finnish sovereignty doctrine was already made in 2000 in the Statement of the Constitutional Law Committee, which stated that 'such international obligations which are normal in today's international cooperation and which have only little effect on the state sovereignty do not mean, as such, an infringement to state sovereignty'.[44]

Many of the changes originating from European integration are not easy to detect as they have spilled over, affecting matters other than clearly within the sphere of the European Union affairs. Membership

[41] See especially cornerstone cases C-26/62 *Van Gend en Loos v Nederlanse Administratie der Belastingen* [1963] ECR 1 and C-6/64 *Costa v ENEL* [1964] ECR 585. The first Finnish case, in which the Court set aside Finnish conflicting law, was the Supreme Administrative Court's case 1996 B 577 which was decided roughly one and a half years after the accession.

[42] P Timonen, 'Sources of Law and Material on the Sources of Law' in J Pöyhönen (ed), *An Introduction to Finnish Law* (Kauppakaari, Helsinki, 2002) 22–30, 23.

[43] See eg, C-106/89 *Marleasing* [1990] ECR-I41 [8].

[44] Statement of the Constitutional Law Committee (11/2000).

has also created certain factual constitutional dynamics, of which the fast and fluid process of total reform of codified constitutional law was a prime example. There has been surprisingly little criticism against the broad reach of EU law even while Finnish people are known to be critical towards the Union. Yet, the doctrine of direct effect and primacy of EU law has not met any remarkable resistance by the courts of law.

However, in the legal academia and in political life there have been some dissident opinions regarding the doctrine of direct effect and primacy as manifestly unconstitutional. The political, judicial and academic elite has not questioned these, instead, they have been almost embraced. This, if nothing else, highlights fittingly the pragmatic and legalistic but simultaneously oddly flexible Finnish constitutional mentality. However, the majority of Finnish people seem to be considerably less enthusiastic about the developments reducing the importance of the national Constitution. Moreover, this also indicates the much less pleasant fact that for some reason the undeniable legitimacy problem relating to the European Union and its institutions has not gained any significant constitutional relevance. Possibly, this tells also something about the nature of Finnish academic public law: it seems to assume ideas and attitudes which are close to those of the political elite.

In a constitutional system in which democratic process and democratic accountability have pronounced constitutional status, the lack of constitutional critique related to the constitutionally democratic dimensions of the European Union does look somewhat puzzling. From a Norwegian, and certainly from a Danish point of view, the Finnish legal elite may appear somewhat conformist in relation to EU law and specifically its constitutional requirements. However, on the other hand, Finnish courts have not been very eager to refer directly to the European Court of Justice's case law.[45] This, again, appears to indicate Finnish constitutional pragmatism: 'actions speak louder than words'.

So, both international law and EU law affect the Finnish Constitution in many ways. However, even the Constitution Act 2000 fails to clearly admit this de facto state of affairs. It has been said that the Finnish Constitution 'reflects a minimalist approach to the regulation of the European Union'.[46] The first subsection of section 1 of the Constitution

[45] However, between 1995–2008, Finnish courts did send 56 requests of preliminary decision to the ECJ.
[46] T Ojanen, 'The Impact of EU Membership on Finnish Constitutional Law' (2004) 10 *European Public Law* 531.

Act boldly declares that 'Finland is a sovereign republic'. From the point of view of living constitutional law, this declaration should certainly not be understood in the literal sense. So, to truly read section 1 'constitutionally correctly', one must know also the constitutional practice and doctrine. Alongside these, the role of well documented *travaux* of the Constitution Act is also underlined. If a nation state is a state that does not recognise any higher decision-making power outside itself, the sovereign state, then Finland is not a nation state.[47] However, things do not need to be this simplistic: constitutional issues tend to be complex.

Furthermore, it should be stated that in February 2010 the Committee proposed that a new explicit sentence should be added to section 1 of the Constitution Act (coming into force possibly in 2012) which would state the following: 'Finland is a Member of the European Union'. However, the future of this proposed amendment remains unclear until 2011 when the post-elections Parliament will meet in session in a new composition.[48]

Today's constitutional understanding conceives the sovereignty to be qualified by the EU membership in a sense that sovereignty connected to the European Union is to be regarded something more than mere conventional international organisation. Further, it is also assumed that Finland may gain via the European Union a possibility to participate and influence the decisions of EU institutions which may concern Finland. In other words, the loss of traditional state sovereignty is justified by this possibility to influence (ie shared sovereignty).[49] Factual constitutional sovereignty is today defined so that it must be interpreted in a manner which takes into account the membership in numerous international organisations and especially in the light of EU membership. Prevailing interpretation no longer regards treaties giving powers to international organisations as being automatically contrary to the Constitution. The possible reform of the Constitution Act will not affect this basic state of affairs.

There has not been a single case in which Finnish supreme courts have scrutinised the constitutional aspects of the European Union. It is not

[47] See J-E Lane and S Ersson, *Comparative Politics* (Polity Press, Cambridge, 1994) 30–33.
[48] *Perustuslain tarkistamiskomitean mietintö* (Report of the Committee for Checking of the Constitution, *Komiteanmietintö* 2010:10) also known as 'The Taxell Committee' (see chapter nine).
[49] See Opinion of Foreign Affairs Committee (18/2001).

difficult to understand that this is due to the fact that the primacy of EU law has been quietly accepted by the domestic judiciary. However, this is not the whole picture. Obviously, also the judicial decisions by the ECJ and the ECtHR are effecting both on Finnish judicial human rights and national constitutional rights case law. As a result, the Finnish Constitution has important overlapping international and European elements. It has been argued by Finnish constitutional expert Liisa Nieminen that 'in fact, general doctrines of constitutional law of EU and Finland may not be separated completely'.[50] Moreover, the Finnish Constitution has been in difficulties in the 2000s because it has struggled to keep the international and European in separate constitutional compartments. As we will see later, this division is all but easy to draw and uphold.

CONCLUSION

In this first chapter we have observed that the Finnish Constitution is mainly based on written enacted law (it is mostly codified), but it also contains some limited customary elements. The constitutional system is that of a republican unitary state mixing both presidential and parliamentary elements. Despite its rigid written character the constitutional system has been acting rather flexibly, making use of exceptive Acts and constitutional interpretation by one of the Parliament's special Committees. But today the use of exceptive Acts is minimised in a manner which seems to be a permanent feature of the constitutional system. The system has evolved during the Swedish and Russian periods, but even during the independency the system has retained a remarkably high level of material continuity reaching to the present constitutional system. In general we might describe the Finnish Constitution as a success. Comparative political scientists have argued that constitutions are likely to be successful if their rules and principles 'accord reasonably well with dominant social interests and values', which probably has been and is the case with the Finnish Constitution and its proven ability to yield without fully breaking.[51] Frankly, nothing else would really explain its success.

---

[50] L Nieminen, *Eurooppalaistuva valtiosääntöoikeus—valtiosääntöistyvä Eurooppa* ('*The Europeanisation of Constitutional Law—The Constitutionalisation of Europe*') (Suomalainen lakimiesyhdistys, Helsinki, 2004) 617.

[51] R Hague, M Harrop and S Breslin, *Comparative Government and Politics* (MacMillan, Houndmills, 1994) 267.

We also noticed the importance of constitutional history in comprehending Finnish constitutional law. Here, however, we need to be careful. Clearly, it would be an exaggeration or at least a serious misunderstanding to describe the development of the Finnish Constitution as a gradual process starting from the seventeenth century and ending in 2000. Yet, we may very well claim that in general continuity has been typical for Finnish constitutional thinking. There has been and still is an invisible but inherent element of slowness of the movement, consistence or a certain kind of inertia against drastic changes.[52] The inertia arises partially due to the codified rules of the Constitution Act, according to which every reform must have the support of the biggest political parties: the constitutional amendment threshold leads to change-blocking consensualism. This inertia has involved also constitutional law and constitutional lawyers: normative legal argument in the area of constitutional affairs has been and still is highly relevant. This is very much different from Sweden, where constitutional questions have been regarded as political and, thus, only concerning political scientists but not really lawyers. From the 1800s, Finnish constitutional culture has been much more normative and legal as to its character than has been the case in Sweden.

One of the typical features of Finnish constitutional mentality, which has been part of it for 200 years, is the high yet pragmatic respect towards law in general and the Constitution in particular. The most important transformations of the system from the 1990s have been the slow decline of presidential power, remarkably strengthened constitutional rights system and classical sovereignty eroding European integration. Even though the majority has accepted the constitutional restrictions stemming from the European Union, there is, especially among the public, explicit resistance to some of the most fundamental EU law doctrines.

Finally, we must note a certain practical significance that the Constitution has in Finland. Clearly, it is not customary for Finnish MPs to go around carrying a copy of the Constitution Act in their back pockets so they can occasionally take it out to cite the rules in public, as might be the case in the United States. Instead, it is commonplace that as soon as someone seriously appeals to the Constitution, all sorts of constitutional materials must be sorted. Rules, principles and doctrines become

---

[52] A Jyränki, *Our New Constitution Act* ['*Uusi Perustuslakimme*'] (Iura Nova, Turku, 2000) 4.

relevant, and statements from the Constitutional Law Committee or a small number of precedents by the supreme courts are consulted, and the learned opinions of public law professors become suddenly relevant and interesting. None of this would take place if the Constitution did not matter: all users of public power are considered as being constrained by the constitutional norms. In short, this might be labelled as traditional Finnish constitutionalism.

FURTHER READING

Husa, J and Pohjolainen, T, 'Prospects of Reforming the Finnish Constitution' (1997) *European Public Law* 3, 45–56.

Husa, J, *Nordic Reflections on Constitutional Law* (Peter Lang, Frankfurt am Main, 2002).

Jussila, O, Hentilä, S and Nevakivi, J, *From Grand Duchy to Modern State: a Political History of Finland since 1809* (Hurst & Co, London, 1999).

Jyränki, A, *Our New Constitutional Act* [in Finnish *Uusi perustuslakimme*] (Iura Nova, Turku, 2000).

Kirby, D, *A Concise History of Finland* (Cambridge University Press, Cambridge, 2006).

Kastari, P, 'The Historical Background of Finnish Constitutional Ideas' (1963) 7 *Scandinavian Studies in Law* 73–77.

Ojanen, T, 'Europeanization of Finnish Law' in P Luif (ed), *Österreich, Schweden, Finnland. Zehn Jahre Mitgliedschaft in der Europäischen* Union (Bohlau, Wien, 2007) 145–78.

Pöyhönen, J (ed), *An Introduction to Finnish Law* (Kauppakaari, Helsinki, 2002).

Scheinin, M (ed), *The Welfare State and Constitutionalism in the Nordic Countries* (Nordic Council of Ministers, Copenhagen, 2001).

Sakslin, M (ed), *The Finnish Constitution in Transition* (Finnish Society of Constitutional Law, Helsinki, 1991).

Sakslin, M (ed), *Constitutionalism in Finland* (Finnish Society of Constitutional Law, Helsinki, 1995).

Saraviita, I, *Finland—Constitutional Law*: International Encyclopaedia of Laws (Kluwer, Alphen, 2009).

Selovuori, J (ed), *Power and Bureaucracy in Finland 1809–1998* (Edita, Helsinki, 1999).

2

Institutional Design

Introduction – General Structure and Division of Power – Conclusion

INTRODUCTION

Most parts of constitutional law deal with the central public institutions: this is the classical core of the *politeia*. However, it is not always clear how much institutions and their workings are based on written legal rules and how much on customs and doctrines. According to Jyränki, 'political constitution—meaning factual political decision-making—is never fully identical with written constitution'.[1] This is especially true when we deal with the central institutions of a state. As in other countries, a great deal of the Finnish Constitution deals with such bodies as have gained democratic legitimacy through the method by which they are elected, that is free general elections. In this general sense we may also broadly characterise the Finnish system as a constitutional democracy. However, the nature of this democracy is indirect and becomes reality through certain quintessential public organs which are constitutional key institutions of the State. This institutional part of constitutional law contains the main organisational constitutional arrangements of the State covering all the main branches of public power. In this chapter we will consider states' institutional design and then outline key institutions and their powers. Throughout the text the general relationship between different branches is highlighted.

---

[1] A Jyränki, *Our New Constitution Act* ['*Uusi perustuslakimme*'] (Iura Nova, Turku, 2000) 41.

GENERAL STRUCTURE OF THE STATE AND
DIVISION OF POWER

It is commonplace in today's living constitutions to uphold either parliamentarism or presidentialism. From the point of view of this book, here lies an obvious difficulty. Curiously, the Finnish system is a real parliamentary system with a surprisingly strong President. But what kind of constitutional regime is this? Finland does not belong to either of the above basic models of organising government, but combines them in a manner that can be labelled a mixed form of government. In other words, there is no single leading constitutional principle or doctrine, but instead there is a general model of parliamentary democracy based on a general idea, according to which legislative, executive and judicial powers are separated functionally and institutionally. However, the executive power is shared with two different organs which derive their constitutional legitimacy from the political will of the people through means of democratic elections. At a slight risk of oversimplification, we may claim that this creates a certain unavoidable basic tension *within* the constitutional system. This tension is characteristic of the Finnish system.

In the light of comparative constitutional law, it is generally accepted that the separation of powers (*vallanjako*) is an important element of modern constitutionalism. Normally this idea is connected with Charles Louis Secondat de Montesquieu (1689–1755) who placed different branches of power against each other, claiming that 'power stops power'.[2] For Montesquieu, the combined power of legislative and executive was equal to the oppressor. According to this thinking, the freedom of a man in society could be secured only if the different branches of public power were separated so that there would be defined areas of separate competence and these branches would monitor and balance the actions of other branches. In this original scheme the focus was on legislative and executive branches. Later, after the constitutional experiences in the United States, the third branch has been understood as equal with the other two branches of public power. Now, we may claim that in the United States the original balance has been shifted in practice towards the judiciary due to the expansion of constitutional judicial review which, however, cannot be freely entertained in the Finnish sys-

---

[2] 'Pour qu'on ne puisse abuser du pouvoir, il faut, que par la disposition des choses, le pouvoir arrête le pouvoir', C-L Montesquieu, *De l'esprit des lois* [edition Lauren Versini] (Flammarion, Paris, 1995) livre XI chapitre IV.

tem. In constitutional theory, separation of powers is also regarded as a constitutive element of modern rule of law.[3] As the principle of separating the powers appears to be a prime feature of most modern constitutional systems, it seems preferable to focus on the specific manner in which this principle has been implemented in the Finnish Constitution.

Dividing Powers

Today this fundamental constitutional principle or doctrine is conceived as dividing the public power of the state into three main branches: passing the laws (legislator); enforcing the laws (executor); and interpreting the laws (judiciary).[4] These branches exercise *mostly* the tasks which are inherent in their principal function even though separation does not work purely anywhere. Even the Finnish Constitution contains the quintessential idea of three main branches of power monitoring and balancing each other. Roughly, the Finnish system seems to fit reasonably well with the paradigmatic definition of a separation of powers type of government.[5]

In the authoritative constitutional interpretation made by the Constitutional Law Committee (see chapters three and six), it was in the 1940s when the separation of powers under the Form of Government 1919 was first officially referred to.[6] However, the Finnish system also has other fundamental principles of which some are to an extent even contradictory to the principle of separation of powers. This is, undoubtedly, a part of the legacy of hasty post-Civil War constitutional engineering. This legacy can be seen in the institutional arrangements concerning the executive power. Namely, the highest executive authority is vested in *both* the Government and the President so that responsibility for government in general is placed with the Government, whereas the President specifically deals with foreign policy and also uses power to issue statutory decrees (*asetus*), appoints high public officials, and acts as a formal Commander in Chief of the armed forces.

[3] See C Schmitt, *Verfassungslehre* (Duncker & Humblot, Berlin, 1928/1983) 39, 27 (saying that the other constitutive part is the system of fundamental rights).
[4] Today we should rather speak of *division of functions* than actually separation of powers. See I Saraviita, *Finland—Constitutional Law*: International Encyclopedia of Laws (Kluwer, Alphen, 2009) 71.
[5] See MJC Vile, *Constitutionalism and Separation of Powers* (Oxford University Press, Oxford, 1967) 13.
[6] Statement of the Constitutional Law Committee 1/1946 (PeVL 1/1946).

Even though our discussion concerns specifically the Finnish Constitution, it is helpful to note that 'Constitution-makers do borrow provisions they find in other constitutions, and constitutional ideas do migrate' as Mark Tushnet states.[7] From the point of view of non-national constitutional theory, the contradictory elements that contradict the separation of powers principle are linked with the specific conception of the sovereignty of the people. This latter idea is normally linked with Jean-Jacques Rousseau (1712–78). However, these principles are not completely contradictory as they both basically state that government should be authorised by the people. In practice, whereas stressing popular sovereignty seems to lead to some form of parliamentary system, the separation of powers appears to lead to some form of presidential model. So, the general constitutional theory is not very informative: it seems to leave the Finnish system in a strange constitutional twilight zone.

If observed from the strict point of view of assigning different powers to distinct branches of government, then surely the parliamentary system looks more like a fusion of powers than a separation of them. However, today, both parliamentary and presidential governments seem to be in many cases somehow hybrid and yet, like the French system during a situation of *cohabitation*, the Finnish system appears to be a genuine hybrid form of presidential-parliamentary government described sometimes as a semi-presidential model.[8] Reasons for this description are easy to conceive; there is both the popularly elected President of the Republic and a Prime Minister-led Council of State (ie Cabinet of Ministers) selected and supported by a majority in Parliament. As such, this is not unheard of. Similar types of mixed elements may be seen, besides in the Finnish and French systems, also in the systems of Austria, Greece, Iceland, Ireland, and Poland. Of these systems with presidential organs, the French system seems to be, at first glance, closest to the Finnish system. While describing these systems as mixed it refers to the general institutional design which combines parliamentary features and certain presidential features as the Finnish system does.

In Finland, legislative powers are exercised by the Parliament (*Eduskunta*) which also decides on state finances, ie the state budget.

---

[7] M Tushnet, 'Comparative Constitutional Law' in M Reimann and R Zimmermann (eds), *The Oxford Handbook of Comparative Law* (Oxford University Press, Oxford, 2006) 1225–57, 1229.

[8] M Duverger, 'A New Political System Model: Semi-Presidential Government' (1980) 8 *European Journal of Political Research* 165.

Governmental powers are exercised in a dual manner: by the President and by the Council of State (ie Government in the narrow sense). These two are partially fused together through their functions. Of these the members of the Council of State, ministers in other words, must enjoy the confidence of the majority of the Parliament. The judicial branch is vested in independent courts of law, headed by the general Supreme Court (*Korkein oikeus*) and Supreme Administrative Court (*Korkein hallinto-oikeus*). It is typical of the Finnish system that courts of law stay at a visible constitutional distance from the other branches. This is easy to demonstrate with a quick comparison: such a high profile US Supreme Court case as *Bush v Gore* would be completely out of the question in the Finnish constitutional climate because courts do not have this significant constitutional role.[9] However, this does not mean to say that Finnish courts would not also have a political significance; obviously they do, as do all courts within the sphere of Western legal culture. In Finland this significance becomes visible when courts exercise judicial review of legislation (see chapter six).

The tripartite basic organisation of the State is written in the important section 3 of the Constitution Act which paradoxically binds together the parliamentary system and presidential style separation of powers. Nevertheless, it makes sense to note that the tripartite design assumed in section 3 is rather weakly reflected in the more detailed stipulations elsewhere in the Constitution Act. Yet, this provision is one of the most important fundamental provisions in the Constitution Act. Thus, it is a part of the national constitutional basic solutions which have more authoritative constitutional significance than other provisions in the Constitution Act: it is a fundamental rule. This rule must be, however, conceived in connection with the popular sovereignty rule (section 2.1), according to which powers are vested in the people, and the people are represented primarily by Parliament. This latter provision is regarded as a written rule which resolves in the level of codified constitutional law the question of how the government by the people should be ultimately conceived. For an outsider to the system, it is important to realise that the system includes two colliding constitutional principles. The constitutional practice described in the following passage takes shape in mediation between the two fundamental principles. Now, why this curious dimension is a permanent feature of the Finnish constitutional

---

[9] *Bush v Gore* 531 US 98 (2000).

landscape can be explained only through the constitutional history; no clear-cut constitutional principle or doctrine bears true significance while trying to comprehend this (see chapter one). No single constitutional theory will explain this internal normative collision.[10]

Basic Structure of Constitutional Design

The 1919 Form of Government was written to emphasise the status of the formal head of the State, the President. Without a shadow of doubt, this was a result of the victory of the Whites in the 1918 Civil War. However, there is more to it, something which has to do with Finland's constitutional past rooted in monarchy. From the point of view of political conservatives, the core problem of 1919 for constitutional engineering actually came from the reform of 1906 when a strong one-chambered Parliament managed to slip into the Finnish Constitution. What to do with it in 1919 when a risk was assumed to exist of losing the majority to the political left, ie radicals? It does appear viable to claim that those who held power looked back to the eighteenth century with a longing and romanticising gaze and thus were scared of the radicalised political left.

What resulted was a strong executive power united under one person; de facto monarch dressed up in a republican garment. In a way, the republican-style President was in fact a powerful monarch in republican disguise. Whereas the first President KJ Ståhlberg (1919–25) stressed the parliamentary elements of government and was using presidential powers somewhat reluctantly, all the presidents after the Second World War felt much less restrained by the parliamentary dimensions of the Form of Government.

There have been various and differing practices depending on the sitting president. The years after the strong President with an Agrarian Union (today's Centre Party) background, Urho Kekkonen (after 1982), were marked by slow steps toward stronger parliamentarism, tolerated to an extent by the Social Democrat President Mauno Koivisto (1982–1994). Today, the President's position is formally clearly weaker than what it was during 1919–90. This is not however the whole picture as the Social Democrat President Tarja Halonen (2000–12) has shown.

[10] However, see G Sartori, *Comparative Constitutional Engineering. An Inquiry into Structures, Incentives and Outcomes* (MacMillan, Chippenham, 1994).

She has occasionally stood in blunt opposition against a united Council of State, perhaps following the letter of the Constitution Act, but not performing quite in accordance with the parliamentary principles of the Constitution. This is but one piece of proof that the system itself contains the ingredients for internal power conflicts which it cannot necessarily resolve as there are really no checks and balances which would facilitate checking the President without upsetting the power balance. On the other hand, the presidential veto of legislation is today only conditional and can be broken by a persistent Council of State backed by the majority of the Parliament (see chapter four).

Tensions Within

The problematic nature of permanent internal constitutional tension flows from the fact that both the President and the Council of State have democratic legitimacy; hence, it is hard to say which one represents more genuinely the will of the people. Their constitutional footing seems rather equal in this respect. This is very different when compared with the United States model, where the executive power 'shall be vested in a President'; whereas the Finnish model consists of a dual executive heading.[11] The main difference between the Government and the President is that only the Government is directly responsible to Parliament. Frankly, the dual nature of executive power is not constitutionally clear. It creates problems even though they are normally kept well away from the public. Actually, on a few occasions it was claimed by Social Democrat President Martti Ahtisaari (1994–2000) that the President held greater legitimacy, but this interpretation was generally rejected as not fitting in with the Finnish constitutional morality which is strongly upheld by the political elite and constitutional experts. However, a certain constitutional logic of the popular backing of the President cannot be denied: the system produces it by the way of elections.

However, has this duality really been severely problematic in actual constitutional practice? The political strength required to oppose the President became clearly visible during the Ahtisaari period. This phenomenon had its background not in clear-cut constitutional norm or principle, but rather in the fact that the Finnish parliamentary system had been changed during the last years of the 1980s. The decisive

---

[11] The Constitution of the United States (1787) article II section 1.

factor was the change of political culture which became gradually less and less willing to uphold strong presidential powers. The change in political culture was caused by the variable and short-lived government coalitions being replaced (already since 1983 actually) by large majority coalitions which remained in office for a full four-year inter-election period without being weakened by internal conflicts. The political system itself became more stable, but not due to any constitutional reform. The cultural change of political life was combined with membership in the European Union and the prior fall of the Soviet Union; both diminished the President's personal power and transferred de facto power to the Government, leaving more and more room for the increasing power of the Prime Minister.

To summarise, the system is institutionally based on the separation of powers, even though it has a dual governmental power system headed jointly by the President and Prime Minister-led Council of the State. This dual legitimacy is not only constructed upon the nineteenth century constitutional legacy of legalism, strong bureaucracy and executive powers, but also on the direct monarchical legacy of the 1772 Form of Government. Institutional design has been working well in practice even though there have been the occasional minor collisions between parliamentary and presidential powers. Whereas the political and constitutional elite have backed up parliamentary elements of the system, presidents have been able to defend their position due to the electoral system which enables them to claim popular democratic legitimacy. The slow institutional change from semi-presidentialism to full-parliamentarism (or if you prefer to three-quarters parliamentarism) or a nearly parliamentary one, has not been completed even by the Constitution Act of 2000. It was generally thought that the reform of 2000 would make the problem go away, but it is not so easy to change deep-rooted constitutional mentality simply by changing a formal constitutional document. Mental images of a constitutionally strong president are far more difficult to eradicate than amending the text of the Constitution Act.

Obviously, the public popularity of presidents in office has played an important role in slowing down constitutional transformation by offering people-derived legitimacy to presidents. Psychologically it is not hard to see why presidents themselves want to maintain a firm grip of their constitutional powers or powers that they themselves regard as having constitutional status. Indeed, why on earth should a seasoned, skilled and highly popular politician cease doing politics merely because 'the dignified constitutional nature' of the President's office. However, this is just what all the presidents have tried to demonstrate in their relation to the public: creating and upholding an image of apolitical neutrality and constitutional stability. And, so it seems, the public has received this populist message well, while parliamentarians, constitutional lawyers and political scientists have been far less impressed by this image-building which masquerades certain constitutional realities: the President is a political actor and takes part in political decision-making even while the President can hide behind the Government and appear as apolitical.

CONCLUSION

In this chapter it was seen how the Finnish Constitution has maintained many of its classical key characteristics and core spirit which took birth in the dialogue between the Swedish past and the Russian-ruled reality of the 1800s. Later, independence and Civil War added certain twists to the heritage from earlier centuries. In 1919, monarchy was seemingly abandoned in favour of the republican form of state, and yet there has been remarkable continuity concerning most of the key doctrines and even key institutions. Accordingly, it seems that there is a certain element of respect toward constitutional traditions or at least an inborn reluctance to engage in such innovations as it would alter the constitutional traditions too radically. The case of joining the European Union in 1995 is the most striking exception to this traditionalism concerning the high organs of the State.

As was stated earlier, the main state organs having a democratically derived nature are the Parliament, the Government coalition which relies on the political support of the Parliament, and the President. Besides these, local government has also a democratic basic nature. From a constitutional point of view, the Parliament is clearly the institution with the greatest degree of popular sovereignty, but even other branches of power are not void of this feature. However, executive power is shared between two key institutions. Of these we will first analyse the one which is in practice more important as a high organ of the State, the Government. However, even though the Government is the central executive organ, the following discussion is slightly shorter than the one concerning the President. This is due to the fact that the Government can act more freely than the President and in most cases the constitutional powers of the President are exercised through governmental machinery. These institutions are functionally and organisationally very much intertwined.

FURTHER READING

Arter, D, 'Finland' in R Elgie (ed), *Semi-Presidentialism in Europe* (Oxford University Press, Oxford, 1999) 48–66.

Hidén, M, 'The Constitution of Finland' in J Uotila (ed), *The Legal System of Finland* (Finnish Lawyers Publishing Company, Helsinki, 1985) 39–59.

Jyränki, A, 'Finland: Foreign Affairs as the Last Stronghold of the Presidency' (2007) *European Constitutional Law Review* 3, 285–306.

Nousiainen, J, 'From Semi-Presidentialism to Parliamentary Government: Political and Constitutional Developments in Finland' (2001) *Scandinavian Political Studies* 24, 95–109.

Nousiainen, J, 'The Finnish System of Government: From Mixed Constitution to Parliamentarism' in *The Constitution of Finland* (Parliament of Finland, Vammala, 2001) 5–42.

3

Legislative Power—the Parliament

Introduction – Parliamentary Elections – Parliament's Key-Functions – Conclusion

INTRODUCTION

Without any doubt the main function of the Finnish Parliament (*Eduskunta*) is to exercise legislative power. In a word, it is a legislature. Of equal importance is to stress that the Parliament passes laws but does not draft them. There is no machinery to take care of law drafting in the Parliament. In an elementary sense, the Parliament may be paralled with the constitutional position of the United States Congress in which 'all legislative powers . . . shall be vested'.[1] *Eduskunta* has been for a long time a typical deliberative organ of elected persons who are empowered to pass, change or repeal Acts of the State, ie it is very much a branch of specialised public power distinguished from the executive and judicial branches. Accordingly, it cannot directly have any effect on courts of law nor can it affect directly the President by any means. However, as we have seen earlier, the Finnish Constitution does not fully follow the separation principle which, in turn, means that even though the main function of Parliament is to pass legislation, there are other dimensions within it too. Once again, the discussion should start from a brief constitutional history which provides the essential pieces of relevant contextual knowledge.

During the 1800s, the Finnish constitutional system started to appear antiquated and helplessly unmodern. The reason for this was clearly visible: it was a remnant from the previous century (but even then it was considered old-fashioned). The position as a Grand Duchy of Russia and the corporate basis of Diet of the Estates were simply constitutionally out of date as the nation entered the 1900s. Mounting political and

---

[1] The Constitution of the United States (1787) article I section 1.

administrative pressure from Russia and the awakening nation of Finland were constantly opposed to each other. Russia's defeat in the war with Japan in 1905 opened access toward constitutional reform. Actually, the radical reform of 1906 is significant and rare in Finnish constitutional culture; instead of continuity there was an inevitable yet highly democratic friction in the constitutional continuity. Instead of the old-fashioned Diet of the Estates, Finland got a brand new democratic Parliament. At its birth the novel Finnish Diet (ie the Parliament) was something of a rarity. It was a completely novel and highly modern institution; it was unicameral and elected by universal suffrage, women included (not only to vote but also to serve in Parliament). For the later development it was of lesser relevance that the Russian Czar effectively blocked the decision-making of this new democratic organ. From 1906 continuity has been well preserved since the basic elements of parliamentary organisation have remained unchanged for the past 100 years.

If we look merely at the constitutional outline of Parliament we might argue that nothing of relevance has changed over 100 years. Nevertheless, because the constitutional landscape has been changed, we may, instead of static features, underline the constant process of slow and gradual change: from the Diet of the Grand Duchy to the relatively weak Parliament of the First and Second Republic; from the 1970s a more and more significant Parliament; and from 1995 a new kind of Parliament with growing European constraints but diminishing domestic presidential restraints. However, even the present system may not be described as a Westminster-type democracy but rather a consensus-type of democracy with executive power being shared, a separation of powers, and a multi-party system.[2]

As the Finnish Constitution and constitutional thinking regard Parliament to be in such an important position, sometimes called the 'Flagship of Democracy' (*demokratian lippulaiva*), from the point of view of democratically transmitting popular sovereignty into laws, the following discussion starts from the way this body is elected. The election mechanism is the channel through which the Diet receives its democratic-constitutional legitimacy and ultimate justification. In the classical sense, even the Finnish Parliament is a kind of a constitutional instrument which forms and utters the general will of the public in the spirit

---

[2] See A Lijphart, *Democracies: Patterns of Majoritarian and Consensus Government in Twenty-One Countries* (Yale University Press, New Haven, 1984).

of article VI in *Déclaration des droits de l'homme et du citoyen du 26 Août 1789*: 'La loi est l'expression de la volonté générale.' This characterisation may appear somewhat grand but it seems to encapsulate the bare essence: the Parliament is important because it formulates and utters the will of the people through legislation.

PARLIAMENTARY ELECTIONS

Finnish constitutional democracy entrusts an extra position of popular sovereignty-based trust to the Parliament because the powers of the State 'are vested in the people, who are represented by the Parliament' (Constitution Act (CA) section 2.1). Accordingly, it is constitutionally important how the will of the people is democratically transmitted to the Parliament. We cannot genuinely speak of the Parliament in a modern constitutional sense when we were dealing with the Diet of the Estates. After 1906 this obstacle was removed and a modernised elected legislature took birth. There are two important dimensions in this: first, power holders must be elected and there must be open competition between politically differing groups seeking power through public institutions. Second, the extent of participation or at least having the possibility to take part in free elections must be high when dealing with democracy. Neither of these criteria was fulfilled in the Diet of the Estates.[3]

The first general parliamentary elections were held in spring 1907; of the elected members (200 altogether) 19 were women. At that time the eligible age for both voting and for office was 24. Today, suffrage is still universal in Finland provided the citizen is aged 18 or older. Even today the body consists of 200 representatives (MP ie *kansanedustaja*) who are elected for a term of four years. There are three leading constitutional rules (CA section 25) covering the electoral system, which are: a) the direct nature of election, b) proportionality, and c) secrecy of voting. These rules are stipulated in great detail in a regular Act of material constitutional nature, since the Constitution Act offers only general guidelines.[4]

---

[3] See T Vanhanen, *Prospects of Democracy—A Study of 172 Countries* (Routledge, London, 1997) 35–36.

[4] Act on Elections (*Vaalilaki* 714/1998, with later amendments). This Act also contains rules concerning presidential elections, communal elections and European parliamentary elections. It also stipulates on division of parliamentary seats between electoral districts.

'Direct nature' refers to the fact that in electoral districts (constituency, *vaalipiiri*) voters vote directly for the person they support. This differs from the Swedish model where people vote for the party and it is the party which puts candidates on a ranking list before the actual elections take place. In Finland no such lists are used which makes the elections clearly more person-focused than party-oriented, even though voters are normally well aware of what party they support or oppose. The right to nominate candidates in elections belongs constitutionally to registered political parties, but also a group of people (at least 100 persons) may do this provided that they have themselves the right to vote. The candidates are set by political parties but also by these electoral associations (*valitsijayhdistys*); however, of those who actually get elected, normally all belong to established political parties.

There are in practice hardly any limits to the eligibility and qualifications of a representative; everyone who has the right to vote and if not under guardianship may be a candidate in parliamentary elections; however, if a person is holding military office he or she cannot be elected as a representative (after retirement this is possible, and in practice there usually are former officers serving as elected MPs). Voting takes place anonymously and the secrecy of voting is highly respected and guarded in a meticulous manner. In practice secrecy of voting is taken care of professionally throughout the country and there are hardly ever any real problems with this. The biggest voting problems lately were experienced in the 2009 communal elections when in a few smaller communities the test-used technology failed resulting in new local elections.

Proportionality means that the country has been divided into electoral districts from which all MPs are chosen. The votes are counted and proportionality is secured by applying the d'Hondt system. The electoral system is an open-list proportional system in which votes are cast for individual candidates only. The country is divided into 14 multi-member and one single-member (Åland Islands) districts. Candidates are listed according to the party (or joint list or electoral alliance) they belong to. Proportionality is secured by applying the d'Hondt system, which applies in a number of European countries. This means that first the total number of votes for each list is calculated, which corresponds to the sum of the votes for the individual candidates in that list. In the second stage the candidates in each list are placed in ranking-order according to the number of votes each candidate has received. In the third stage each candidate is assigned a reference figure (*vertausluku*, ie comparative index). The reference figure for the candidate with the most votes in each list is the total for that list; the figure for the candidate ranked second is half that total; the figure for the third-ranked candidate is a third of the total; and so forth, ie following the electoral dividers of the d'Hondt formula. In the final stage, the prescribed number of MPs is filled by placing all the candidates in the electoral district in order according to their reference figures.

This system, however, seems to favour large parties to an extent. The system is under constant discussion and criticism; accordingly, from time to time, various ideas to reform the system are voiced. Nevertheless, because changing the system is both politically and constitutionally complicated, no great changes are to be expected. Yet, in the late spring of 2009 a political deal between major political parties was made concerning the three per cent national threshold to be used in future parliamentary elections. This would mean that a party needs three per cent of votes to be able to get even one MP.

It is probably one of the outcomes of the proportional representation system that Finland has a multi-party system. This has been the case from the very early days of the democratically chosen national Diet. In the latest parliamentary elections (spring 2007) the parliamentary seats were divided as the following table shows:

Name of the Party	No of Seats
Centre Party (*Keskustapuolue*) [Political right, conservative]	51
National Coalition Party (*Kansallinen kokoomus*) [Political right/conservative]	50
Social Democratic Party (*Sosiaalidemokraattinen puolue*) [Moderate political left]	45
Left Wing Alliance (*Vasemmistoliitto*) [Political left]	17
Green League (*Vihreät*) [Environmental party, moderate political left]	15
Swedish Peoples Party (*Ruotsalainen kansanpuolue*) [Swedish speaking people's party, conservative]	10
Kristillisdemokraatit (*Christian Democrats*) [Conservative, religious party]	7
True Finn Party (*Perussuomalaiset*) [Populist, conservative]	5
	(200)

After negotiations, the Government was formed in April 2007 by the Centre, National Coalition, Greens and Swedish parties. Other parties outside of these formed the opposition. Of those elected, 84 were women.

Each term of Parliament starts when the results of the elections have been officially confirmed. The term lasts until the next parliamentary elections have been held. The four-year electoral term is divided into four parliamentary sessions (*valtiopäivät*) and it is at the end of the last session that Parliament concludes its work. The President has here a symbolic role of officially declaring the work of Parliament to be finished for the past electoral term. However, the Speaker of Parliament is entitled to reconvene Parliament before elections if a pressing need should arise (CA section 33.2). This has not taken place but in the Finnish system there has always been some distrust between the President and the Parliament and this rule makes it possible for the Parliament to keep guard should the President try to do something when the Parliament is not convening.

Position of MPs

If a member is elected as a Member of the European Parliament, then membership of the Finnish Parliament is suspended for that period of time and a deputy replaces the MP (CA section 28.1). It is also possible for the Parliament to grant release from office upon a member's request if there is deemed to be an acceptable reason. Normally these reasons have to do with nominations to high public positions or serious medical reasons. According to constitutional custom, merely political reasons are not deemed as qualifying as an acceptable reason. However, there are examples of frustrated or disillusioned MPs trying to get away from the Parliament without succession.

There is also the possibility that if an MP seriously and repeatedly neglects parliamentary duties, Parliament may, after having received a de facto constitutionally-binding opinion from the respected Constitutional Law Committee of the Parliament, either dismiss or suspend the MP (CA section 28.4). However, this decision requires at least two-thirds of the votes cast which obviously sets the criteria constitutionally at a very high level. Besides, if an MP is sentenced to imprisonment for committing a serious crime, he or she may not continue as an MP.

With regard to dismissal, Parliament must request a constitution-ally authoritative opinion from the Constitutional Law Committee. Should the opinion be in favour of dismissal, the decision requires at least two-thirds of the votes cast. All in all, it is an important feature of the Finnish Constitution to regard MPs with respect; they enjoy par-liamentary immunity and have the right to speak freely in Parliament on all matters under consideration. Immunity means that an MP must not be prevented from carrying out parliamentary duties. In the Finnish thinking the right to have liberty to express opinions is especially impor-tant. From a comparative point of view Finnish MPs have very broad and unrestricted freedom to speak and this right may be restricted only due to practical reasons and in such a manner that it concerns all MPs equally. However, what political parties choose to do and how their MPs choose to act is left out of formal constitutional rules.

Should the member be arrested or detained by the police, the Speaker of Parliament must be notified without delay. The rationale behind these constitutional prerogatives is not to grant any special position, privilege or to protect MPs from the law, but to safeguard the political freedom of an MP who has been elected in free and general elections to represent the people. So, the special status of an MP has stable constitutional justi-fication even though from time to time the public regards these constitu-tional rights of MPs as excessive, disproportionate or elitist. This picture of elitism is normally transmitted only too well by the media.

There are no genuine checks and balances which can be targeted towards Parliament from the outside. Parliament is constitutionally in a very special position because courts of law, the Government, or the President for that matter, have no competence to intervene on the position or internal management and procedures of Parliament. On the other hand, Parliament may change the position of other branches simply by using its fundamental constitutional power; it holds what the German doctrine calls *Kompetenz-Kompetenz*. This means that it is the only organ of the State legally capable of changing the Constitution Act itself because it has *pouvoir constituant*.[5] Obviously, there are many important dimensions in this element. For example, the right of MPs to express their opinions is specifically safeguarded (CA section 30.2). The right to speak is mainly limited by 'dignity and decorum' and there must be

---

[5] See eg, C Schmitt, *Verfassungslehre* (Duncker & Humblot, Berlin, 1982/1983) 76–81 (*verfassunggebende Gewalt* which includes power to decide over the powers of other state organs).

avoidance of offensive behaviour. Upholding these rules depends on the Speaker, but there are certain customary principles according to which the behaviour of the MPs is conceived. It must be underlined that all parliamentary organs are elected by the MPs themselves, and no other power may interfere with this, although it is clear that political parties have their say concerning this. On the other hand, parties can act only through their elected MPs: they have no direct access to the Parliament.

Groups

In the actual working of the constitutional system, the parliamentary groups (*eduskuntaryhmä*) are in a central position; they form the Government coalition block and the opposition block. Even though the Constitution Act speaks of 'groups represented in Parliament', it actually refers to political parties.[6] All in all, the party-system is part of the living constitutional system itself: parties actually link free political action of civil society with constitutional processes and institutions. This is the bread and butter of the Finnish living Constitution and daily politics (debate, discussion, interpellations, etc). It gives genuine content to the system and injects an element of direct popular sovereignty into the Constitution. This, of course, also requires that ministers have the right to attend the plenary sessions of Parliament and they may—indeed they are expected—to participate in its discussions. Ministers are expected to follow the handling of such matters in Parliament which coincide within their own ministry.

Now, it must be underlined that the parties have a strong grip on the workings of Parliament even though, formally, MPs ought to follow only 'justice and truth' and they should 'abide by the Constitution and no other orders are binding' on them (CA section 30). This written rule has very little to do with constitutional realities since almost all the parties require their representatives to follow group discipline (*ryhmäkuri*), which ensures that the Government can at all times enjoy the confidence of the majority of Parliament. This practice, or rather a true *e contrario* interpretation, is explained by the constitutional doctrine maintaining that this provision applies only to formally legal norms, ie an MP cannot be legally bound to follow any command concerning his or

---

[6] Political parties are specifically mentioned in sections 25.3 and 54.4 of the Constitutional Act.

her actions in parliamentary work.[7] According to this generally accepted line of interpretation, parties' inner rules that require group discipline are not regarded as 'other orders' as referred to in section 30 of the Constitution Act. Again, this proves the existence of constitutional conservatism as this provision was explicitly kept in the new Constitution Act even though those well informed know perfectly well that this rule follows actual constitutional practice rather poorly. However, when it comes to group discipline the Finnish system is hardly alone.

Speakers

Constitutionally important elements of Parliament are the Speaker (*Eduskunnan puhemies*) and the Speaker's Council (*Puhemiesneuvosto*). The Speaker and two Deputies are elected from amongst MPs by secret ballot. The ballot is not however blind; the parties negotiate before the ballot actually takes place. The Speaker and two Deputies form the Speaker's Council which issues instructions concerning the practical organisation of parliamentary work. The Council also decides on the procedures to be followed when matters are considered by Parliament. Besides, the Council can also make initiatives for the enactment or revision of Acts which govern Parliament's officials and its Rules of Procedure. The Council and especially the Speaker have a formally high and visible constitutional position; however, in practical decision-making the Council's and Speaker's role are very limited indeed. Nevertheless, the Speaker (and partially Deputy Speakers also) holds a constitutionally symbolic position which is regarded as not being really powerful but constitutionally honourable.[8] According to constitutional custom, the Speaker always comes from a different party than that of the Prime Minister. Speakers are normally elected in a consensus-like manner, even though in 2010 there was a large number of MPs voting against Sauli

---

[7] By *e contrario* is meant here a conclusion which is not formally proper because 'legal rule according to its content is applied only within a certain limitation', as Alf Ross defines this type of interpretation. Ross, *On Law and Justice* (California University Press, Berkeley, 1958) 150.

[8] This can be seen in the oath which the Speaker (and Deputies) makes before the Parliament: 'I affirm that in my office as a Speaker I shall to the best of my ability defend the rights of the people of Finland and of the Parliament in accordance with the Constitution.' (Parliament's Rule of Procedure section 4) It may be noted that the oath speaks of the Constitution and not only of the Constitution Act.

Niinistö (National Coalition Party) who was elected with a surprisingly low number of votes.

Parliament's Bureaucracy

Political decision-making concerning proposed legislation is the key function of the Finnish Parliament. Nevertheless, there is also a certain inner civil-service dimension in Parliament which concerns its own administration. The inner administrative organisation of Parliament consists mainly of the Parliamentary Office, the Secretary General (*pääsihteeri*), the Committee Secretariat, the Central Office, and the Administrative Department. The Parliamentary Office is generally responsible for creating decent conditions for Parliament to carry out its main functions, and the other pieces in the organisation are all situated in this head office. The work of the Parliamentary Office is led by the Secretary General. The Committee Secretariat is the organ that handles preparations and arrangements for Committee meetings. The Secretariat is expected to prepare matters for the discussion, different accompanying documents and minutes.

The actual legislative function is carried out by the committees which prepare government bills and reports and other possible matters for consideration in the parliamentary plenary session. Committees also issue statements when they are requested by Parliament to do so. There are presently 15 committees in Parliament, of which four are such that their position and functions are directly stipulated by the Constitution Act (section 35): the Grand Committee, the Constitutional Law Committee, the Foreign Affairs Committee, and the Finance Committee. Other committees are, in practice, established on a customary basis but also have a formal position based on stipulations in Parliament's Rules of Procedure (*Eduskunnan työjärjestys*). Even though the plenary sessions are open to the public, the committees work behind closed doors and only their official reports are published.[9]

The other two abovementioned organs, the Central Office and Administrative Department, have a more purely administrative nature. The first mentioned has to do with practical work concerning prepara-

---

[9] See for a concise description of standing Committees, I Saraviita, *Finland—Constitutional Law*: International Encyclopedia of Laws (Kluwer, Alphen, 2009) 154–58.

tory work, execution and service-related tasks which all provide technical service for plenary sessions (eg keeping minutes, publishing documents, etc). The Office also takes care of translating the most important parliamentary documents into Swedish (which is the other national language of Finland, CA section 17.1).[10] The Administrative Department takes care of such mundane things like finance, real estate, and information technology and personnel administration.

Constitutional Role of the Opposition

The opposition has no codified constitutional position, but clearly plays a very central role in the parliamentary system. This can be seen indirectly in many of the constitutional rules and practices. Obviously, the opposition normally *per definitionem* opposes the Government by raising objections to the Government's bills and criticising the Government's political performance. It is the natural role of all high profile opposition politicians to constantly challenge and question the policy and performance of the sitting Government coalition. However, because of the multi-party system the opposition gains strength best when it is united and raises reasoned objections backed up by large popular opinion. In practice this takes place every now and then, but not necessarily always due to the internal fragmentation of the opposition itself. Only seldom do the right wing and left wing opposition parties unite due to sharing a similar political interest. In most cases they join together only due to short-term interests and for strategic reasons: the will to harm and if possible even overthrow the Government coalition is what binds opposition parties. Accordingly, in Finland there is no such institution as the United Kingdom's 'Shadow Cabinet'.[11] The actual direct constitutional instruments for the opposition are interpellations, handling of Government statements, questions, announcements and debates.

---

[10] Constitutional Act section 51.1 stipulates that both Finnish and Swedish are to be used in parliamentary work. In practice, most of the work takes place in Finnish even though many of the formal documents are produced in both languages. Moreover, even the Swedish speaking MPs deal with most of their functions in the Parliament in Finnish (ie they are practically bilingual).

[11] See P Leyland, *The Constitution of the United Kingdom* (Hart, Oxford-Portland/ Oregon, 2007) 90.

Interpellation

Interpellation (*välikysymys*) is addressed to the whole Government or just an individual minister if the subject matter is solely situated within the competence of a certain ministry. To raise an interpellation, a group of no less than 20 MPs is required. Then, the Government collectively or the minister alone is required to reply orally in a Plenary Session within two weeks. After the debate, there is normally a vote of confidence because the opposition hardly ever fails to present a motion of no confidence (CA section 43). However, as the governments of today have a parliamentary majority, these interpellations do not actually lead to the resignation of a minister or the Government. In the Finnish system, if governments are to resign at all it is normally due to them collapsing internally due to the tensions and disagreements within the Government coalition itself. However, interpellations do raise popular interest and when used sparingly they seem to provide a constitutional platform for the opposition to criticise the Government, obtain information and focus public debate toward themes and areas not favourable to the sitting Government. Before the 1980s interpellation had much more significance as coherent majority-governments were rare. This weakness of governments then gave more political weight to the President. Today, government coalitions sit for a full four years. This is yet another factor which today weakens the position of the President and it does not depend on what the formal constitutional rules say; the transformation is rather derived from the change in the political culture. Long-standing majority coalitions are not dependent on the President's support.

Statements

The handling of the Government's statements (*valtioneuvoston tiedonanto*) also offers the possibility for the opposition to challenge the Government and to measure its confidence in Parliament. Like interpellation, it may be followed by a vote of confidence. There are really no constitutional restraints concerning the topic of such a statement; it suffices that the matter relates to the 'governance of the country or its international relations' (CA section 44). This leaves much room for the Government coalition to decide when it chooses to wield this constitutional instrument. So, this method is initiated by the Government itself when it wishes to measure its confidence, ie it may turn a political question into a Government statement and by doing so it forces the MPs of the Government block parties to choose. The choice is clear: to back the Government's position or to break up the Government. Normally, this imposes discipline even on the reluctant 'back-benchers' to vote for the Government. Group-discipline is applied practically by all MPs, even though there are voices of internal opposition group-discipline.

Additionally, when a new Government enters into office, it must without delay submit the Government's Programme to Parliament in the form of a statement; and also when the composition of the Government is being essentially altered (CA section 62). The latter situation allows some interpretative space for the Government because it is not clear what the expression 'essentially altered' precisely means. However, it may be safely assumed that when one party decides to abandon the Government coalition, leaving the Government politically weaker but still having the majority of MPs, such a vote ought to be organised. However, when only ministers change and the coalition remains intact does not constitute 'essential alteration'.

Reports

The Government's Annual Report (*hallituksen kertomus eduskunnalle*) bears some of the characteristics of the Government's statement, with the difference that these are provided automatically according to the rules in the Constitution Act (eg Report on State Finances, *kertomus valtiontalouden hoidosta*) and other Acts, or in the Parliament's Rules of Procedure. Like interpellation and statement, debate concerning the report may also end up in a confidence vote.

Questions and other Instruments

Questions (*kysymykset*), announcements (*ilmoitukset*) and debates (*keskustelut*) do not lead to decisions concerning confidence in the Government. These, however, offer possibilities for the opposition to criticise the Government's policy. The same applies to the Government's reports (*valtioneuvoston tiedonanto*) which are in all other respects identical with the Government's statement. All of these, however, offer different ways for the MPs to gain information on topical issues and other questions of interest.[12] The Constitution Act and Parliament's Rules of Procedure stipulate in detail how these constitutional instruments are to be used. They have practical meaning for the work of the opposition, but because they may not lead to a no confidence vote, they are not to be regarded constitutionally as being so central to parliamentarism. Nevertheless, they facilitate parliamentary business and public political debate and in this sense they serve de facto very much the same political purpose as interpellation.

To summarise, the opposition has an important role in the functioning of the constitutional system; however, this fact can only scarcely be deduced from the written constitutional stipulations. Yet, the interplay between the majority and the opposition is a quintessential part of constitutional life in Finland: it animates the whole system.

PARLIAMENT'S KEY FUNCTIONS

According to the written constitutional provision and generally accepted constitutional principle, Parliament is the most central of state organs. According to the Constitution Act (section 2.1), the Finnish people 'are represented by Parliament'. Even though the Act later (section 3) separates different functions, we may regard the functions of Parliament to be in principle constitutionally the most important ones. Generally, the functions of Parliament are precisely the same political functions that are typical in other parliamentary democracies: acting as a public discussion forum, training of political leaders, and upholding a workable Government. A constitutionally important piece of statutory legislation, without the formal position of an Act, is the Procedure of Parliament which contains the most practically relevant provisions relating to actual operation of Parliament. It contains mostly such rules as were deconstitutionalised in 2000.[13]

Besides these there are certain obvious constitutional functions or powers that belong to Parliament. These are legislative power, finance power, power to control and supervise the Government (ie Council of

---

[12] Section 47 of the Constitutional Act gives the Parliament the right to receive information from the Government. Also, private MPs enjoy this right of gaining such information which MPs need for parliamentary duties. However, this information may not be secret nor may it pertain to a state budget under preparation.

[13] Parliament's Rule of Procedure (*Eduskunnan työjärjestys* 40/2000).

State), administrative power (which does not fit in with the separation of powers principle), the power to take part in foreign policy, and quasi-judicial powers (which also do not fit within the separation of powers principle). Of these functions there are clearly two which are constitutionally of quintessential importance: legislative power, and budgetary power which is a key element of Parliament's power over finance.

Legislating

In practice, legislative proposals are presented to Parliament in the form of Government bills (*hallituksen esitys* (HE)) even though individual MPs also have the right to present their own legislative initiatives. In practice, nevertheless, this is not quite the case. Generally speaking, each year the Government submits some 200–300 bills to the Parliament, whereas MPs submit some 100–200 bills. The overwhelmingly large majority of legislative amendments or new Acts are introduced as government bills and only a handful, if even that, of MP initiatives lead to actual legislation.

Finnish Acts are drafted in ministries by professional civil servants even though it is the Government (here the Council of State and the President together) which actually represents bills to Parliament. The handling of bills in Parliament begins with a preliminary debate (*lähetekeskustelu*, literarily 'accompanying discussion') in a plenary session. Plenary sessions are open to the public and high-profile plenary sessions are sometimes broadcast on national television. At this stage no actual decisions are made regarding the content of the bill. The preliminary debates' sole rationale is to provide a basis for committee work, so, after this preliminary debate the bill is referred to a special standing committee. The meetings of these committees are not open to the public unless it is specifically decided. After the committee handling, a bill returns to the plenary session, where it is processed in two stages. In the case of major legislative projects, the committee chairperson generally takes the floor first to present the committee's report. This is followed by a general debate. After this, the actual content of the bill is decided on section by section, with votes being conducted as necessary. Typically, amendments or changes are generally proposed, with devastatingly poor success, by opposition MPs. Formally, the Parliament can refer a bill to the Grand Committee after the first reading, but in practice this is rare.

The committee which handles a bill often hears from outside experts and interest groups and organises non-public discussion on the bill. Then it issues a report (*valiokunnan mietintö*) to the plenary session. The constitutional core of committee work is easy to pinpoint: will it approve the bill or not or what changes does it deem necessary? Basically, the committee may recommend that the bill should be approved with or without changes. It is also possible, even though rare, that the committee recommends that a bill be rejected; the composition of the committees accurately reflects the power-relations of the opposition and the Government coalition. In most of the cases, even the changes that are proposed tend to be very restricted in their scope. Rarely, a highly unpopular bill is drawn back.

The second reading can begin no earlier than the third day after the end of the first reading. Other matters than bills are considered in the plenary sessions only in a single reading (CA section 41). At this time the bill must be either approved or rejected, but it can no longer be amended or changed. In fact, the majority of the bills are handled in two to four months, but large legislative projects may be digested over several years. The bills (and MPs' own bills) that have not been processed by the end of the electoral period automatically lapse according to the present system.

Changing the Codified Constitution

When the Parliament handles enacting of constitutional Acts, the process is more complex (see chapter eight). A simple majority of votes is required to approve or to reject ordinary Acts. So, even a majority of one vote is sufficient. However, a more complicated procedure must be followed if a bill concerns the Constitution Act. This kind of bill must first be approved by a simple majority of votes on its second reading. The bill is then left in abeyance until after the next general parliamentary election. The newly elected legislature continues discussion of the bill and must approve the bill by a two-thirds majority of votes, in order for it to become an Act in force. However, even here there is, nonetheless, a possibility for expedited procedure. Expedited procedure (*kiireellinen säätämisjärjestys*) means that a constitutional bill need not wait until after the next general election if, and only if, it is declared urgent by a five-sixths majority of votes.[14]

---

[14] Originally, it was thought that the question concerning the urgency and the question concerning the approval of the bill were different things. However, of course those who oppose the bill see it as being easier to stop the bill already at

After the Parliament has approved an Act, the legislative document in question is signed by the Speaker and the Secretary General and is then sent to the President for formal ratification. Only after the President has signed it is the Act published in the *Suomen säädöskokoelma* (The Statutes of Finland). This is the official series which consists of printed, consecutively numbered leaflets containing official legislative material (Acts, decrees, official orders, etc).[15] As already stated, the President can also refuse to ratify an Act with a conditional veto: if Parliament again approves the Act, it comes into force without ratification. If it is not approved again by Parliament, the matter is regarded as having lapsed. However, presidential veto is a true rarity these days. Decrees by the Council of State or its ministries do not require presidential ratification.[16]

Finally, it should be noted that the Finnish Parliament has some important restrictions concerning its powers in the legislative area. Some of these are practical and derived from political facts: no parliament is fully ready to go radically against the clear political consensus of the public majority, even though this would be constitutionally possible. Some of the restrictions are legal, of which two topics should be mentioned: international obligations including the European Union in general and human rights in particular (European Convention on Human Rights (ECHR)). Both of these mean that Parliament is not all-powerful because it cannot free itself easily from international obligations and it cannot deprive the individual of his or her constitutional rights by means of an ordinary Act. Europeanisation has diminished the sovereignty of Parliament.

Finance Power

The Constitution Act does not only locate legislative powers in Parliament but also the power to 'decide on State finances' (CA section 3.1). This power contains two main elements, taxes and state budget (*valtiontalousarvio*). In

---

this stage when only one-sixth of MPs is needed (in contrast with the later needed amount of one-third) to stop the bill.

[15] See Act on the Statutes of Finland (*Laki Suomen säädöskokoelmasta* 188/2000). The series also has a separate part for international treaties (*Treaty Series/Sopimussarja*).

[16] Key Finnish legal material and especially legislation can also be found as English translations from the FINLEX database (www.finlex.fi). These unofficial translations are in fact rather scarce.

Finland, state tax must be governed by an Act which prescribes provisions on the grounds for tax liability and the amount of tax payable. Tax Acts must also contain rules and legal remedies which are available for such persons or legal entities as are liable to taxation (CA section 81). The system of tax Acts goes back to the Swedish era; it is very much an old constitutional tradition in Sweden (thus also in Finland) that the people have the power to decide on taxes through their parliamentary representatives. Originally, the acceptance was given by four estates, and the Monarch was unable to order taxes by other means (eg decrees). Even today, the power to decide on taxes remains with the people, represented in Parliament. The power to decide on taxes by legislating Acts is an important portion of the constitutional finance power.

The power over the budget is used every year, ie one budgetary year at a time. The budget, which is not formally an Act, is published in the Statutes of Finland. The Government's proposal (*budjettiehdotus*) is submitted to Parliament well before the next budgetary year. The State's budget includes estimates of the annual revenues and appropriations for the State's annual expenditures. Importantly, the basis for the appropriations and other justifications must be included in the Budget. There is also a possibility, frequently used, for a supplementary Budget (*lisäbudjetti*), provided that there are justified reasons for amending the Budget. Now, even while the Budget is an important device for Parliament, two factors limit its practical significance: 1) majority coalitions can always defend their Budget proposals against any attack of the opposition no matter what reasons are presented, and 2) most of the contents concerning expenditure are in fact bound to certain purposes already before the Budget is made, so that much of it is just a formality.

The actual debate takes place within the Government coalition, not within Parliament which has de facto a very formal role in this. The Government coalition debates and discusses over budgetary questions and brings the negotiated outcome to Parliament, thus binding the coalition MPs before the parliamentary procedure is carried out. And yet, the public debates in Parliament offer a good chance for the opposition to challenge the policy of the Government and to criticise its policy choices as reflected in the budget.

Public Accounts and Financial Accountability

As already stated, along with its legislative role, exercising budgetary power is one of Parliament's basic tasks. Many times it is the use of this power that has a greater effect on society than the numerous Acts that Parliament passes. Now, Parliament exercises this power by approving the State budget, which outlines revenue and expenditure during the following year. However, the use of this power is closely connected with Parliament's ability to check public accounts and, in general, the State's financial accountability. Today, in practice, the role of the National Audit Office (*Valtiontalouden tarkastusvirasto*) is important. From a constitutional point of view, auditing is an important instrument which is directly connected with one of Parliament's key competences. The National Audit Office's role is constitutionally crucial because in fact it is Parliament's watchdog concerning public accounts and financial accountability. However, in national constitutional debate this financial dimension is surprisingly underrated, and academic constitutional experts especially tend to overlook it. Notwithstanding this, for anyone looking from the outside and trying to grasp the fundamentals of the Finnish constitutional system, it makes perfect sense to obtain a basic comprehension of this dimension too.

The formal constitutional position and tasks of the Office are prescribed in the Constitution Act (section 90) and they provide that the Office is an 'independent body affiliated with the Parliament; the National Audit Office exists to audit the financial management of the State and compliance with the budget'. The Constitution Act also stipulates that the 'Audit Committee and the National Audit Office have the right to receive information needed for the performance of their duties from public authorities and other entities that are subject to their control'. More detailed provisions concerning the Office are given in specific parliamentary Acts. These more detailed constitutional provisions are contained in two key Acts which are the Act on the National Audit Office and the Act on the Right of the State Audit Office to Audit Certain Credit Transfers between Finland and the EU.[17] As to their substance they are part of constitutional law.

---

[17] Act on the National Audit Office (*Laki valtiontalouden tarkastusvirastosta*, 676/2000) and the Act on the Right of the State Audit Office to Audit Certain Credit Transfers between Finland and the EC (*Laki valtiontalouden tarkastusviraston oikeudesta tarkastaa eräitä Suomen ja Euroopan yhteisöjen välisiä varainsiirtoja*, 353/1995).

National Audit Office: Parliament's Financial Watchdog

The National Audit Office is historically the key financial monitoring organ in Finland. It plays a significant role in the parliamentary supervision of the Government and the whole executive machinery of public power. Its constitutional roots go far back. In fact, it is the oldest Finnish State institution responsible for auditing the Government's financial management and the State economy. The history of the Office goes back all the way to 1695. It was then when an independent body was set up to monitor financial administration under the Swedish Crown. However, even though the history of this body may be traced back to Swedish rule, it must be said that in practice the genuine forerunner of the Audit Office was established in 1824 as a part of the Financial Department of the Finnish Senate. During the era of the Grand Duchy under the Russian Empire, and in the early years of independence, state audit activities remained largely unchanged. The *modus operandi* assumed during the 1800s meant in practice concentrating on numerical audits of Government accounts and narrowly understood legality of public administration. The constitutional foundation for the present dual system of external supervision and auditing of state finances was created by the Form of Government in 1919. The Audit Office started to function within the Ministry of Finance in 1924.

In the next phase, after World War II, legislation was passed in 1947 which reformed the State audit system; the National Audit Office started to operate in a reformed shape in 1948. The latest reform removed the Office from the Ministry of Finance. In 2001, the Office started to operate in connection with the Parliament. It is of importance to grasp that even though the Office is situated within Parliament, it is in fact an independent and neutral public expert body. In accordance, it cannot be regarded as a mere instrument of Parliament even while it certainly may be regarded as its financial watchdog, having constitutional significance. The Office's prime task is to audit the legality and propriety of the State's financial management and specifically its compliance with the State Budget. While doing this, the Office also seeks to provide reliable information concerning the State's financial management, compliance with the Budget and administrative activities for Parliament, the Government and also the lower levels of public administration.

In a broad sense, the Office also has undeniable democratic legitimacy; it protects citizens' and taxpayers' interests by auditing the collection of state revenues, the use of state funds and the general management of state property. The idea is to promote economy, efficiency and in general effectiveness in state administration by conducting audits and other expert tasks connected with the control of financial management. As a result, in a broad sense the Office protects an important dimension of the Constitution.

While fulfilling its functions, the Office has certain specific competences including the right to obtain information which it requires to perform its task. Moreover, all state authorities and business enterprises must report any abuse of funds to the Office without delay. The Office is obliged to report improprieties to the appropriate body and it sees that any improprieties and shortcomings observed in audits are also corrected.

The organisation of the Office is rather simple. It is directed by the Auditor General (*pääjohtaja*), who is elected by Parliament for a term of six years. From the point of view of its constitutional function, the Office consists of two main elements, which are the Financial Audit Unit (*tilintarkastuksen toimintayksikkö*) and the Performance Audit Unit (*tuloksellisuustarkastuksen toimintayksikkö*). Besides these, there are also the Administrative and Communications Services Unit and Executive Management Support. The Office has today some 150 employees of which most are divided rather evenly between the two main units. The Financial Audit Unit performs audits and related expert activities in order to ensure compliance with the State Budget and the provision of correct and adequate annual accounts by the State and its agencies. This unit also promotes the exercise of the Parliament's budgetary power, proper arranging of internal control, and application of good financial management principles and effectiveness of administration. These are economic dimensions of modern constitutionalism not confined to narrow legality.

In its turn, the Performance Audit Unit produces fresh information on the effectiveness of administration and compliance with regulations and the principles of good governance, which is also an important constitutional right (see later in chapter seven). This unit struggles to fulfil the various information needs of the Parliament and central public administration but also of citizens by assessing the economy, efficiency and effectiveness of the management of tasks, reliability and adequacy of external information regarding results, setting of objectives and their grounds, efficiency of control, monitoring and evaluation systems. Besides these, the Performance Audit Unit deals in general with the legality of the management of tasks and compliance with objectives and compliance with the State Budget.

The Office's scope and watchdog-competences cover the Government and ministries, state agencies, funds outside the State budget, state business enterprises and state-owned companies, state grants and aids to local authorities, enterprises and other organisations and the transfer of funds between Finland and the European Union. However, the Office does not audit the Parliament's finances, funds under Parliament's control, the Bank of Finland (*Suomen pankki*) and the Social Insurance Institution (*Kansaneläkelaitos*). These constitutionally curious entities are controlled by other means.

In the Constitutional Shadow-land: the Bank of Finland and Social Insurance Institution

The Bank of Finland was originally established in 1811 as a public office under the supervision of the Economic Division of the Senate (*Senaatin talousosasto*). This makes it one of the oldest central banks in Europe. One may well assume that the endurance of this institution can be explained possibly because of its old age: it has become a part of the traditional Finnish constitutional landscape, an institution in itself having a place in the hearts and minds of politicians and lawyers alike. Now, according to the Constitution Act (section 91), the Bank of Finland ought to operate 'under the guarantee and supervision of the Parliament' as provided by a separate Act.[18] Parliament elects the Bank's governors in order to supervise the operations of the Bank. However, in fact it is hard to claim that Parliament would genuinely supervise the Bank, because in practice most of the regulation concerning the Bank does not originate from Parliament but from the European Central Bank which is situated in Frankfurt.

From the point of view of constitutional reality, European integration had already in the late 1990s bypassed national legislation on this matter, constitutional or otherwise. As Jyränki has described, the written text of the Constitution Act concerning the Bank is 'without meaning-

---

[18] Act on the Bank of Finland (*Laki Suomen pankista* 214/1998). According to this Act, the Bank is the central bank of Finland and an independent institution governed by public law but the Bank also acts as part of the European System of Central Banks (section 1).

ful content': it does not really mean what it says.[19] Indeed, the Treaty on European Union demands independence from national governments and parliaments as well as from the Union itself. Perhaps only constitutional conservatism prevented section 91 of the Constitution Act from being re-written in 2000, thus, leaving a visible gap between constitutional reality and codified rule.

The Social Insurance Institution (mostly known by its abbreviation KELA) is a large body situated in the area of indirect public administration, but because it uses the State's power it is included within the constitutional sphere of 'exercising public power'. So, the Institution functions under the supervision of the Parliament. In practice this means that the administration and operations are supervised by 12 trustees (*valtuutetut*) appointed by Parliament and eight auditors chosen by the trustees. In addition, the Institution has also a 10-member Board of Directors that manages and develops its operations. Parliament-chosen trustees approve the financial statements and accounting principles based on the recommendation of the Board of Directors, and issue decisions on releasing the Board from liability. The trustees also submit a report on their operations to Parliament annually. Even though the Constitution Act indirectly deals also with the administration of the Institution in practice, the precise legal position, actual responsibilities and administration of the Institution are stipulated in an Act on the Social Insurance Institution.[20]

Basically, the Institution's responsibilities concern the area of social protection which is defined in a range of Acts of Parliament concerning specific benefits. Standard situations in which customers contact the Institution deal with childbirth, study, sickness, unemployment and retirement. From a constitutional point of view, we may note that in practice the possibilities of the trustees to really supervise this huge administrative body are somewhat limited. And yet, the fact that Parliament chooses the trustees and provides them with certain functions gives at least a semi-constitutional status to the whole Institution. From an organisational point of view, the Institution is quite removed from other branches of governmental power. Yet, it also has another constitutional dimension: it fulfils certain constitutional economic and social rights obligations through its activities.

[19] A Jyränki, *Uusi perustuslakimme* ['*Our New Constitution Act*'] (Iura Nova, Turku, 2000) 198.
[20] *Laki kansaneläkelaitoksesta* (731/2001).

Parliament and Broadcasting

Freedom of expression is a key element of modern constitutional democracy. It is also a protected constitutional right (see chapter seven). In Finland this constitutional right contains the right to express, disseminate and receive information, opinions and other communication without censorship. Basically, this right covers all forms of media. In contemporary constitutionalism the role of the media is important: it can offer a healthy democratic counterweight to public power. It is for this reason that we need to say something about the constitutionally interesting role of the 'Finnish BBC', ie Finnish Broadcasting Company (*Yleisradio*, most commonly known by the abbreviation *YLE*). The Company is 99.9 per cent state-owned and supervised by an Administrative Council appointed by Parliament, and operates under the Act on Finnish Broadcasting Company.[21] According to this Act, the State must own and control at least 70 per cent of the share capital of the Company and of the votes generated by all the shares in the Company. The Company's task is to be responsible for the provision of comprehensive television and radio programming with the related additional and extra services for all citizens under equal conditions. So, there is clearly an element of democracy involved here.

The Company has a constitutional dimension through Parliament: the Company has an Administrative Council which consists of 21 members. These members of the Administrative Council are elected by Parliament in its first session of the parliamentary term. Members must include representatives from the fields of science, the arts, education, business and economics, as well as different groups based on age, mother tongue (Finnish, Swedish, Sámi) and area of residence. The profile of YLE differs from those broadcasting companies with a clear commercial profile: YLE produces more news and documentaries and other such programmes which are generally regarded as useful and lacking clear commercial interests. The Act on YLE holds it responsible for the provision of comprehensive television and radio programming aimed at all citizens under equal conditions. In general this public service includes, in particular, support for democracy and an opportunity for society to participate by offering a wide variety of information, opinions and debates. Furthermore, the educational aspects must be taken into account in the programming (Act on YLE section 7).

---

[21] *Laki yleisradiosta* (1380/1993).

Controversial Role of National Referendum

Some rather recent constitutional ideas have proved difficult to incorporate into a system with roots in a parliamentary-type of democracy and indirect popular sovereignty. The question that deals with other forms of democracy and especially direct democracy is one of those: how to inject direct democracy into the parliamentary system? This question has exceptional relevance in the Finnish scene: 'Finland has always been state-centred society, in which most organisations have been contacted with the machinery of the State', as Kauko Sipponen, a former Professor, high civil servant and a long time constitutional expert, has described.[22] The basis of his critical remark is the fact that in Finland there has been very little expression of the idea of a true counter-force to state-centred power. It has been paradigmatic to conceive constitutional democracy primarily as parliamentary-channelled democracy without direct plebiscite decision-making.

Basically, the Finnish Constitution transforms the will of the people into forms of institutions and functions by using elections which are based on the principle of proportional representation. This same idea is followed in all constitutionally important elections (Parliament, President, local government, Euro-Parliament). Notwithstanding this, the Constitution Act also makes stipulation with regard to referenda which are as to their nature merely consultative or advice-giving (*neuvoa-antava*), not constitutionally binding or decisive. The wording of section 53 is very sparse and only states that the 'decision to organise a consultative referendum (*kansanäänestys*, literally 'peoples vote') is made by an Act'.[23] This Act must contain provisions concerning the time of the referendum and the choice which is presented to the voters. So, the use of this instrument of direct democracy is at the mercy of MPs.

The national consultative referendum was for the first time included in the constitutional system in 1987 when a specific section containing the core of this institution was inserted into the 1919 Form of Government. The written formulations in 1987 and in 2000 are similar, so in the full reform of the Constitution Act the referendum was not changed as to

---

[22] K Sipponen, *Citizen—Master or Servant?* ['*Kansalainen—isäntä vai renki?*'] (WSOY, Helsinki, 2000) 34.

[23] There is also the possibility to organise a local consultative referendum. This is not dealt with here. For a comparative view see M Sutela, 'Comparative Aspects of Local Direct Democracy' (2001) 7 *European Public Law* 651.

its foundations. However, even before 1987 it was deemed to be constitutionally possible to organise a consultative referendum by means of an ordinary parliamentary Act.[24] In this sense the 1987 reform only transformed previous constitutional customary law (or at least a common understanding) into codified written law. In 1987, a specific Act concerning the Procedure on Consultative Referenda was enacted. This normal parliamentary Act, of material constitutional nature, stipulates in a detailed manner how consultative referenda must be organised.[25] However, this Act is general and it does not make stipulation with regard to each individual type of referendum, only on the general conduct of a referendum.

Basically, it is the State that must inform the voters of the alternatives which are to be presented to them. Further, the State must also support the dissemination of information relating to the alternatives in the referendum. Even though the Finnish Constitution contains the instrument of referendum, it must be understood that it is not an alteration in the established division of powers or in other constitutional decision-making structures. What was originally aimed at was to supplement representative democracy by allowing citizens to express their opinion and to partially participate in decision-making. This was intended, however, to take place in such a manner that the constitutional authority and political responsibility of the elected organs would not be compromised.

Indeed, quintessential constitutional principles have weight here: representative democracy may be regarded as one of the leading Finnish constitutional ideas. In other words, the supremacy of the Parliament has been preserved: the Finnish political elite seem reluctant to give more room to direct democracy. The key idea has been and still is to preserve the use of referendum under the control of the Parliament which decides if and when referenda are going to be held.

This kind of national referendum has been held only once in Finland. This took place in October 1994 and it concerned the question of Finnish membership of the European Union. This referendum had only two alternatives: yes/no. The result of the referendum was favour-

---

[24] In 1931, a consultative referendum was held concerning the highly unpopular Prohibition Act of Alcohol (so-called *kieltolaki*), which was abandoned because of the outcome of the referendum. This was done without a specific section in the Form of Government, and a normal parliamentary Act (340/1931) was used instead. Besides, also the much later statement of the authoritative Constitutional Law Committee (PeVM 3/1994) considered the referendum, although, not binding as such so that it should have important meaning in parliamentary procedure.

[25] *Laki menettelystä neuvoa-antavissa kansanäänestyksissä* (571/1987).

able to membership (56.9 per cent voted for the yes option, 43.1 per cent against).[26] It was of specific constitutional interest to define the true nature of the EU referendum because, strictly from the point of view of written constitutional law, the referendum was not binding. In Parliament, after the referendum, the yes decision was reached in a vote 152–45. Judging by the numbers in Parliament, one may find support for the idea of de facto constitutional bindingness of this referendum. Accordingly, in terms of the living Constitution, the outcome was regarded largely as psychologically binding. Of course, from the point of view of individual members of the Finnish Parliament, this was problematic because it was Parliament that was responsible for making the final decision and the referendum had nothing more than persuasive constitutional power. Curiously, this referendum concerned only the possible accession to the European Union but nothing was asked concerning the changing of the Constitution (which was sure to follow).

From a general point of view, it is largely regarded in Finland that the referendum instrument should be retained as a kind of back-up possibility. However, most of the experts and other concerned parties seem to think that it is of the utmost importance to give special consideration to two questions: how the alternatives are presented to the voters, and what kind of constitutional significance should be given to the result of the referendum. In sum, the consultative referendum is a part of the Finnish Constitution but it is regarded with a certain suspicion because it does not really fit into the system of representative democracy.[27] And yet, most would keep this possibility for such special occasions like EU membership or possible membership of the *North Atlantic Treaty Organisation* (NATO). As of now, the referendum may be regarded as a constitutional appendix which does not seem to have a proper place in the constitutional framework.

However, it is quite likely than in the future the significance of the referendum may grow, but this seems to be a slow process because of political and constitutional inertia. The younger generation seems to be more open to the idea of stronger elements of direct democracy. Of political parties, however, only the Green League has consistently supported elements of direct democracy. In the discussions of 2008–2010 concerning the reform of the Constitution, the issue of referendum was

---

[26] The percentage of those taking part was 70.8%.

[27] See M Suksi, 'The People as the Advisor' in Hollo (ed), *Finnish Legal System and Recent Development* (Edita, Helsinki, 2006) 177–200.

once again on the agenda of the Government coalition. The Committee for Checking of the Constitution proposed in February 2010 that popular initiative should be made possible in the future if 50000 voters make such a motion. However, the nature of the referendum would not be changed: it would still remain consultative only.[28]

Parliament and the Control of Constitutionality

In most countries, it is the courts not the legislator that takes care of the constitutionality of Acts, but this is not the case in Finland. Once again, to understand the present system one must look back to the past. According to the earlier system applied in most part of the twentieth century, courts and other public authorities had no legal competence to review the constitutionality of parliamentary Acts; however, such control concerning norms lower than parliamentary Acts was allowed. The emphasis on control was solely located on the preventive and abstract norm-control executed by one standing committee of the Parliament, the Committee for Constitutional Law (*Perustuslakivaliokunta* (PeV)). From the point of view of comparative constitutional law, Finland basically adheres to the system of preventive, centralised and abstract form of control, where the main controlling organ is not a court of law, not even a special constitutional court.[29]

Already in 1882 a legislative initiative was sent to a special Committee of the Diet of the Estates in order to receive an opinion concerning the constitutionality of the bill. The Committee (then the Legislative Committee, ie *lakivaliokunta*) declared that its review was carried out strictly from the point of view of constitutional law. Later, this declaration was to become a crucial part of the Finnish constitutional landscape. The cunning idea was to make the control of constitutionality an internal affair of the Grand Duchy and, thus, keep it out of Russian hands. In 1906 a new Diet Act transformed the Legislative Committee into a special Committee for Constitutional Law which inherited the role of interpreter of the Constitution, although this role was based on practice and had no direct basis in the wording of constitutional documents. Independence changed surprisingly little in this respect. The

---

[28] *Perustuslain tarkistamiskomitean mietintö* (*Komiteanmietintö* 2010:9).

[29] See J Husa, 'Guarding the Constitutionality of Laws in Nordic Countries' (2000) 48 *American Journal of Comparative Law* 345.

most important development took place in the 1920s when the practice of listening to outside experts became an accepted *modus operandi.*

According to the 1919 Form of Government, a public authority could not apply a lower regulation, ie decree (*asetus*) which was incompatible with a parliamentary Act or the Constitution. No authority had the formal or even informal competence to observe the constitutionality of a parliamentary Act after it had been ratified by the President. Notwithstanding this, there was some scholarly opposition (notably from Paavo Kastari) claiming that courts should have the right to leave an Act unapplied, when the conflict situation would have been deemed indisputable or obviously beyond doubt (as in the Danish model). It was allegedly assumed by hesitant *doctorum opinio* that an Act which would have been 'manifestly and beyond any doubt whatsoever' contrary to the Constitution should not be applied. This doctrine was never realised, unlike in Denmark in 1999 in the *Tvind* case, yet at the beginning of the 1990s it started to gain more impetus because Finland ratified the ECHR.[30]

In practice, control was concentrated in the Constitutional Law Committee, which controlled the legislative process of bills for new Acts and gave authoritative opinions to other committees of the Parliament and, if necessary, on request to the Speaker of Parliament, concerning whether the legislative process regarding the draft bill was correct. The proceedings were formally based—after the reform of constitutional rights in 1995—on the Parliamentary Procedure Act, section 46, according to which the task of the Constitutional Law Committee was to deliver authoritative opinions about the constitutionality of Government bills and a bill's relation to international human rights. Before 1995 the system was mainly based on constitutional customary rule, but after the reform of 2000 the function of the Committee is also defined in writing in the Constitution Act. Nonetheless, this system has not changed institutionally at any significant rate.

Authoritative Interpretation through Statements

The Committee issues statements or opinions on the constitutionality of legislative proposals and other matters brought for its consideration, as well as in relation to international human rights treaties. Statements

---

[30] In 1996, an Act was passed cutting public funding from Tvind schools and barring any challenge to this decision legally. In 1999, the Danish Supreme Court judged that the Act was unconstitutional; it violated the separation of powers.

(*Perustuslakivaliokunnan lausunto* (PeVL)) made by the Constitutional Law Committee are in practice authoritative interpretations concerning the substantive content of the Constitution. The opinions, outlining the living Constitution, are constitutionally binding in compliance with customary constitutional law, ie by the nature of constitutional convention the statements of the Committee are considered as binding during the legislative process: no codified rule expresses this. The interpretations of the Committee are transmitted as normative standpoints in connection with legislative arrangements, and if the draft bill is considered constitutional it can be legislated in the normal order of enactment. If the draft bill law contains contradictions with the Constitution Act, the Constitutional Law Committee can propose a change so that the controversy is removed or suggest that the law should be legislated in the same order as the Constitution Act.

The Constitutional Law Committee can also approve a draft bill that is suspected as being constitutionally controversial; to be legislated in the normal order of enactment, but it is then presumed that the courts and other authorities *must* interpret the law in conformity with the Constitution. Under the law-in-action doctrine of the sources of law, the interpretations made by the Constitutional Law Committee are of considerable importance when courts seek to avoid controversy through interpretation.[31] Also, when estimating the quality of a controversy in a possible conflict situation between an ordinary Act and Constitutional Law, the Committee's statements are given considerable importance; at least this has been the case up to the present day.

Besides the Constitutional Law Committee, both the Speaker of the Parliament, the Chancellor of Justice and the President (at the ratifying stage) were and are able to control the constitutionality of the bills. However, the most authoritative nucleus of the control was and is de facto concentrated in the Constitutional Law Committee. So, it makes sense to ask what really changed in 2000 with the new Constitution Act concerning the institutional position of the Constitutional Law Committee.

Reformation of 2000—To change or Not to Change?

The reform did not change the institutional features concerning control of constitutionality; nevertheless, it included one novelty. Today,

---

[31] See eg, Supreme Court case 2006:71 in which the Court relied heavily on the statements of the Committee in a complicated tort case.

the Constitution Act's section 106 enables limited judicial review of the constitutionality of parliamentary acts. The written rule allows rejection to apply to a provision of an act, where the application of the provision would result in a clear contradiction (*ilmeinen ristiriita*) with the Constitution.[32] This innovation was not truly a national innovation but rather a constitutional transplant from Sweden. The Finnish model is a modified transplant from the Swedish system (close to Danish doctrine also) with one significant exception: limited review of constitutionality is possible only in courts, not in other public organs.[33] Section 106 of the Constitution Act complemented the preventive and abstract control-model so that the emphasis of the control is still preserved in the advance control done in conjunction with the legislative process of the Parliament. This outcome was clearly a compromise between international pressures pushing towards clearer judicial review and Finnish traditional reluctance against judicial review of parliamentary legislation.

Under the present system, the control exercised by the Constitutional Law Committee is centralised to safeguarding the *correct legislative procedure*, so attention is paid mainly to the formal constitutionality, whereas the substantive constitutionality has been left as a subordinate part. The interpretations of the Committee are considerably influenced—according to established custom—by the opinions of the constitutional experts, which, if they have consensual opinion, are principally followed.[34] The fact is that the Committee does not systematically give statements about all bills, neither can the controlled bills be independently chosen by the Committee. Attention is paid, only, to those bills, of which the relation to the Constitution Act is conceived as problematical and the question of unconstitutionality cannot be answered simply by leaning on the Constitutional Law Committee's earlier praxis. In practice, interpretations made by the Committee, which have been mostly linked to protection of property, are highly respected and the source-of-law-position of opinions of the Constitutional Law Committee is even

[32] The exact wording says that 'If in a matter being tried by a court of law, the application of an Act would be in evident conflict with the Constitution Act, the court of law shall give primacy to the provision in the Constitution Act.'

[33] See J Husa, *Nordic Reflections on Constitutional Law* (Peter Lange, Frankfurt am Main, 2002) ch 5.

[34] Also, the practice of hearing from constitutional experts (mainly public law professors) must also be regarded as constitutional custom having a practically binding force. See M Scheinin, 'Constitutional Law and Human Rights' in J Pöyhönen (ed), *An Introduction to Finnish Law* (Kauppakaari, Helsinki, 2002) 40–41.

considered equal to that of a constitutional court. However, from time to time there has been occasional criticism against the Constitutional Law Committee's role. Also, it is interesting to note that in 2001 the Supreme Court challenged for the first time, although indirectly, the supremacy of the Constitutional Law Committee in the area of a priori constitutionality control in the so-called Åland-saga. On July 2001, President Halonen decided not to ratify the proposed Gambling Act. The Act would have banned Finnish money-lenders from gambling at the internet site maintained by the Ålandic Slot Machine Association. The President asked the Supreme Court to investigate whether the Act would be in conflict with the autonomy of the Åland Islands. On August 2001, the Supreme Court stated that the Gambling Act was not compatible with the Constitution even while the Constitutional Law Committee had accepted the Gambling Act in its own review.[35]

Previously, the occasions in which constitutional rights were to be applied involved predominantly the protection of property rights. This, again, may be at least partially traced back to the victory of Whites in 1918: the idea of protection of property against any public infringement was boosted because of the fear of the potentially radical political left. However, when the constitutional rights system was completely reformed in 1995 there was some kind of expansion of constitutional rights which reached almost every sector of legislation. After the 1995 reform, the Constitutional Law Committee has gradually taken on more of a role as a controller of the substantive constitutionality, too.

The Constitutional Law Committee has put into use the principle of 'Constitutional Rights Conformity Rule of Interpretation' (*perusoikeusmyönteinen laintulkinta*) which is set forth in its influential Report 25/1994. The idea is to choose from the legally possible interpretations the one which best enhances the intention of constitutional right(s) and eliminates those interpretations which could be seen as colliding with the intention of constitutional right(s). While estimating the nature of a contradiction, opinions are given considerable importance. This has been proved in the case law by the supreme courts in a handful of cases

---

[35] Formally Supreme Court did not evaluate in its statement (*lausunto* 29 August 2001, OH 2001/68) the constitutionality of the bill (HE 197/1999) on the President's request, but its incompatibility with the semi-constitutional Autonomy Act of Åland (1144/1991). The Supreme Court's statement was not de jure binding the President or Parliament, but its de facto effect was that it actually 'overruled' the Constitutional Law Committee's interpretation (PeVL 22/2001).

where the Constitution Act section 106's right to overrule parliamentary Act has been used.[36] Most of these cases have received markedly critical reception from public law specialists on the basis of poor constitutional reasoning. Actually, largely because of this critique, in 2008–2009 the Ministry of Justice started to ponder over the possibility of eradicating the criterion of obviousness.

In sum, compared with many other systems, the control of the constitutionality is different, because it is emphasised as being preventive, abstract, and it is moreover executed through the activity of the Parliament itself. This partly explains why there has been no political desire to change a proven and seemingly well functioning system; this basic model has been used from the end of the nineteenth century.[37] From a non-national comparative perspective, attention is drawn to the fact that the Constitutional Law Committee is de facto a quasi-judicial organ that uses legal discretion and argumentation in its interpretations. The strong emphasis on preventive control was, nevertheless, weakened by the present Constitution Act, in addition to which the membership of the European Union and ECHR increase the pressure for consolidation of the ex post facto court-control (ie standard constitutional judicial review) in the future. However, the traditional reluctance to change any of the inherent basic features of the Constitution sets obstacles for any significant growth of judicial activism. The institutional position of the Constitutional Law Committee seems quite secure as of now.

Constitutional Solitude?

In an EU context, Finland is a rare representative of such a control model, where the control power of the constitutionality of the Acts is mainly in the hands of the democratically-elected legislator. In a sense, the Finnish constitutional system has for a long time nurtured a deeply embedded Montesquieu-type suspicion toward the court's constitutional role. Moreover, Finland is one of the last representatives of a system, where the emphasis on a priori control lies with Parliament. So, the deci-

---

[36] For example, Supreme Court Case KKO 2004:24 and Supreme Administrative Court Case KHO 2008:25.

[37] See also V-P Hautamäki, 'The Question of Constitutional Court—On Its Relevance in the Nordic Context' in J Husa, K Nuotio, H Pihlajamäki (eds), *Nordic Law—Between Tradition and Dynamism* (Intersentia, Antwerp—Oxford, 2007) 153, 166–69.

sion-making power concerning constitutionality of Acts has been kept *within* the legislative body itself but today this tradition is under slowly growing criticism by constitutional lawyers, many of whom would like to see a stricter system of judicial constitutional review. The Committee has met recently growing critique from academic experts claiming that the Committee does not function properly anymore.

Pressures of a similar nature are felt elsewhere too. The French system was reformed in 2008 and now article 61-1 makes it possible to claim that legislative provision infringes constitutional rights, and, the matter may be referred to the *Conseil constitutionnel* by the *Conceil d'Etat* or Court of Cassation. Yet, the party cannot directly challenge the constitutionality of an Act; only a request to refer the case to the *Conseil* can be made. This model, though not similar, parallels the Finnish development of the 2000s: movement towards stronger judicial review.

However, there are still obvious counter-arguments familiar from other systems too: that courts are not directly accountable, judges being unelected; the capacity of the judiciary to undermine democratic decision-making; and the lack of constitutional expertise of standard judges.[38] Up until now Finland has signalled typical Nordic resilience in its willingness to reject the expansion of judicial power within the area of constitutional law.[39] This proves that Finland is not free of the more general trend of the last 20 years in constitutional law globally, in which the transfer of power from representative institutions to judiciaries has taken place.[40]

CONCLUSION

The Finnish Parliament does not differ from typical legislatures of parliamentary system. It uses legislative power and also decides on financial matters. All that can be said is that during the last 30 years the parliamentary features have been strengthened and this trend seems to continue. Simultaneously, the role of Government has also grown because it leans on the political support of parliamentary majority. On the other hand

---

[38]   *cf* P Leyland, *The Constitution of the United Kingdom* (Hart, Oxford, 2007) 182.

[39]   See also A Follesdal and M Wind, 'Introduction—Nordic Reluctance towards Judicial Review under Siege' (2009) 27 *Nordic Journal of Human Rights* 131.

[40]   R Hirschl, *Towards Juristocracy—The Origins and Consequences of the New Constitutionalism* (Harvard University Press, Cambridge Mass, 2004) 211–23.

the significance of the President has gone downwards even while presidents enjoy greater popularity than prime ministers. However, in some sense the Parliament has also lost some of its earlier powers. Alongside strengthening parliamentary features, constitutional judicial review has started to gain more legal-cultural ground.

Waves of the new judicially-oriented constitutionalism have reached the shores of Finland. The system of constitutional control of laws seems to be very slowly moving away from the legislator toward the courts of law. In this sense Finnish constitutional culture appears to be losing some of its traditional character as it gets closer to continental European constitutional models. Nonetheless, the system contains certain special features which are rather unusual in a comparative perspective: constitutional control of Acts and the resulting special role of the Constitutional Law Committee of Parliament. Also, the remaining small role of the referendum seems to prove a certain sustained constitutional mentality regarding the Parliament as the primary organ within the field of the Constitution.

FURTHER READING

Jyränki, A, 'Die neue Verfassung Finnlands'. *Zeitschrift für öffentliches Recht* 56 (2001) 113–127.

Jääskinen, N and Kivisaari, T, 'Parliamentary Scrutiny of European Union Affairs in Finland' in M Wiberg (ed), *Trying to Make Democracy Work—Nordic Parliaments and the European Union* (Gidlunds, Stockholm, 1997) 29–47.

Länsineva, P, 'The Constitutional Committee of Parliament: the Finnish Model of Norm Control' in M Sakslin (ed), *The Finnish Constitution in Transition* (The Finnish Society of Constitutional Law, Helsinki, 1991) 68–80.

Nousiainen, J, 'The Finnish System of Government: From Mixed Constitution to Parliamentarism' in *The Constitution of Finland* (Parliament of Finland, Vammala, 2001) 5–42.

Raunio, T and Wiberg, M, 'Finland: Polarized Pluralism in the Shadow of a Strong President' in K Strom, WC Müller and T Bergman (eds), *Delegation and Accountability in Parliamentary Democracies* (Oxford University Press, Oxford 2003) 301–24.

Saraviita, I, *Finland—Constitutional Law*: International Encyclopedia of Laws (Kluwer, Alphen, 2009).

Suksi, M, *Bringing in the People: A Comparison of the Constitutional Forms and Practices of the Referendum* (Martinus Nijhoff, Dordrecht, 1993).

Sundberg, J, 'The Electoral System of Finland: Old and Working Well' in B Grofman and A Lijphart (eds), *The Evolution of Electoral and Party Systems in the Nordic Countries* (Agathon Press, New York, 2002) 67–92.

Sutela, M, Comparative Aspects of Local Direct Democracy: The Municipal Referendum in Finland, Sweden, Germany and Switzerland (2001) 7 *European Public Law* 651–70.

WEBSITES

All of the following websites also contain information in English.

www.eduskunta.fi [Parliament's official website].
www.virtual.finland.fi/politics_society/ [General information of Finland and useful links].
www.vtt.fi [National Audit Office's official website].
www.sp.fi [Bank of Finland's official website].
www.kela.fi [Social Insurance Institution's official website].

4

Executive Power

———➤•◦◄———

Introduction – Government – President – Conclusion

INTRODUCTION

Executive power in Finland is divided into two organs which are using this constitutional competence. In this sense the system of government is dualistic: the focal question is how the power is divided between these organs. This chapter examines the roles of the Government and the President of the Republic. These have been and still are the institutions which sit at the heart of Finnish constitutional debates. In consequence, particular attention is devoted to discussing the relationship between these two top institutions wielding executive power.

GOVERNMENT

Historically, the Government in Finland is a high state organ that originates from the era of the Grand Duchy and it was first established in 1809 to oversee the central administration in Finland. To be more precise, the Government's predecessor was the Economic Division (*Talousosasto*) of the Senate, containing subordinate administrative departments which were, of course, the predecessors of today's ministries. However, during the Russian period governmental power was actually wielded by two organs of which the Finnish Senate was only one, ie the 'national' user of executive power. The other half of this power was in the hands of the Committee of Finnish Affairs in St Petersburg (1811–26). Obviously the Senate used its power which was actually delegated to it by the Russian Czar. Hence, during the Russian period the ultimate source of public power was the Emperor Czar himself. Later, a new organ called the Office of Secretary of State (*Valtiosihteerinvirasto*) was established to deal with Finnish affairs in St Petersburg.

When the system was reformed during 1917–19, the old system served as a basis from which the central administration of the independent state was also constructed. Senators became ministers. As a matter of fact, surprisingly little was changed even though novel separate ministries for things such as defence and foreign relations were needed. In the Grand Duchy, these branches were taken care of by Imperial Russia. Again, this pragmatism underlines the characteristic feature of Finnish constitutional culture which contains a certain constitutional conservatism and a pragmatic will to preserve constitutional continuity even during times of drastic social and political change. Finnish constitutional thinking and mentality has always shown little enthusiasm for grand theories; instead the axiom 'if it is not broken do not fix it' has always been closely followed, if not outspokenly expressed.

Government and its Structure

To begin with, in the Finnish multi-party system all governments are multi-party coalitions with different political views, even though all the member-parties are committed to the Government Programme by persuasive constitutional custom. It is also useful to note that in this book Government refers first and foremost to the Prime Minister (PM)-led Council of State unless stated otherwise.

In the current Finnish system, the Government's powers and duties are only partially stipulated in the Constitution Act and regular Acts, and lower decrees. This is because the Government takes care not only of what is specifically provided by the Constitution Act but also various administrative duties which are not specifically attributed to the competence of the President or some other public authority. Finnish constitutional law regards the Government as having a general competency (*yleistoimivalta*) which is not enumerated in a detailed manner (see Constitution Act (CA) section 65.1). This, in turn, has a far-reaching constitutional effect strengthening the position of the Government in general. It is easier to say what the Government does not do than to say what it does. And vice versa, if it is not clearly stated anywhere then it is a duty of the Government coalition.

As so often in comparatively oriented international analysis, terminology produces some problems. Polysemia lurks behind every corner. The Finnish concept of Government, for example, may be understood in many ways. Even the Constitution Act of 2000 is quite unsystematic in its usage of the term. First, Government means the ministerial body which convenes for the general governing of the country, consisting of PMs and other ministers (formally Council of State, *valtioneuvosto*). Second, Government also refers to the larger decision-making body for various governmental and central administrative matters which covers not only the Government as a Cabinet of ministers but also ministries and their public officials. Third, the Constitution Act uses the concept of Government to also mean the combined organ consisting of the Council of the State and the President together.[1] So, this collegial body of ministers has two main dimensions: a) combined decision-making with the President (Presidential Session, *presidentin esittely*) in which decisions are based on ministerial presentations/reports, and b) Council of State decision-making (where the President has no role or presence) covering matters belonging to the wide area of governmental power. The Constitution Act does not stipulate in detail the number of the ministries, but just states that the 'Government has the requisite number of Ministries' (CA section 68.1). The number of ministries and other forms of organisation of the Government, as well as the distribution of matters, are more specifically laid down in other acts or decrees. The Openness Act concerns all of the Ministries.[2] According to this Act, all official documents shall be in the public domain unless specifically provided for in an Act.

Even though the ministries work under a coalition government, it is crucial to understand that the Government is certainly not without inner tensions: both political and bureaucratic. Often there are tensions, conflicts and even clashes over power and prestige between politicians but also between different ministries and their departments. A classical collision is the yearly one between the powerful Ministry of Finance (*Valtiovarainministeriö*) and such soft ministries as Education and Social Affairs and Health. Unsurprisingly, the main dispute is over money.

---

[1] For example, in section 70 of the Constitution Act it is said that the proposal for the enactment of an Act is initiated in Parliament through a Government bill (*hallituksen esitys*). This proposal is 'submitted by the Government'. Here, the concept of Government covers also the President.

[2] Act on the Openness of Government Activities (*Laki viranomaistoiminnan julkisuudesta* 621/1999).

In the Grand Duchy there were no ministries but small administrative departments which retained their administrative structure even after 1918. Currently, there are 12 ministries of which each one is mainly responsible for preparing administrative matters within their specified field of competence. The Ministry of Justice has the main responsibility of drafting legislation even though all ministries have their own smaller law-drafting departments. It is worth noting that constitutional legislation is prepared and drafted solely in the Ministry of Justice. Besides, each of the minister-led ministries has general responsibility for the proper functioning of administration in its field. Ministries have the following specified competency-areas, as the following table shows:

Ministries
Foreign Affairs
Justice
Interior
Defence
Finance
Education
Agriculture and Forestry
Transport and Communications
Employment and Economy
Social Affairs and Health
Environment
(PM's Office)

Besides, the PM's office is constitutionally equivalent to a ministry even though it does not have a specific defined administrative field; but it aids the PM in the work of directing governmental activities in general and overseeing such matters as are situated within the mandate of the whole Government. In addition, the PM's Office is considerably smaller than the actual ministries. However, politically and constitutionally, the PM's Office has a key function within the executive branch. Led by the PM personally, it is constitutionally a ministry which is responsible for the monitoring of the implementation of the Government coalition's political programme. It also assists the PM in the general management of Government functions, coordinates EU policy and handles issues which are related to the development of the European Union. The Office also seeks to promote cooperation not only within the Government coalition but in a more general sense between the various branches of public administration. In practical terms, it seeks to ensure that the activities of the PM and Government coalition in general are problem-free in all circumstances. For these reasons we may claim that the PM's Office plays a much greater constitutional role than its small size suggests.

Today, ministers may assign political state secretaries (*poliittinen valtiosihteeri*) to assist them or to act as substitutes for them in preparatory work. Political state secretaries have a limited term of office which covers no more than the minister's term of office. They are responsible to a minister, ie this position is based on the confidence of the minister. The political state secretary-system is a recent novelty, being introduced only in 2005.

Ministers have also their own political advisers who vacate the formal position of temporary public officials. The standard civil service is different from political staff. Within each of the ministries a permanent secretary (literally office chief or staff chief, ie *kansliapäällikkö*) is the most senior official in a ministry. An office chief's main task is to oversee the functioning of the whole ministry. It is crucial to underline that the position of *kansliapäällikkö* is not equivalent to that of political state secretary because an office chief is the highest civil servant in the ministry and not a political confidant of the minister. Normally, a permanent secretary directs and monitors the actual operations within the ministry and brings much needed continuity to the work of the Government. There are also other means by which to try to secure continuity and legality of government business. One of these is the Official Oath of Affirmation (*virkavala*) which all ministers must take before they can act in their posts as ministers. The Oath is judicial as to its nature and clearly stresses the legalistic dimensions of Finnish constitutional heritage. This Oath places judges and ministers formally in a similar legal position, although there are obvious differences too. Nevertheless, ministers are constitutionally more in *political responsibility* before the Parliament. Actual legal responsibility takes place only very rarely, the last occurrence was in 1993 (see chapter six).

Resignation of a Minister

It is not only strictly legal grounds which compel a minister to resign. Resignation due to losing political reliability has also taken place in the

2000s. In 2002, Minister of Culture Suvi Lindén resigned due to a controversy involving her participation in a decision to approve a state subsidy for the expansion of a golf course in which she was a shareholder. Even though it was not proven that she had committed an unlawful act, the political pressure became too strong to resist. However, this did not prevent her becoming an MP and a minister again. The latest resignations took place when the Minister of Foreign Affairs (Ilkka Kanerva) had to resign in 2008 due to sending SMS texts to an erotic dancer who sold these messages to a glossy magazine. Both of these ministers tried at first to defend themselves against public pressure, stating basically that, 'I have done nothing wrong and nothing explicitly against the law'.

All in all, ministerial responsibility on a political basis seems to be constitutionally imprecise. Yet, the constitutional rationale behind all this is clear and generally acknowledged: ministers as persons and as heads of their departments are responsible and answerable to Parliament and to the general public. These elements are today much more significant than they used to be some 20 years ago. However, these developments have also stirred criticism against the uncontrolled power of the media. However, on the other hand, top politicians themselves frequently seek to use the media when it fits their purposes. During the second Government coalition of PM Vanhanen (2007–2010), there were constant clashes between the media and the PM. Not surprisingly, these clashes have dealt with the PM's private life rather than politically or constitutionally significant questions. Actually, one of these ended up in court as a libel case in which the PM requested compensation from his former girlfriend.

PM and Government

It has been rightly stated recently that the 'PM has stepped out of the constitutional shadow of the President'.[3] Today, the PM is in an important position in the constitutional system. The nucleus for the PM took birth in the Russian period when the Governors-General were Russians and could not speak Swedish (or Finnish): the Governor's role as a chairman of the Senate was formal and minimal and in fact it was the Vice-Chairman of the Economic Division who took a more significant

---

[3] A Myllymäki, *Suomen pääministeri—valtiosääntövarjoista valoihin* ['*PM—from constitutional Shadow to the Light*'] (Talentum, Helsinki, 2010).

practical role in governing the Grand Duchy. From this rather modest position later grew a relatively weak PM, eventually becoming the strong PM of today.

Of the politically chosen ministers, the PM is the most important. The PM's position as the most senior originates from different sources: constitutional and political. One important reason for this is the fact that the PM is first elected (after a general Parliamentary election that is) and chosen directly by the Parliament and then formally nominated by the President. Other Ministers are appointed by the President to their posts in accordance with a specific proposal from the PM. Before this takes place different political parties must first negotiate on the Government programme (*hallitusohjelma*) and political composition of the Government. These negotiations form the background against which an internal election of the PM is held in Parliament. If the nominee gets more than half of the votes, then he or she is elected PM. This system leaves very little possibility for the President to intervene, although under certain special circumstances (when no majority coalition seems to emerge naturally) there is still some potential room for presidential influence. After the elections of 2003 and 2007 there was no presidential influence, but this possibility cannot be excluded completely.

In sharp contrast with earlier semi-presidentialism, the PM is formally and practically elected directly by the Parliament, not by the President. To step into office, the Government coalition needs a Parliament which is elemental in the formation of the Government. Normally, after a general parliamentary election, the leader of the major party regarded to be the winner of the election (according to practice this seems to mean the party with the largest number of seats) takes an active role in forming the next Government. Commonly, ministers are themselves Members of Parliament, but constitutional law is not clear on this, and from time to time coalitions also contain ministers that are not Members of Parliament. For example, in the Government coalition 2007–11 there was a minister (2007–09) who was not an MP, even though she was leader of the Green League during her time as a minister. No constitutional custom or rule requires the minister to be also an MP although this is usually commonplace.

The election procedure shortly described above provides the PM with the strongest political legitimacy within the Government. It is only in its first plenary session that the Government actually makes a decision concerning the division of labour between the ministers. The

Government Programme defines what the main tasks and policy guidelines are facing the incoming central administration. Generally speaking
the programme is a written and rather general plan of action agreed
by all the parties participating in the Government. For the actions of
the Government and Parliament it is a highly important, although not
a constitutionally-binding, document since it defines the lines of the
Government's policy during the electoral period (*vaalikausi*) before
the next general parliamentary election which is held every four years
(the latest of which took place in Spring 2007). In today's political culture governments sit in office a full four years, so the Government
Programme is of importance in multi-party coalitions as it ensures their
adequate inner political cohesion. In 2003, however, the first female PM,
Anneli Jäätteenmäki, was forced to resign because she lost the confidence of the Parliament after only two months in office (see later in this
chapter). However, the actual vote never took place because she resigned
before it. However, the coalition stayed intact after the Centre Party
reshuffled ministerial posts by lifting one of the ministers into the position of PM (Matti Vanhanen). Since other coalition members accepted
this reshuffle, there were no constitutional or political obstacles. Clearly,
a key factor is the trust of the parliamentary majority.

The PM's strong constitutional position is also derived from the
directing and oversight of government business in general. In these
functions are included the important monitoring and implementation
of the Government Programme and coordinating the preparation and
consideration of various issues that are decided in the European Union.
Perhaps most importantly, nonetheless, the PM is the political leader of
the Government which includes reconciling between differing views on
government policy, which are sure to appear. However, there are also non-
constitutional factors that explain the heightened position of the PM.[4]

From a more formal point of view we may also note that the President
of the Republic may dissolve Parliament, but only if there is a reasoned
request from the PM (CA section 26). Also, on the proposal of the PM
the President may accept the resignation of a minister. Even though the
majority of ministers stay for the whole four years, individual resignations do occasionally take place. In a more critical tone it must be said
that political accountability of individual ministers is not fully working in

---

[4] See H Paloheimo, 'The Rising Power of Prime Minister in Finland' (2003) 26
Scandinavian Political Studies 219.

the Finnish system because ministers are not necessarily MPs. From the point of view of a pure parliamentary system, this may be regarded as a blow against genuine constitutional executive accountability.

Making Decisions—Plenary and Committees

Some of the working habits from the Russian period exist even today, although of course they have been transformed. Formally, the Council of State makes decisions in bureaucratic plenary sessions which are chaired by the PM. However, as we will see later, this is only the formal side of the decision-making process. This rigid form of decision-making originates from the period of Russian rule and as to its nature it is formal and allows very little space for any true discussion: each item on the official agenda is presented and decided on the basis of a reporter (*esittelijä*) from the concerned ministry. This way of making decisions is manifestly outdated (as is well known by everyone), but once again the constitutional history explains its existence and survival. Legalistic and bureaucratic nineteenth century heritage is clearly reflected in the fact that each minister is legally responsible for any decision made unless expressed explicit objection has been entered into the formal minutes (CA section 60.2).

The *modus operandi* is based on the presentation of an official list (*esityslista*) distributed in advance, including draft decisions of the reporter who is always a civil servant. In practice, most decisions taken in plenary sessions merely provide a kind of official finishing touch or a rubber stamp. This is easy to understand when one takes into account that in each session some 40 matters are handled within a short period of time. However, in the practical workings of the Government, it is sub-organised into Cabinet committees (*ministerivaliokunta*) which play a more important role in the actual governmental decision-making. For the constitutional organisation and actual decision-making of the Government, the Cabinet committees play a crucial role. Importantly, there is not much legal regulation concerning these committees. This is explained by the fact that these committees do not make formal decisions in a legal sense.

Presently, there are four such committees which should all be chaired by the PM. These are the Committee on Foreign and Security Policy (presently chaired by the President Halonen; the Cabinet allowing her to do so), on European Union Affairs, for Finance and the Committee on Economic Policy. It is relevant to note that in the area of foreign policy power is divided between the Government and the President. The Constitution Act stipulates (section 93.1) that foreign policy 'is directed by the President of the Republic in cooperation with the Government'. In practice 'cooperation' (*yhteistoiminta*) has worked rather well, but since there are no constitutional means to resolve possible power-conflicts concerning foreign policy between these two institutions, there is always a potential danger for constitutional crisis. Moreover, there has been very little information coming to the public concerning the realities of this constitutionally forced cooperation; possible tensions are not generally known about outside the top political elite. During the old system, such a conflict actually arose in 1994 when Social Democrat President Ahtisaari took a firm stance against the Government in regards to the interpretation of presidential powers within the area of foreign policy.

Ahtisaari actually made a rare statement that was recorded to the official minutes (no 144/1994 para 3) of the Government. The President was keen to see EU matters as also belonging to the scope of foreign policy. After the Parliamentary elections, the problem went away as new PM (also a Social Democrat) Paavo Lipponen yielded to the President, whereas his predecessor Centre partisan Esko Aho (PM 1991–95) tended not to yield. Largely due to these happenings, section 93 was enacted in the Constitution Act (see later in this chapter). However, section 93 does not genuinely solve the problem should the President and Government- backed-up PM should really stand in conflict concerning EU representation. So, this problem still remains today (see also chapter nine).

Straight after the Constitution Act came formally into force in 2000 (the same day as President Halonen took office), the general feeling was that the dominant role of the Government in EU matters would turn the President into an opinion leader and representative figure rather than a political-decision maker. This parliamentary-centred constitutional vision has not been completely realised, even though the President's power has clearly diminished. A further aspect is the lack of a Vice-President: the PM is a substitute for the President should he or she be prevented from carrying out presidential duties (CA section 59). This is not the same as having a Vice-President but rather a system for substituting the President temporarily if genuine need arises. In a symbolic sense it seems to hint that the PM is ranked after the President.

Other Divisions

The abovementioned division of powers concerning foreign policy is shadowed by the fact that the Government is in principle using all the competencies when it comes to EU policy. It was one of the main motives behind the Constitution Act's institutional reforms to confirm division of competences between the President and the Government that had already taken place in the constitutional practice during the 1990s mainly due to Finnish EU Membership. Finnish constitutional law separates EU issues from the presidential competence concerning foreign affairs in the classical sense, and deals with EU matters as if they were domestic matters. This also explains why EU matters are regarded as being situated within the domain of the Government which has the general competence to govern the country: if EU matters are domestic in their nature, then the preparation and monitoring of these matters belongs to the Government coalition, and not to the President. Be that as it may, it has often proved arduous to define what remains within the scope of EU policy and what stays within traditional foreign policy.[5] Written constitutional law offers very little means by which to resolve this demarcation. What follows is constitutional practice which resolves this division created by the Constitution Act. Unfortunately, this question is anything but clear: the President and Government coalition seem to argue about this on some rare occasions even publicly.

There is something curious in this. Even though the Constitution Act was planned to enhance parliamentary dimensions, this traditional presidential power concerning foreign policy was not fully stripped away. In the main, constitutional experts and actors themselves seem to think that in the case of controversy the opinion of the President ought to be decisive. This hardly fits in with the long-time development of parliamentarism. To put it more dramatically, one might see here the effect of the Civil War and the desire to have 'strong power' in the form of the President casting his or her overshadowing figure upon today's constitutional life. Finnish governance has its deep roots in Swedish practices, which continued even after 1809. In the 1800s they were transformed by the help of German doctrines of public law brought to the country

---

[5] This is difficult even for the expert-organ which is the most authoritative interpreter of constitutional law in Finland, namely the Constitutional Law Committee of the Parliament (see later in this chapter). See Statements 54/2005 and 6/2006.

by certain high profile law professors. There was no particular relation-ship between Germany and Finland: academic lawyers simply went to German universities because German legal science was regarded to be most developed during that time. One thing led to another and Finnish constitutional lawyers (for example influential Robert F Hermanson 1846–1928) started to use what they learned from German doctrines of thinkers like Paul Laband (1838–1918) and applied these ideas creatively to the Finnish circumstances of that time.

When it comes to the Government coalition, ministers, except of course the PM, have a dual role in the system as they handle a remark-able number of issues within their ministries; but when it comes to more important or more principled questions the matters are decided on in the Government (ie Council of State) and the ministry in ques-tion merely provides the preparation for the basis of decision-making. This is different from the Grand Duchy where there was no ministe-rial model of government. The workings of government are partially based on written rules, by the Constitution Act, Government Rules of Procedure (*hallituksen työjärjestys*) and numerous separate decrees stipu-lating the workings of different ministries. Established practices are also followed where the written legal rules leave room.

Only the working of the stiff Government Plenary Session (*hal-lituksen täysistunto*) is densely regulated. The politically and practically more important Government Evening Session (*hallituksen iltakoulu*) and other extraordinary meetings are constitutionally less restricted in their functioning. Even though the formal decisions are made in the Plenary Session, it must be said that actual political decision-making and nego-tiating takes place on occasions which provide more freedom of pro-cedure and genuine discussion. Here we can see the characteristic dual nature of the Finnish Constitution: forms are followed to the detail, but within the rigid written forms the living Constitution has come up with various informal and unregulated means in governing the coun-try. By only reading the formal rules of written constitutional law the picture of the workings of the system would be poor and inadequate indeed. It is only in combination with the context, political culture, lim-ited amount of constitutionally relevant case law, and accompanying legal doctrine that comprehension of the constitutional system can be attained. However, does this not sound like UK constitutional law also? So, how can this fit to a non-common law and a non-monarchical state like Finland?

Even though British and Finnish constitutional law have obviously no formal or historical connections and they are situated within different constitutional-culture spheres, we may very well quote here FW Maitland when he struggled with trying to define constitutional law. Maitland stressed the importance of conventions and practice and said that a constitutional question could 'not be solved by appeal to authority'.[6] This fits just perfectly with the Finnish Constitution's institutional design concerning the executive power: there is no judicial organ to resolve possible constitutional power conflicts between high state organs. In this sense much of the constitutional law of Finland is not law at all in Hans Kelsen's narrow sense, ie in most cases there are no legal sanctions at all or other methods of enforcement in order to bend the constitutional actors to abide to the constitutional rules.[7] This does not, however, mean that constitutional arguments would be meaningless or without considerable weight. Typically, strong discontent against political actors by the media, public law experts and public opinion are in many cases the only sanctions that exist. For a legalist this may sound very odd indeed. In practice, nevertheless, these unofficial sanctions may have a huge constitutional impact; for example, strong public discontent may force a minister or high public official to resign. Strong and decisive public majority opinion may change the actions of the PM as well as that of the President: the constitutional sphere is constantly highlighted by the media.

Civil Service

The Finnish system follows particularism concerning employees of the public administration: there is a basic division between labour law and public law governing the civil service. The Constitution stresses the importance of public officials who exercise the State's public power; this is conceived as a key guarantee of ensuring the constitutionality and general legality of the use of public power. Civil servants have an important position in the working of the State and it is through their hands that

---

[6] FW Maitland, *The Constitutional History of England* (Cambridge University Press, Cambridge, 1908) 527.

[7] According to Kelsen's pure theory of law, the legal system is necessarily always based on enforcement; it is *Zwangsordnung*. See H Kelsen, *Reine Rechtslehre* (Verlag Österreich, Wien, 1960/2000) 34–59.

public power is actually used. No modern government functions without administrative machinery.

There is no general recruitment in Finland for civil service posts, nor does there exist a preferred school for the training of civil servants. There are no such elite institutions in Finland as the *École nationale d'administration* in France for instance. To be sure, a system in which the civil servants would come from only one or two top universities is quite unthinkable, and, there are no such institutions in Finland as the universities of Oxford and Cambridge in the United Kingdom. In most cases, the recruitment is done on an individual basis for a vacant or a newly created post which means that the recruiting system is open and competitive.

Normally, an applicable university degree is the only formal requirement. So, the examinations/degrees which are required are normal university examinations. Constitutional general qualifications for public office are very flexible: 'skill, ability and proven civic merit' (CA section 125). Of these, the last mentioned has very limited practical significance. From a general point of view we may say that the legalistic tradition and lawyers have previously dominated the public service and, perhaps even the whole civil service system. Today also a social science or political science background is very much typical for a civil servant. The overall qualification structure of the civil service is evidently higher than in the private sector. In fact, there are two to three times more university graduates in the public sector than there are in the private sector.

Those who are employed as civil servants enjoy a rather secure tenure in their posts. It is noteworthy that even top civil servants are not changed after elections: positions are normally stable. However, civil servants may be dismissed for poor performance or for disreputable behaviour on or off the job. During the 1970s there was a certain politicisation of public positions, especially concerning the highest positions. Today, however, only the very top positions are clearly political in the sense that political affiliations play a crucial role in the recruiting and nominating process. At the local governmental level the importance of politics is far greater than for State civil servants. In practice, the political reasons are not openly stated; thus, we may speak of 'hidden political appointments'. Yet, the Finnish civil service has a reputation for professional competence, and it enjoys legitimacy in the eyes of most citizens. Moreover, civil servants have played a strong role in Finland as a force which has defended the interest of individuals, sometimes even against the public interest of the State.

The Constitution Act (section 2) requires the civil service and any exercise of public powers to be based on statute law. This can be seen in various places. For example, ministers have to announce their own liabilities (for example ownership of corporation or membership of interest organisation) which might harm their status in the Council of the State. Similar types of regulations under the State Civil Service Act also concern the highest civil servants and executives.[8] Basically, legal principles and rules concerning the working of public officials have remained relatively unchanged for several decades. This tradition gives great weight to legal arguments and the constitutional points of view. For example, civil servants must provide public (in writing) argumentation for decisions. In most cases a large part of these arguments tends to be of a legal nature. Actually, the classical referendary or reporting system, in which the reporting civil servant researches the matter under scrutiny, presents alternative proposals and suggests a final proposal to the decision-makers, is still largely in use today.[9] Many of these features are still part of the working of civil servants especially in those parts of the State's administration which are situated close to the Government, ministries and central agencies. A certain bureaucratic legalism seems to linger in spite of various reforms toward more flexible public administration and such ideologies as so-called New Public Administration.

When the Finnish Senate began it had some 30 civil servants in 1810, and 100 years later there were still less than 100 officials. In the beginning of the 1980s the Government already had more than 4,000 civil servants, and in the middle of the 1990s there were more than 5,000 such officials. Today, the whole central administration of the State (which is much larger than the Government and its officials) employs some 120,000 persons in various duties, of which some 80,000 are civil servants in the legal sense. Yet, in practice the legal status and general terms of service of civil servants are very close to those of other public

---

[8]   *Virkamieslaki* (750/1994). This Act is aimed at ensuring that State responsibilities are carried out efficiently and justly. The Act also aims to ensure that the State's civil servants receive just treatment from their employers. This Act is complemented with the State Civil Servant Decree (*Valtion virkamiesasetus* 971/1994) which stipulates on State civil servants' duties, nominations, leaves and other similar things.

[9]   In the Finnish system of public administration and also in the judicial system, official decisions are made on the basis of written proposals. Referendary is an official whose duty it is to make independently written proposals for decision. If a minister makes a decision against the proposition, the civil servant may release himself from legal responsibility by writing a response. See also chapter six.

employees. During recent decades the trend has gone towards diminishing the amount of civil servants and the proportion of public workers, without the legal position of civil servants, has risen.[10] This trend is very likely going to continue in the coming years. However, not all public functions can be carried out by non-civil servants: if a public task includes a significant exercise of public power, then, such a task may only be carried out by public authorities (ie civil servants). When something is privatised, constitutional rights and other constitutional requirements of good governance (*hyvä hallinto*) may not be endangered (CA section 124). The term public authority in Finland includes all parts of the central administration and various different agencies, as well as local authorities whose position is based on statutory law.

Public Power and Liability

Finnish civil servants have been mostly neutral politically and loyal to the sitting government coalitions: legalism as a mental attitude has largely prevailed. Civil servants are held legally responsible for the lawfulness of actions; this includes such decisions as are made by an official multi-member body if the civil servant has supported the taken decision. Besides, a referendary is also held responsible for such decisions as are based upon his/her presentation unless he/she has not specifically filed an official objection to the decision (CA section 118.1). Obviously, the operations of public administration are always under judicial scrutiny when individuals make appeals to administrative courts. From time to time, prosecutors press charges against civil servants if they have committed crimes. In addition, there are normally always numerous lawsuits going on in general courts of law concerning questions such as contracts and torts in situations which are connected with civil servants and public administration. If cases do not end up in courts of law, the general overseers of legality have an important position in supervising the actions of civil servants and the administrative culture and spirit of constitutionalism more generally.

Both the Chancellor of Justice and the Parliamentary Ombudsman are expected to ensure that civil servants, public employees, and other

---

[10] A civil servant's position differs slightly from the position of worker. Basically, civil servants have a higher legal responsibility for their actions but also have a more secure employment relationship and independent position.

persons performing public functions observe the law and fulfil their legal obligations. These top organs share many duties even while there are some clear differences too (see chapter six). However, since these overseers of legality cannot clearly supervise effectively the vast machinery of public administration they, instead, concentrate on giving general signals to all public officials while they deal with individual complaints. Besides, the overseers of legality are not able to decide over tort compensation. In practice, tort questions are left completely to the courts of law.

There is also civil law responsibility if a private party has suffered a violation of rights or sustained a loss through an unlawful act or by an omission of a civil servant. Civil servants, besides being possibly punished under the rules of penal law, are also held liable for damages (CA section 118.2). However, there may also be other types of problems than those which are legally conceived. In the Tort Liability Act there are provisions which limit the liability of public authorities: liability normally arises in the exercise of public power only if the *modus operandi* used does not meet the requirements of reasonableness.[11] Previously, the tort law was far away from constitutional dimensions but today it is deemed largely that assessment of negligence of public authority is based not only on the Tort Act but also on the requirements of constitutional rights and European human rights: these rights may have an interpretative role when tort law is applied to the use of public power. In some cases, liability of public power may arise from the breach of EU law.[12]

Corruption

It has been said earlier that Finland adheres to the rule of law principle and that generally speaking it also acts according to the core ideas of constitutionalism. This seems to be also reflected in the area of the mentality of the civil service because corruption, the misuse of entrusted public power, seems so rare. First of all, the judiciary seems to be practically completely incorrupt; there are no cases on this at all. When it comes to civil servants, Finland has done well in international comparisons when it comes to corruption. Finnish civil servants have

[11] *Vahingonkorvauslaki* (412/1974).
[12] See Case C-5/94 *The Queen v Ministry of Agriculture, Fisheries and Food, ex p Hedley Lomas Ltd* [1996] ECR I-2553.

been found to take fewer bribes than their colleagues in most other countries. This seems to prove that public power and its officials are not corrupt. However, the truth may be more complex. Now, even though Finland has often been regarded as one of the least corrupt countries, it has been pointed out that Finland's impeccable record has been slightly tarnished as a consequence of a few bribery scandals that have surfaced in recent years.[13] From a constitutional point of view, in 2008 and 2009, a few embarrassing facts concerning the funding of political parties for elections were brought to light. This information became public and resulted in a debate about demanding the opening up of the funding system so that the funding of political parties would be more transparent.

However, it is possible that there are some forms of corruption which are difficult to study and to expose in public. The infamous 'Dear-Brothers' or 'Old-Boys' networks (*hyväveli verkostot*) are at the core of Finnish corruption, and yet, nobody seems to know precisely who these people are. Yet, it is crucial to understand that instead of cash in a brown envelope, the system instead produces something more subtle, as for example, honorary titles, jobs, and other ways of promoting a person's social esteem. So, it seems that Finnish small-scale corruption involves mainly covert social cooperation and debts of gratitude, rather than any blatant money exchanges. For example, in connection with the public debate on election and party funding, it became clear that private companies had paid considerable sums in support of the election campaigns of parties. The problem with public power may arise from the fact that politicians and high officials (who often also have political connections or backgrounds) actually make public decisions on town plans, building permits, and the use of land, for example. However, these connections are covert in nature so it is very difficult to prove that such links genuinely exist. However, sometimes there is some amount of doubt about hidden foul play.

The size of the Finnish State and society also plays a role in this. Namely, close personal social relations inherent to a small country make it difficult to prove that such things like inappropriate exchange of favours actually exist. On the other hand, one should not go too far in making conclusions about corruption, as customary small gifts and other benefits with sentimental value are generally not experienced nor regarded as corruption. We may perhaps claim that these problems are

[13]   See Transparency International (www.transparency.fi/english.htm).

more typical at the local government level where many kinds of dual roles (conflicts of interest) may occur. However, these roles are sometimes impossible to avoid in a small country and especially in small local communities.

Obviously, the problem is how to distinguish between corruption and normal networking. Clearly, not all networking may be coined as being negative and ending in the false use of public power. For private companies amicable social connections are a kind of social capital. Moreover, in a democracy it is constitutionally obvious that everyone is allowed to promote their own interests. The fact that decision-makers, politicians and high civil servants alike know each other, and that private citizens may have direct contacts with them, is valuable to a working democracy. Finland, however, has not been very successful in drawing the lines between what is acceptable and what is not: blatantly illegal behaviour is easy to detect but more subtle behaviour is not.

At the end of the day it seems, anyhow, that there is no widespread and structural corruption in Finland: governance works professionally. In this sense the system works well and the democracy functions according to the core ideas of constitutionalism. However, an exception to this rule seems to be the Election Funding Act which leaves plenty of room for various interpretations and even some loopholes.[14] From a critical point of view we may note that the recent problems concerning the transparency of political funding have been so notable, that the Council of Europe's Group of States against Corruption has compared Finland with such a country as Belarus.[15] Understandably, this has not brought about very enthusiastic comments in Finland.[16]

---

[14] The purpose of this Act was to 'increase the transparency of election financing in order to clarify the possible personal interests of the candidates' (section 1.2). In fact, the Act has not worked very well at all: it leaves room for interpretations and it has no sanctions. The Act on the Disclosure of Election Financing (*Laki ehdokkaan vaalirahoituksesta* 414/2000). The Act was amended in 2009 but it still does not seem to do what it should (273/2009).

[15] Evaluation Report, Finland. Political Funding (7 December 2007) available at: www.coe.int/Greco.

[16] For example, *Helsingin Sanomat*, the biggest newspaper in Finland, titled its story in June 2009 'Finland's Corruption Parallel with Belorussia', this stirred angry reactions from the ranks of politicians as well as from the general public.

PRESIDENT

It has been said by comparative constitutional lawyers that 'one can read a constitution sometimes as an autobiography of the nation'.[17] Surely the Finnish presidency suggests that this is very much true. The institution of President was created only in 1919 by the Form of Government, so it did not have deep institutional roots in the Finnish constitutional heritage, unless one compares a strong president with a monarch with powers. Actually, this would not be too far-fetched a characterisation at all. In 1919, Finland had no republican tradition whatsoever. In spite of this a presidency is always a republican institution and has something of a profoundly alien nature to monarchy. And yet, only history makes it intelligible as to why the institution of President was adopted and became rooted so deeply in the mental constitutional landscape.

From the viewpoint of constitutional history, it appears that the only plausible explanation for the powers of the Finnish President is the fact that this institution actually inherited many of the powers granted to the Grand Duke during the Russian period prior to independence. In other words, the Finnish President is not truly a republican institution. As a matter of fact it is a monarchical remnant, a living constitutional ruin, from the earlier constitutional layers, later facilitated by events of history providing a surprisingly firm rooting in an otherwise republican and parliamentary system. Further, it seems also evident that nothing else than the victory of the Whites over the Reds in the Civil War of 1918 explains why there has been such a long road toward the predominance of a parliamentary system. Without the Civil War it might all have been very different from the beginning.

It was the Civil War which made many of the Centrist (then Agrarian Union, *Maalaisliitto*) Members of the Parliament join the supporters of the semi-presidential governmental model. Before the war it had looked like Finland would have assumed a much more clearly parliamentary type of government. A famous right-wing liberal lawyer, who would later also become the President of the Republic, KJ Ståhlberg (1865–1952), had a strong influence on the constitutional reform of 1919. Yet

[17] A Harding and P Leyland, 'Comparative Law in Constitutional Context' in D Nelken and E Örücü (eds), *Comparative Law: a Handbook* (Hart, Oxford, 2007) 313–38, 316.

the outcome was not truly surprising if we take into account the fact that according to him what was needed was 'lawful but solid and strong governmental power'. Ståhlberg was clearly aware of different constitutional models and he sought explicitly to combine the separation of powers model with restricted parliamentarism. The dilemma was clear: how should constitutional oil and water be combined, ie a strong executive single-person organ and the requirements of a parliamentary form of democracy. This problem reflected the constitutional past and challenged (then) contemporary Western legal-ideology.

Without a shadow of a doubt, those who drafted the final 1919 constitutional document were not thinking any *pouvoir neutre* according to French constitutional theory, but rather a strong governmental organ taking part in political life on a constant basis. Very little came from constitutional theory, but much was taken from earlier practice and experience. Much has changed since and yet this basic dual executive structure is still present because many of the steps toward a parliamentary system have been somewhat unambiguous. Moreover, it is crucial to understand that sometimes overlapping presidential executive powers are partly based on constitutional culture and they are binding provided that the actors themselves regard them as binding, ie as a part of the practically significant constitutional morality. Importantly, political scientists have reminded us that the classification into parliamentary and presidential systems 'cannot be based entirely on constitutional formalities'.[18] This is very much true in the case of Finland.

Surprisingly in many accounts other constitutional players (ministers and high public officials) have shown clear reluctance to challenge the President. This, however, is not due to any constitutional thinking but rather due to political opportunism: it is not politically wise to challenge such an institution as the challenger's own political party may have the possibility to get the seat in future elections. A fitting example of this is the Social Democratic Party which for decades resisted the strong powers of the President, but after having several presidents coming from its own ranks it has, simply, cynically changed its earlier stance on this.

Basically, the President's constitutional and democratic legitimacy flows from a democratic election process. In a genuinely democratic and constitutional system there is genuine competition between those who seek power through governmental institutions. Elections are important:

---

[18]   J-E Lane and S Ersson, *Comparative Politics* (Polity Press, Cambridge, 1994) 160.

they are the key channels providing constitutional-political justification for this executive institution. Here the development has been somewhat internally contradictory. Between the years 1919–87, presidents were elected indirectly by an electoral college (300 in number, although in 1981 there were 301). This system was abandoned in 1988 when a two-stage electoral system was used. However, this model was used only once because from 1994 the current system of popular election over two ballots has been used. This method of direct popular election strangely collides with many codified constitutional rules and more importantly some of the quintessential constitutional principles and doctrines.

Electing the President

It is a commonly held opinion by constitutional experts (lawyers and political scientists alike) that the method of choosing the President does not fit well with the system in which most of the governmental power is used by the Government coalition and to a growing extent specifically by the PM. Simply put, voters can easily get a false impression of the powers of the President. The publicly held popular mental-constitutional image of the President's constitutional dignity has disproportionate measures from the point of view of constitutional law. This certainly makes the system more difficult to understand, especially as the Presidential election gains high profile when compared to the parliamentary election. It seems highly likely that the media play a decisive role in this; it is simpler to concentrate on a couple of strong candidates than to follow thousands who take part in parliamentary elections as candidates. Drama is easily constructed in a presidential election setting where a one-on-one battle between opponents takes place.

Paradoxically, while the Constitution has been parliamentarised, the mass-media driven political culture has been presidentialised. This constitutional irony creates a tension between the President-loving general public and Parliament-oriented constitutional experts and parliamentarians. The present author knows this from personal experience as a university teacher of constitutional law: time and time again fresh students are genuinely puzzled to hear the constitutional facts concerning the position of the President.

From a more technical point of view, the President is elected by a direct vote for a term of six years and he or she must be a native-born

Finnish citizen. After the long years of powerful President Kekkonen, it has been a feature (adopted in written constitutional law) of the Finnish system from 1991 onwards that the same person may be elected to no more than two consecutive terms in office (CA section 54.1). President Ahtisaari was the first president to whom this constitutional rule applied, even though he was not a candidate for a second term. In case of such an event where the President would die or would become permanently unable to carry out the presidential duties, a new President must be elected as soon as possible (CA section 55.2).

In sum, as has already been stated, the Finnish system was previously classified as a presidential-style parliamentarism, but today it is more like a parliamentary-style of presidentialism. Yet, the ambiguity has not disappeared. The written constitutional law provides a still rather strong position for the President as section 3 of the Constitution Act clearly demonstrates: 'governmental Powers are exercised by the President of the Republic and the Government'. It comes hardly as a surprise that President Halonen has given strict relevance to the order of the words in the Constitutional Act: first the President and only then the Government coalition. However, whereas the Government's powers are general as to their nature, the President's duties are enumerated by the Constitution Act and other Acts and decrees. It is also important to note that the President may use powers mainly in the Government and on the basis of proposals for decisions that are put forward by the Government. This is clearly different from the French semi-presidentialism in which the President actually presides over the Government coalition, although more weakly under the *cohabitation* situation.[19] In a word, the Finnish President's powers are more closely checked. Let us consider next the competences and duties of the President. This discussion also sheds light on the competences and duties of the Government and thus completing the earlier discussion.

Competences and Duties of the President

Under the scheme of separation of powers the President takes part in using the executive power.

---

[19] La Constitution du 4 octobre 1958 article 9: 'Le Président de la République préside la Conseil des Ministres'.

According to the Constitution Act, governmental competences are vested in the President and the Government, of which only the Government coalition (ie Council of State) must enjoy the confidence of the Parliament.[20] In practice this means that the President uses power mainly in conjunction with the Council of State in different forms while dealing with governmental proposals for new legislation, decrees, and appointment of certain high public officials. Importantly, the Government with its ministries both facilitates and implements the decisions of the President. Now, even though the President clearly has a certain share in using executive power, it must be stated that EU membership has enhanced the development which has transferred the use of executive power toward the Government. Very likely, this trend will continue in the future too despite the popularity of the presidential institution among the public. Moreover, this trend does not depend on written provisions of the Constitution Act but, rather, from a change of political life and especially the growing importance of the European Union.

Nominating and Discharging the Government

The President may also order a premature parliamentary election. This sounds like a very strong power to have but in practice it is no longer so. During the years of President Kekkonen this was indeed a strong competence which formed an instrument of political power that the President was able to use when he wanted to create pressure towards governments. During the period 1919–91 this power was virtually constitutionally unrestrained. Actually, the President could order premature parliamentary election if the act was 'deemed as necessary'; there was really no binding constitutional rule, principle or custom that would have clarified the true reach of this power. The power was not left unused since presidents have ordered premature parliamentary elections on several occasions: Ståhlberg did this in 1924, Relander in 1929 and 1930, Paasikivi in 1953 and Kekkonen in 1961, 1971 and 1975. Clearly this was one of the strongest powers of the President carrying the legacy of the Civil War ('solid and strong governmental power') all the way up until 1991.

[20] The Constitution Act requires that (section 3.2) the members of the Government 'shall have the confidence of the Parliament'. The Act also stipulates (section 60.2) that '[m]inisters are responsible before the Parliament for their actions in office'.

Today, the power to order extraordinary parliamentary elections is remarkably more limited as the President can do this only upon 'reasoned proposal' (*perustellusta aloitteesta*) from the PM (CA section 26.1). There are also other restrictions here because first the President must consult parliamentary groups, and Parliament must be in session. Only after all these conditions are fulfilled can the President order the holding of a premature parliamentary election. This constitutional rule has never been used, although in 2003 it was seriously considered when the PM Jäätteenmäki was forced to leave her post after just a couple of months in office due to the fact that the parliamentary majority regarded her to have compromised her credibility as PM. Even though no actual voting took place, it was clear that she lost political trust of the other main party in the coalition (SDP).

During the heated electoral campaigns in the early spring of 2003, Jäätteenmäki (then in opposition) received a great amount of secret information concerning Finnish foreign and security policy from the Presidential Office. She used this delicate information for her benefit in public debates with the main rival (at that time PM) Lipponen. When it became known a few months later that she got this information in a highly questionable and utterly clandestine manner from an inside source, her credibility as a PM was completely eroded—she was not trusted anymore by the majority of the Parliament: she had to go before she would have been eventually forced to go (and thus causing serious harm to the political coherence of the Government coalition).

The President also has a role in appointing and discharging ministers; however, this power is today a mere formality leaving very little room for the independent use of presidential discretion (CA section 64). After general parliamentary elections or in some other situation where the Government has resigned, the President submits to the Parliament a nominee for PM.[21] When doing this the President must follow the result of consultations between the parliamentary groups (ie parties) and must also hear the view of the Speaker of the Parliament (*Eduskunnan puhemies*). In addition, if the nomination is confirmed by the Parliament with a majority of the votes cast, the President must then proceed to appoint the PM

---

[21] It is relevant to note that the Government must always resign after parliamentary elections. A resignation at any other time can result from a vote of no confidence by the Parliament or because the preconditions for continuing co-operation between the coalition partners have ceased to exist, ie the inner political cohesion is simply lost.

and other ministers according to the proposition of the PM. Immediately following this and after the composition of the Government has been agreed upon, the new Government coalition is appointed in the last session of the resigning Council of State. The President formally relieves the outgoing ministers of their duties and immediately appoints the new ones. The President may also dismiss any minister upon the proposal of the PM, ie this power cannot be wielded solely by the PM. The President is constitutionally required to dismiss a government or any minister as soon as they have lost the confidence of Parliament, even if no such request would have been presented (CA section 64.2).

Foreign Policy—Difficulty of Drawing the Lines

As already stated, the President has had a stronghold of power in the area of foreign policy which is directed by the President in cooperation with the Government. In fact, there is no clear constitutional rationale behind this: development after World War II brought about the position that the constitutional rule (ie Section in the Form of Government) concerning the President's competence was understood and interpreted in a very broad manner. This power, however, was not and certainly is not complete in that the parliamentary features constrain the President's powers in this field. Parliament accepts international obligations and their denunciation and decides on the bringing into force of the State's international obligations. Moreover, the President decides on matters of war and peace, with the consent of the Parliament.

European Union affairs are a delicate issue in conjunction with the President's power. In 1995 the accession to the European Union turned the tables and actually elevated the PM's position and role as the leader of politics. This is because the Government is mainly responsible for the national preparation of the decisions to be made in the European Union. It is the Government which decides on the concomitant Finnish EU measures, unless the decision requires constitutional approval of Parliament (CA section 94.2). The Parliament also participates indirectly in the national preparation of decisions to be made in the European Union. This covers consideration of proposals for acts, agreements or other measures which are decided in the European Union and would otherwise (ie without EU membership) be situated within the competence of Parliament (CA section 96.1).

According to the Constitution Act, the President takes all significant decisions in relation to foreign policy in cooperation with the Government, which is responsible for the preparatory work. In fact, the President's own machinery of public officials is very limited if compared with the resources of the ministries. Different formal decisions relating to foreign policy guidelines, initiatives and instructions to official representatives of Finland in questions of importance are situated within the competence of the President. The President also formally decides on recognition of foreign states, the establishment or severance of diplomatic relations, on Finnish diplomatic missions, on joining or withdrawing from international organisations, on delegations to international negotiations, and on the signing, ratification and entry into force of international conventions (this may sometimes be regarded as subject to parliamentary approval).

Besides these competences within the area of foreign affairs, the President assigns the highest officials in the foreign affairs administration and the heads of Finnish diplomatic missions (ie ambassadors). Accordingly, foreign diplomats accredited to Finland present their credentials to the President.[22] In this regard, the President functions as a kind of super-diplomat of the republic very much in the same manner as the constitutional monarch acts, for example, in Sweden. In fact, it is possible to divide the President's foreign policy powers into two blocks: formal decision-making with the Government and the actual decision-making which takes place in and through the Committee for Foreign and Security Policy.

President and Legislating

Separation of powers proves yet again to be partly blurred because the President actually takes part in legislating power mainly because new legislation is virtually always initiated by a government (Council of State and President together) bill. However, it goes even deeper than this. Formally it is the President who introduces government bills and may also recall them. The Committee for Checking of the Constitution proposed in February 2010 that in the future it would be solely the Government (meaning here narrowly the Council of the State) which would use this

---

[22] These are all specifically enumerated competences in the Constitution Act.

power to issue bills to Parliament.[23] It remains to be seen whether or not this reform actually takes place.

It is important to stress here that Parliament determines the final content of all Acts, so it may amend or reject legislative proposals. In practice, the President plays a minor role in this because government bills are drafted by the relevant ministry. These drafts are first approved by the Council of State and only then submitted to the President. Now, if the President does not approve the draft bill, he or she can return it for redrafting. However, on the second reading the President must issue the bill on the basis of the Cabinet's new draft (CA section 58).

The President must sign and approve for promulgation all bills adopted by Parliament before they formally become Acts. Should the President refuse assent or fail to decide on the matter within the space of three months, Parliament reconsiders the bill and may readopt it with a majority of votes cast. The resuscitated bill will then enter into force without the President's ratification (power of *veto* is conditional). However, if Parliament fails to readopt the bill, it is deemed to have lapsed. This weakened veto-power came into being in 2000 when the old tradition which lay on a monarchical base was finally transformed into a more republican one. How this works in practice depends not only on written constitutional rules but also on the person who is the President: should the President be highly popular and respected then it is politically difficult to actually break the veto, whereas to do the same with the veto of an unpopular President is much easier. Also, the nature of a government coalition may play a role here: sometimes the fact that the President's own party is part of the coalition may ease the life of a government coalition. Yet, there is hardly any constitutional practice concerning weak veto-power so it would be risky to claim how it does or does not work. The Åland case in 2001 (see chapter three) remains a curious example. Only time will tell.

The President also has some independent minor legislative power in the form of issuing decrees. This clearly displays the fact that even while separation of powers (or at least division of functions) is an important constitutional principle, it is anything but consistently carried out. Matters concerning the rights and obligations of the individual and any other matters stipulated in the Constitution Act as being within the

---

[23] *Perustuslain tarkistamiskomitean mietintö* (Komiteanmietintö 9/2010).

sphere of legislation must be regulated by an Act of Parliament.[24] The
President's power to issue decrees is qualified, and mainly decrees are
issued by the Government. Presidential decrees (dealing exclusively with
international affairs, CA section 95.1) are drafted by the relevant ministry and submitted to the President for approval by the relevant minister
in the presidential session of the Government. However, because the
President does not have large bureaucratic machinery, the President's
Office (which is comparatively tiny in size) does not take care of matters
related to preparing or presenting decrees. Simply, there are no resources
for this to take place. Decrees may be issued only on the basis of authori-
sation in the Constitution Act or in another Act. Government has large
powers to issue decrees because when there is no specific provision on
who shall issue a decree, then, it is issued by the Government (CA section 80).

Appointing Officials and Officers

Of constitutional importance is the President's power in certain official
appointments which are all stipulated in the Constitution Act or based
on written provisions of other regulations. The President appoints, for
example, the Permanent Secretary of the Office of the President and
also other officials with direct access to the President, the Chancellor of
Justice, the Prosecutor-General, the Permanent Secretaries of Ministries,
the Governor and other Members of the Board of the Bank of Finland,
and the officers of the armed forces (ie Defence Forces and the Frontier
Guard). Moreover, the President also appoints the presidents and justices of the Supreme Court and of the Supreme Administrative Court,
the presidents and justices of the Courts of Appeal, other permanently
appointed members of the judiciary and other officials stipulated separately in other Acts.

During the office of President Halonen only a few of her high
profile appointments were widely regarded as not really concurrent
with the spirit of the Constitution, although perhaps black-letter-rule
wise they were impeccable. Oddly enough, these occasions seem to
have gained more public popularity for the presidency: she has been

---

[24] In cases where there is no specific provision in written law (Constitution Act or
normal lower Act), the decree may only be issued by the Government which holds
the general executive competency (CA section 80).

conceived as a counter-balance to 'politicising'. This is one indication of the deep constitutional experience: 'Power to influence is not
depending only from the written Sections expressed in the Constitution
Act', as the most experienced Finnish parliamentarian of the 1900s
and minister in numerous government coalitions, Johannes Virolainen
(1914–2000), once said.[25] Indeed, President Halonen has shown that
even though the Constitution Act 2000 sets limits, the President can
still potentially be an important political player in the usage of public
power. The public mental-constitutional image of the presidency is a
crucial factor behind this.

One of the traditional powers of the Head of State organ is that of
the Commander-in-Chief of the Defence Forces, which in Finland is a
presidential duty. However, this position may be delegated to another
Finnish citizen on the proposal of the Government (CA section 128.1).
This competence of the President is bit unclear: the section does not
state which part of the competence can be delegated, precisely to whom
it may be delegated, or for how long a time it may be delegated. The
previous rule on this (1919 Form of Government section 30) was clear
because it stated that this power may be delegated only during the time
of war. Today, no such limit exists. However, the fact that the President
is bound to the proposal of the Government seems to limit this power a
great deal. In practice, however, it is not to be expected that this competence would really be exercised during normal times. During the old system, the power of Commander-in-Chief was delegated, partially against
the Constitution, to Marshal Carl Gustav Mannerheim (1867–1951) in
1939–44. The Committee for Checking of the Constitution proposed in
February 2010 that the President could delegate this power only during a
state of emergency.[26] It is likely that this reform will be accepted; it does
not appear to be politically controversial.

In the capacity of Commander-in-Chief, the President has the power
to issue military orders concerning rough guidelines for military defence,
significant changes in military preparedness and the principles according to which military defence is implemented. The President also makes
decisions concerning other military matters of importance or great significance, as well as on military appointments and promotions of officers. These powers are used in conjunction with the PM and the Minister

---

[25] J Virolainen, *Defence of Politics* ['*Politiikan puolustus*'] (Helsinki, Otava, 1996) 326.
[26] *Perustuslain tarkistamiskomitean mietintö* (*Komiteanmietintö* 2010:9).

of Defence at a so-called in-camera presentation of business, which generally takes place outside the Government. The President also plays a role in times of emergency because in times of exceptional circumstances the President may issue a decree authorising the Government to exercise emergency powers for up to one year at a time. However, this decree must be later submitted to the Parliament for its approval and no human rights obligations may be breached.

Pardoning—a Remnant of the Past

Military affairs and the powers in this area may easily be traced to earlier constitutional layers of Finnish history. Along a similar line to the 'republican-monarch' line division, the competence to issue pardons (*armahdusoikeus*) is a classical competence of a monarch. Now, in an individual case and after having received the opinion of the Supreme Court (a formal but not binding prerequisite for a pardon being granted), the President may remit, either wholly or in part, a sentence or other criminal penalty imposed by a court. However, a general amnesty may be granted only by an Act of Parliament. In practice, a pardon applies only to penalties imposed for criminal offences. So, the President cannot waive such obligations as administrative duties, taxes or bank loans. Different presidents have had different policies in exercising the power of pardoning.

Moreover, a pardon is possible only after all avenues of appeal in the court system have been exhausted. Petitions for pardons are handled in the Ministry of Justice and submitted to the President by the Minister of Justice in the presidential sessions of the Government. Even though constitutionally of small importance, this power offers a high public media-profile to the institution of President even though its practical importance is utterly minimal from the point of view of the judicial system. Be that as it may, this is yet more proof of the fact that the separation of powers principle is, on numerous occasions, blurred in the Finnish Constitution. When the main principles are looked at (in conjunction with the President) in more detail there are several features that seem to reflect rather fusion than separation of powers.

Constitutionally important is also the power which the President uses in Åland-related matters which are dealt with later in the next chapter.

CONCLUSION

The central question in this chapter has been to consider the top demo-cratic institutions and their main functions from the point of view of divi-sion of powers. Finland abandoned the monarchical tradition reluctantly in 1919 and moved to presidential-style republicanism with parliamen-tary features. The system is built upon a separation of powers scheme, but often there are clear divergences from the tripartite organisation of public power. Importantly, the system is driven in two directions when it comes to the executive-governmental power: the Government Coalition of Ministers and the President of the Republic share some of their pow-ers, thus creating a dualist system in which there is always a potential risk of inner tensions. These tensions, real or fictional, offer constant fuel to political commentators and the press: the media follows presidents much more closely and seemingly with a bit more respect than the PM, ministers or MPs. This is hard to explain by any other thing but through history and the resulting mental image of the presidency.

During the twentieth century the Finnish Constitution has moved gradually toward a more full-bodied parliamentary system, even though in practice the majority government coalitions actually dominate the decision-making of Parliament. It is crucial to conceive that normally only small changes take place in the political culture and only after such changes is the written constitutional document slightly amended. So, the fact that the highly unstable government coalitions of the 1960s and 1970s transformed into stable majority coalitions has had a tremendous impact on the constitutional landscape. The fall of the Soviet Union, European integration and many internal factors have pushed the system toward an ever stronger Cabinet with a PM and, in turn, the President's powers seem to have spiralled downwards. However, the high level of popularity of sitting presidents has slowed down the transformation process. Nonetheless, almost unanimously, expert opinion has stressed the importance of stripping down the formal constitutional compe-tences of the President, especially the foreign policy-related powers which have been largely recommended to be further parliamentarised in order to strengthen the position of the Council of the State in this area.

FURTHER READING

Arter, D, 'Finland' in R Elgie (ed), *Semi-Presidentialism in Europe* (Oxford University Press, Oxford, 1999) 48–66.

Jyränki, A, 'Die neue Verfassung Finnlands' (2001) *Zeitschrift für öffentliches Recht* 56, 113–27.

Jyränki, A, 'Finland: Foreign Affairs as the Last Stronghold of the Presidency' (2007) *European Constitutional Law Review* 3, 285–306.

Nousiainen, J, 'From Semi-Presidentialism to Parliamentary Government: Political and Constitutional Developments in Finland' (2001) *Scandinavian Political Studies* 24, 95–109.

Nousiainen, J, 'The Finnish System of Government: From Mixed Constitution to Parliamentarism' in *The Constitution of Finland* (Parliament of Finland, Vammala, 2001) 5–42.

Temmes, M, 'Finland and New Public Management' (1998) *International Review of Administrative Sciences* 64, 441–56.

WEBSITES

The following websites also contain information in English.

www.tasavallanpresidentti.fi [President's official website].
www.valtioneuvosto.fi [Council of State's official website].

5

Decentralised Government

⊶⊷

Introduction – Local Government – Åland Islands: Federal Feature in Unitary State – Conclusion

INTRODUCTION

In such a unitary state as Finland, state administration tends to be rather centralised. Regions have no legislative powers and state administration has various regional bodies which have duties and responsibilities based on statute law. This state of affairs has stayed largely intact for a longer period of time. However, at the end of the 1990s and in the 2000s regional state bodies underwent several reforms. These features seem to undermine the unitary nature of the State as they bring evident elements of decentralisation to the otherwise unitary basic structure of the State. This chapter sets out to explore two forms of constitutional decentralisation which are local government and the Åland Islands.

LOCAL GOVERNMENT

It was in the seventeenth century that local government took shape; Sweden had, from very early on, a rather uniform and centralised governmental structure and the Russian years never changed these basic features. So, when the far-reaching reform of communal government, the basis of local government even today, took place in 1865, the ideas were transplanted from Sweden, not from Russia. Now, today in addition to Government (ie Council of State) and its ministries, there are plenty of other state agencies, institutions and bodies. Moreover, there are also some regional and local state authorities. The Constitution Act (section 119) specifically mentions in a broad manner these possibilities and more detailed concretising provisions situated in ordinary parliamentary Acts and lower decrees. From a constitutional point of view, all these state authorities belong to the broad organisation of the State, and their democratic legitimacy flows from the same source as the Government's, namely from the democratically elected Parliament. In a narrow constitutional sense, Parliament passes legislation and especially Acts which are the legal basis for all exercise of public power by the State or by other public organs, local government included. Besides, state administrative non-central bodies (eg regional administration) there are other organs too, of which by far the most important are municipalities into which Finland is regionally divided (approximately 350).

Administrative Structure

A municipality has an explicit constitutional base. The administration of a municipality (*kunta*) is based on 'on the self-government of local residents' (Constitution Act (CA) section 121.1). Even though Finland has in principle a three-layer model of public administration, it may be stated that traditionally the regional mid-level has remained relatively weak in comparison to municipal administration. Yet, mid-level government (*lääninhallitus,* ie State Provincial Office) had some important control powers and licensing powers in various fields. These offices functioned as the regional authorities of the State and were administrative experts in several domains. From the beginning of 2010 Finland abandoned her traditional county model (*lääni*) and new regional administrative agencies (*aluehallintovirasto*) started their work. The rationale behind this reform was to make the roles, duties, steering and regional division of all regional state administrative authorities clearer. The object was to enhance the citizen and customer orientation of regional administration, as well as increase efficiency and productivity. It remains to be seen whether or not these objectives are actually reached. These agencies are in fact kinds of administrative continuations of ministries and they are situated within the State in a constitutional sense. This is why the following text concentrates on municipalities which differ from the State's organs in a constitutional sense.

The constitutional position of municipalities was first formally guaranteed by the 1919 Form of Government (section 50) which provided a written constitutional base for municipal administration and it was kept even in the 2000 reform. It is of importance for anyone who looks at the Finnish system from the outside to understand that in a quantitative sense municipalities form the largest sector of all public administration in Finland (eg greatest number of civil servants and public functions). So, in fact, the State is smaller in this quantitative organisational sense.

However, achieving a clear line of demarcation between the State and other public organs seems somewhat unattainable. In general public law perception, municipalities are in a sense part of the State, provided that the concept of state is used in a rather broad sense. However, there is more to it. Municipalities are perhaps the clearest evidence of Finnish constitutional decentralisation (ie devolution) of public power. In fact, a municipality is not genuinely or formally directly subject to state administration; however, it takes care of some of the duties and functions which in other countries are taken care of directly by the organs of the State. However, obviously a municipality differs from state organs because its administration is democratically based on its residents: the most important local administrative organ (Municipal Council, *kunnanvaltuusto*) is chosen by the local people in democratic elections (every fourth year). Actually, the municipality is perhaps best understood as a decentralised form of representative democracy which, in turn, is an important constitutional principle itself. Municipality is based, like the State itself, on democracy: key organs are elected by a direct ballot in municipal elections. The State's governmental agencies have no elected bodies at the regional (ie provincial) or local level.

The Constitutional Core of Local Self-Government

The constitutional core of local government is as to its nature defensive: it creates an obstacle for the Government and the Parliament to change the relation between the State and municipalities without first changing the Constitution Act. Namely, the Constitution Act (section 121) specifically prevents the State from interfering with the basic features (ie changes that would alter the constitutional character of local government being genuinely self-governing) of local government by means of ordinary parliamentary Acts. Further, all the provisions concerning general principles of municipal administration must be 'laid down by an Act'. Besides this, the right of municipalities to levy municipal tax is also constitutionally safeguarded. Now, the right to levy municipal tax is highly important for the relative constitutional autonomy of the municipalities; they are not fully financially dependent on the State, even though significant amounts of state subventions are needed. Presently, the most important parliamentary Act concerning the municipalities is the general Municipality Act.[1] This Act covers the general duties and organisation of municipalities, whereas the numerous functions of municipalities are stipulated in multiple separate Acts on, for example, social welfare, comprehensive school, and public healthcare.

Constitutionally, it is also crucial that a municipality can conduct its own administration and finances independently, ie organs of the State may interfere only to a limited extent. These limits are set by the Acts passed by the Parliament.

The Municipality Act (section 2.1) reflects the separation of state and municipality by making a distinction between 'state-delegated-functions' and 'self-generated-functions'. According to this distinction the municipality has a broad sphere of authority (*toimiala*) which is divided into a general sphere and a special sphere of authority. The former contains all such duties as a municipality may take care of in accordance with the law (matters of common interest within its own municipal territory), and the latter concerns such duties as a municipality is obliged to take care of due to parliamentary legislation. There has been, from time to time, constitutionally justified criticism of the fact that an overtly wide scope of special legislation de facto carves a defined sphere of municipal freedom constitutionally empty; so little has been left for the municipalities themselves to genuinely decide over that freedom from state organs is practically limited. However, in the last 15 years or so there has been greater nominal freedom from the State's governmental bodies. However, this development has not been genuinely welcomed as formal growth in freedom has meant more obligations (ever increasing social, health and educational legislation with legal responsibilities) and less financial support. One method to try to overcome these difficulties is the possibility for the communities to create a regional coalition

---

[1] *Kuntalaki* (365/1995). Section 1.1 stipulates that 'Finland is divided into local authorities where the autonomy of residents is safeguarded in the Constitution Act'.

(*maakuntaliitto*) which can carry out more demanding tasks concerning, for example, central hospitals and vocational schools.

So, the constitutional core features of local self-government can be easily placed into four main categories, as follows:

1. The residents themselves elect the supreme decision-making body, the Municipal Council.
2. The Municipal Council has the general decision-making competency in local affairs.
3. The local authorities have the competency to make financial decisions, based on the constitutional right to levy taxes.
4. Local government is organisationally separate from central government, and the municipal bodies are therefore at least partly independent of the State.

Public law doctrine has traditionally regarded the last mentioned dimension as covering a municipality's right to decide over the salaries of its public officials and workers. However, lately local governments have started to apply more market-oriented approaches which have changed the former public law-oriented understanding of municipality.

The financial affairs have also an important constitutional dimension: a municipality has the competence to levy taxes on its members and, importantly, the tax rate is decided legally, independently from the State. In practice, the local authorities can organise municipal administration relatively freely, and only some basic principles must be followed: each municipality must have a Municipal Council, a Municipal Board, an Auditing Committee for auditing municipal administration and finance, and an Election Committee that is responsible for organising elections. A municipality must also have a Municipal Manager (*kunnanjohtaja*), elected by the Municipal Council. However, the municipal manager is not a member of the local council. Since 2006 it has been possible for a municipality to have a Mayor (*pormestari*), but this is very rare.

Other Forms of Self-Government

There are also other forms of self-government than local government even though there are no genuine regional mid-level governments or equivalent. Of these we may mention universities which have some degree of constitutionally defined self-government. However, universities do not have as much administrative freedom as do the municipalities. In addition, the Sámi people have some elements of self-government in their native region (ie most Northern part of Finland, Lapland) concerning linguistic and cultural matters.[2] The Åland Islands (*Ahvenanmaa*) have by far the greatest degree of self-government and are dealt with in the following section as one of the decentralised features of the Finnish Constitution.

Constitutional Autonomy?

The discussion above has already indicated that there are some themes in Finnish constitutional law that appear somewhat peculiar in international comparison. These are peculiarities even in Nordic comparison. Obviously, there are several such dimensions but here only the most important may be dealt with. In this section we will look deeper into one of the institutional special features of the Finnish Constitution. The dual nature of the Finnish Government system has already been described and analysed, but there are other areas which are of specific interest from the point of view of comparison. From the viewpoint of devolution the autonomic Åland Islands are the most relevant.

ÅLAND ISLANDS — FEDERAL FEATURE IN UNITARY STATE?

As it has been stated earlier in this book, Finland is a unitary state. As such, this is true even though there is one special feature regarding this. The Åland Islands (*Ahvenanmaa*) have a constitutionally highly protected position in Finland; in fact, their position is constitutionally unique even in global comparison.[3] In an administrative sense the Ålands are a province (*maakunta*). According to the Constitution Act (section 120), Åland has self-government in accordance with special provisions in the Act on

---

[2] The Sámi (*Saamelaiset*) are an indigenous population living in the area of Northern Fennoscandia. In Finland their total number is less than 7000. The Sámi speak three different versions of the Sámi language: North Sámi, Inari Sámi, and Skolt Sámi. However, today most of the Sámi live outside their natural areas and speak also Finnish.

[3] The islands are situated in the Baltic Sea in between Finland and Sweden. The highly scattered archipelago consists of more than 6,000 islands. There are approximately 25,000 inhabitants.

the Autonomy of the Åland Islands.[4]

The Islands became autonomous in 1920 due to the Autonomy Act and a decision by the League of Nations in 1921. The Council of the League of Nations reached a decision in 1921 according to which Finland should receive sovereignty over the Åland Islands. On this basis the state agreed to guarantee the population of Åland, its Swedish language, as well as culture and local customs. The League of Nations also decided that an international treaty ought to secure that the demilitarisation of the Åland Islands would be confirmed legally. However, the first Autonomy Act (1920) was inadequate and it was replaced by a new Act (1951). After some 20 years of preparation, the present Act on the Autonomy was passed, entering into force in 1993.

Although in the 1900s the Finnish mainland started to demand independence from Russia, the people in Åland, having a large Swedish-speaking majority, turned to Sweden, wanting to be incorporated into it. Like the rest of the country, Åland had been part of Sweden until 1809 but, unlike the mainland, Åland had retained its linguistic and cultural relations with Sweden much more tightly. Sweden was, nevertheless, not overtly eager to have Åland fearing the strategic consequences in the Baltic Sea area. The League of Nations made a decision in 1921 which held the Islands to be part of Finland, even though this decision was not largely accepted by the local people. The feeling on the Islands was that more independence and more self-government were needed. However, after World War II the position of the Islands transformed into an economic and legal link between Finland and Åland; this also gained more support for the autonomous position of the Islands as a part of Finland. The present Autonomy Act guarantees that the 'Åland Islands are autonomous'.[5] Today, the majority of the population seem to want to remain a part of Finland. Yet, there has been a small growth in the number of those seeking to turn Åland into an independent micro-state lately.

From a constitutional point of view, the degree of autonomy may be regarded as very significant. The Autonomy Act of the Åland Islands gives to the legislative body of the Islands the power to legislate on such things like taxation, education, trade, culture, environmental protection, communications and postal services. The Act also provides to the local Government the right to propose negotiations on an international treaty

---

[4] *Ahvenanmaan itsehallintolaki* (1144/1991).
[5] Autonomy Act section 1.

and to participate in such negotiations. Constitutionally, the position of the Islands is special because only partially does the basis and use of public power flow from the Finnish Constitution: it is also partially derived from international law. Further, the Autonomy Act is not a formally constitutional document, but is technically a normal parliamentary Act. However, it can be changed only if (a) the legislative process which is used to enact a constitutional document is used, and (b) the Åland Islands gives its consent to any such change. In fact, the existence of the Åland Islands brings a certain element of a federal state into the Finnish Constitution. Curiously, to change this position is even harder than to change the Constitutional Act itself. This certainly gives the Åland Islands a constitutionally secure position within the Finnish constitutional system. Yet, the slowly weakening position of the Swedish language in Finland seems to be stirring criticism against Finland and raising old ideas of joining Sweden.

There are even more peculiarities concerning the precise constitutional status of the Åland Islands. A very important feature of Åland is the fact that, according to international law, it is a fully demilitarised area. Constitutionally noteworthy is the fact that land acquisition and ownership on the Åland Islands is restricted to only those who are resident; hence even other Finns who are not resident are not allowed to acquire land there. Specifically, from the point of view of Finnish constitutional law, Åland is an example of deeply reaching constitutional devolution which is backed up by specific international law dimensions and linguistic and property arrangements. Furthermore, especially among the Swedish-speaking minority public law experts, there seems to be a tendency to regard the legal material which concerns the Islands as the 'Åland Constitution'. From the point of view of the Finnish State, this characterisation is nonetheless a problematic one.[6] And yet, without a doubt, the Finnish State is genuinely proud of the constitutionally curious autonomic status of Åland which has also aroused a great deal of international interest around the world. This curious constitutional arrangement of extreme devolution seems to inject certain federal features into an otherwise so clearly unitary state. It also seems to indicate how tolerant the Finnish system may be when it deals with such minority questions as those concerning the Swedish-speaking part of the population.

---

[6] M Suksi, *Åland konstitution* (Åbo Akademis Förlag, Åbo, 2005) is a thick legal commentary of what the writer calls literally 'the Ålands Constitution'.

CONCLUSION

Finland is a unitary state and for a long time its administrative organisation has been very much centralised. However, as the examples of local government and Åland Islands show, Finland also has elements of decentralisation and even some dimensions of federal state. The role of the Åland Islands is especially constitutionally curious. The position of the Åland Islands indicates that the Finnish constitutional system is able to also tolerate regional constitutional pluralism even while constitutional culture in all other respects has traditionally stressed the uniform nature of the State. In conjunction with the changes generated by the European integration, it looks likely that the elements of constitutional pluralism and polycentric constitutional organisation are growing in the future. It is not yet clear how these changes will effect local government and their constitutional position.

FURTHER READING

Hannikainen, L and Horn, F (eds), *Autonomy and Demilitarisation in International Law: The Åland Islands in Changing Europe* (Kluwer, The Hague, 1997).

Jääskinen, N, 'The Case of Åland Islands' in S Weatherhill and U Bernitz (eds), *Regions and Subnational Actors in Europe* (Hart, Oxford, 2005) 89–102.

Kunnallistieteellinen Aikakauskirja ('The Finnish Journal for Local Government Affairs') 34 (2006) English Issue.

Saraviita, I, *Finland—Constitutional Law*: International Encyclopedia of Laws (Kluwer, Alphen, 2009).

WEBSITES

All of the following websites also contain information in English.

www.aland.fi [Åland Islands' official website].
www.kuntaliitto [The Association of Finnish Local and Regional Authorities].
www.virtual.finland.fi/politics_society/ [General information on Finland and useful links].

6

Judicial Institutions and their Functions

—➤◆◀—

**Introduction – Finnish Rule of Law – Judiciary and Judicial
Organs – Supreme Courts and Constitutionally Relevant Case
Law – Overseeing Legality – Constitutional Judicial Review –
Conclusion**

INTRODUCTION

The previous chapters dealt with the two main branches of public power
in the Finnish constitutional system. Now it is time to look at the third
branch. Actually, the division of power works most clearly while considering the judicial branch of public power. However, judges in Finland
do not have a visible public role or status: in general they are closer to
civil servants. However, it would be a mistake to think that judges and
courts would not be respected by the general public. On the contrary, the
constitutional relevance of courts and the judiciary is generally deemed
as important. Rulings by the courts of law are faithfully followed by
public organs and, further, their decisions are largely respected by the
public, although not always very much appreciated. It is proposed, in this
chapter, first to describe judiciary and judicial organs, then to discuss the
role of case law, to outline other means of ensuring constitutionality, and
finally to consider constitutional judicial review.

FINNISH RULE OF LAW

In Finland it is deemed that all branches of public power ought to act
in accordance with the rule of law principle. However, because the rule

of law principle is not only celebrated but also complex and even a contested idea, it makes sense to look at what it means in Finnish constitutional law. It appears to have a specific Finnish meaning that is close to the continental European way of conceiving it.

Even though Finnish judicial culture is based historically on Swedish tradition, we may note that in Finland the general legal landscape underlines the principle of strict legality in a slightly sharper formalistic tone, sometimes even in a legalistic manner. Against this background, we might also speak of formal *constitutionalism* as a common constitutional value-base of the whole system. If, however, we look specifically into the division of constitutional functions we must underline the function of the courts of law. Basically, the judicial administration of justice seeks to provide legal security. In short, it secures the rule of law. This is the main constitutional justification for the very existence of judicial machinery. In Finland legal security is regarded as a constitutional right of the people and individuals. The Constitution Act and other relevant lower legislation secures the independence of courts and the structure and functioning of the court system.

Finnish Rechtsstaat?

Under the Constitution Act (section 21), everyone is entitled to have his or her case heard by a court or another independent judicial authority appropriately and without undue delay. In a broader perspective, this national constitutional rule is understood to be closely connected with article 6 of the European Convention on Human Rights (ECHR). In some situations the European Court of Human Rights' (ECtHR) case law has meant a heightened human rights standard as, for example, concerning the length of court proceedings.[1] In fact, the constitutional guarantees for legal security are based simultaneously on the Constitution Act and ECHR (see chapter seven). However, within a larger legal-cultural perspective, the Finnish rule of law principle (*laillisuusperiaate*) is much closer to the German notion of *Rechtsstaat* and the following *Rechtsstaatlichkeit* than what it is to the British and American notion of 'rule of law'.[2] In

---

[1] See eg ECtHR case *Jaanti v Finland* (24 February 2009). This is but one of the cases judged against Finland on the ground of too lengthy court proceedings.

[2] C Varga, *Transition to Rule of Law* (Philosophiae Iuris, Budapest, 1995) 159–68 provides more detailed discussion of the differences between civil law and the common law understanding of 'rule of law'.

practice Finnish doctrine often speaks literally of the 'rule of law State principle' (*oikeusvaltioperiaate*). Following the German nineteenth century public law tradition, law and State are linked together.[3] Instead of the rule of law we might refer to German *Gesetzmässigkeitsprinzip* or even to the French *principe de légalité* which both are closer to the Finnish rule of law than the common law style rule of law. In Finland, the rule of law principle entails commitment to parliamentary democracy, separation of powers and protection of rights that have a constitutional or human rights law anchorage.

It therefore comes as no surprise that the actual wording of the Constitution Act section 21.1 is very close to the German *Grundgesetz*'s formulation.[4] Furthermore, from the viewpoint of German constitutional theory, Finland may be characterised as a State that fulfils the basic requirements of *Verfassungsstaat*, which is constitutional state: predominance of the Constitution, protected fundamental rights, democracy, and separation of powers.[5] These are, of course, very much the same ingredients that were included in the Treaty on European Union.[6] It should be added, however, that in Finland the majority of law that regulates the actions of public authorities is regarded as administrative law which is the other main area of public law. Constitutionally relevant is also the Administrative Procedure Act which seeks to achieve and promote good governance and access to justice in administrative matters. This Act concretises constitutional rules on the principle of good administration, not just access to justice. Most of this Act's principles are of a substantive constitutional character: treating customers of public administration on an equal basis, exercising competences for purposes accepted by the law, impartiality, proportionality and protection of legally legitimate expectations.[7]

As a general constitutional doctrine, the rule of law principle seems to be multidimensional. The Finnish codified constitutional principle conceives the rule of law in two dimensions: 1) use of public power must be

[3] Concerning the German manner to bind the State and morality together in the concept of *Staat*, see D Kommers, *The Constitutional Jurisprudence of the Federal Republic of Germany* (Duke University Press, Durham, 1997) 33–38.
[4] *Grundgesetz* article 19(4) first sentence says that 'Wird jemand durch die öffentliche Gewalt in seinen Rechten verletzt, so steht ihm der Rechtsweg offen.'
[5] See F Venter, *Constitutional Comparison* (Juta/Kluwer, Lansdowne, 2000) 47–52.
[6] See Treaty of European Union (TEU) article 6(1).
[7] *Hallintolaki* (434/2003) section 6.

based on an Act of Parliament (no lower decree will provide an adequate basis), and 2) law—in the broad sense—must be *strictly observed* in all public activity (Constitution Act (CA) section 3.3). Thus, there is always a certain element of legalism—arising partly from domestic political history but also flowing partly from a German doctrinal influence filtered through academic constitutional law. Today, the German influence is weaker than it was during the latter half of the 1800s and is also more clandestine and, thus, more difficult to pinpoint exactly. And yet, it makes sense to note that German ideas flow through academic doctrinal public law (books, articles, case comments, expert opinions, teaching).

It is important to stress that the principle of legality runs through the whole constitutional system and it is adhered to also by the Government and Parliament, as well as by the local governments. Generally, the mentality in Finland can be characterised as being exceptionally law abiding, based on various historical experiences. The darkest hour of the Finnish court system was experienced immediately after the Civil War of 1918; the rule of law principle was not always, if at all, upheld by the courts and there were clear signs of repression clad in judicial garment against those who lost the war, the Reds.[8] Similar types of problems were encountered in the 1930s even though the rule of law principle was followed more closely.

On a more practical level, constitutional rule of legality prevents the Prime Minister and other ministers from creating or reshaping government departments without a clear legal basis in a parliamentary Act. However, following the scheme of separating powers the most important actors within the field of securing the rule of law are courts of law and other overseers of legality: they embody the rule of law principle in visible institutional and functional form. We will first deal with the courts.

THE JUDICIARY AND JUDICIAL ORGANS

In Finland courts are an important part of the public decision-making machinery in contemporary society. However, it would be a mistake to assume that most social conflicts would be resolved by the courts. In

---

[8] Finnish Professor of legal history Jukka Kekkonen has coined these happenings as 'the shipwreck of legality' (*Laillisuuden haaksirikko*, Lakimiesliiton kustannus, Helsinki, 1991).

fact, the great majority of conflicts are resolved outside the courts by various official, semi-official and unofficial resolution organs. In general, the statistics seem to suggest that the so-called litigation-mania within the Western hemisphere has not fully reached Finland. Even though the law's role in general seems to have expanded, society has not undergone a transformation into being fully judicialised.[9]

The core constitutional function of the Finnish judicial system is simple: courts exercise judicial power, ie they decide individual cases. Following the separation of powers scheme the courts are functionally independent, meaning that they are bound only by the law in force. Basically, the constitutional core is clear: judicial power is exercised by independent courts of law. It has been rightly said that 'A judiciary which is in the hands of the government would turn the *Rechtsstaat* into a hypocritical farce.'[10] Accordingly, no outside party may intervene in the decision-making of the courts. This independence is guaranteed by the Constitution Act (section 3.3) and it is also generally held as an important constitutional principle, exceeding the narrow scope of the mere written provision. It is important to grasp that even though the Parliament is the most central constitutional organ, even it cannot directly interfere with the everyday practical functioning of judicial machinery. It goes without saying that this obligation not to interfere judging individual cases concerns also the Ministry of Justice which is, notwithstanding, in a formal organisational sense, steering the courts administratively (eg paying wages, acting as formal employer). The actual administration of the courts is by and large self-management and only very general administrative and budgetary functions are carried out by the Ministry.

The principal function of Finnish courts is adjudication, which is conducted by professional judges, known collectively as the 'judiciary' (*tuomarikunta*). The role of lay-judges, which takes place only in courts in the first instance, is today rather limited and there is no equivalent to common law's jury system in Finland. However, since there is no absolute separation of powers, public officials may also perform some functions that are as to their nature bordering on what is normally deemed as judicial. In turn, courts also have some internal administrative duties to perform. The actual cases with which they deal are divided into three

---

[9] See M Shapiro and Alec Stone Sweet, *On Law, Politics, and Judicialization* (Oxford University Press, Oxford, 2002).

[10] RC van Caenegem, *An Historical Introduction to Western Constitutional Law* (Cambridge University Press, Cambridge, 1995) 16.

main types of procedures: civil cases, criminal cases and administrative cases. There is no need to embark on a deeper analysis of these categories, since these case-types are typically what they are in other Roman-German law countries.

From a comparative point of view, nevertheless, the classification of law into different categories plays a significant role concerning the organisation of judiciary and courts. Public law cases that deal with administrative matters are dealt with by a different body of courts and judiciary than the other two branches. Of Nordic systems only Finland and Sweden follow this continental tradition, whereas Denmark, Iceland and Norway do not have separate administrative courts. In Finland, however, following the continental civil law tradition, there are separate courts for administrative legal disputes. The historical roots of the system may be traced back to the 1734 general Code of Procedure (*Oikeudenkäymiskaari*) of Sweden. From the 1970s there have been various reforms in which the judicial system has been changed to meet the tightened standards of each time.

It must also be noted that the ECtHR and the European Court of Justice (ECJ) have relevance as courts of law. However, since the ECtHR cannot overturn national judicial or administrative decisions, its significance is different from ordinary courts: it may find that the responding state has failed to safeguard the rights and freedoms protected by the ECHR. So, in this sense, the ECtHR has a relevant constitutional role, namely that states may change their legislation in order to prevent future judgments against them in similar situations. Individuals may of course invoke European human rights domestically but the authoritative interpretation of ECHR law takes place in the ECtHR. So, for example, when the ECtHR delivers judgments of the right to a fair trial, it also sets certain general requirements as to how the right to a fair trial must be interpreted in domestic practice.[11] The ECJ operates differently because individuals can invoke EC law before national courts and there is no need to wait for the exhaustion of domestic remedies as is the case with the ECtHR.[12]

If there is a problem concerning the content of EC law, a national court is obliged to ask for a preliminary judgment from the ECJ. A prime example is the case *Siilin* in which the ECJ delivered a preliminary judg-

---

[11] See ECtHR case *KP v Finland* (31 May 2001).
[12] See article 35(1) of the ECHR.

ment in 2002 which gave a basis for the Supreme Administrative Court to make a decision later that year, and, in the following year the Finnish Act in question was changed to meet the requirements of EC law.[13] As both of these non-domestic judicial elements are incorporated in various ways into Finnish law and because case law by both European courts is integrated into the working of national courts, they will not be separately dealt with in what follows.[14] Simply put, their precedents are Finnish precedents in a substantive constitutional sense.

The organisation of the courts follows the systematic separation between branches of law and it is rather straightforward. As already stated, there are two jurisdictional lines: general courts of law and administrative courts of law. The district courts (*Käräjäoikeus*) deal with criminal and civil cases and they are the courts of first instance. These courts are the only ones to also have lay-judges, who take part especially in civil law cases. Lay-judges, who must be Finnish citizens, must be over 25 years of age but not older than 63.

The decision of a district court can normally be appealed to a court of appeal (*Hovioikeus*). Today, there are six such courts spread out geographically throughout the country. In turn, the decisions of the courts of appeal may be appealed in the Supreme Court (*Korkein oikeus* (KKO)), provided that the Supreme Court grants leave to appeal. The regional administrative courts (*hallinto-oikeus*) review the decisions of public authorities. Typically, administrative disputes concern environmental matters, social welfare and tax disputes. The decisions of the administrative courts may be appealed to the Supreme Administrative Court (*Korkein hallinto-oikeus* (KHO)). Besides these there are certain special courts, including the Market Court, the Labour Court, the Insurance Court and the constitutionally interesting High Court of Impeachment. From a general point of view, all courts are part of the constitutional branch of judicial power. As the supreme courts are constitutionally the most relevant judicial organs, we will concentrate on them in the following discussion.

---

[13] Case C-101/00 *Siilin* KHO 2002:85. Act (266/03) was changed in 2003.

[14] In short, there are very seldom—if any—such cases that would deal only with the EU or only with the ECHR. These elements are intertwined with national legal questions: separations are hard to maintain.

SUPREME COURTS AND CONSTITUTIONALLY
RELEVANT CASE LAW

After World War II and after the collapse of socialism, continental Europe saw an extraordinary proliferation of specialised constitutional courts. In most of the systems this judicial body was created as a guardian against the possibility of sliding back into the earlier political culture, such as fascism or socialism. In Finland, as in other Nordic systems, there is no such constitutional court or even anything that could be regarded as an equivalent organ. Even the very possibility of such an organ has always been met with scepticism and inborn constitutional suspicion. Instead, at the apex of the judicial system there are two supreme courts, both having the last judicial say in their respective fields of jurisdiction.

Finland has two supreme courts divided along the lines of the legal system. Both of these courts have historical roots in the Russian era: in an historical sense they grew from the autonomy period's Senate. Both Finnish supreme courts deal with the facts and questions of law. Accordingly, they are not courts of cassation in nature, as in some other European countries (eg France, Greece and Italy). So, these courts do not only judge on the basis of the law and nor do they look exclusively at whether the lower courts have applied the law in a correct manner. However, it must be stated that most of the cases are decided on written documents only. There are, however, some cases in which supreme courts also organise new oral hearings even though these are quite rare.

Supreme Court

Background of the Supreme General Adjudication

The Supreme Court of Finland, which sits in Helsinki, was officially established in 1918, but its beginnings go back much further. The first superior courts in Sweden-Finland were the courts of appeal, which were originally intended to exercise the royal prerogative to adjudicate on the Monarch's behalf. The first of these courts was the Svea Court of Appeal, established in 1614. However, in practice, these superior courts became rather a kind of intermediate judicial instance because the old tradition of appealing directly to the King still remained in place (in Swedish '*gå till kungs*', ie 'to go to the King'). As a separate judicial organ, the Swedish Supreme Court was established in 1789. The Finnish situation changed in 1809 when Finland was annexed to Russia. The judicial duties of the Supreme Court were entrusted to the Justice Department of the Imperial Finnish Senate. This Department had a crucial role in developing the legal system in the first half of the Russian period. This role was assumed simply because the estates did not convene during that time.

From a modern point of view, this system was deeply problematic because it lacked a separation of powers. Accordingly, the senators of the Justice Department participated both in the exercise of executive power and legislative power. However, it should be mentioned that actually many of the senators were legal experts and many served also as university professors. However, these senators represented, at least in a formal sense, the Russian Emperor and the power of the Senate to adjudicate was in a constitutional sense ultimately the power of the Russian Czar. In practice, however, the Czar did not normally interfere with the use of judicial power. Nevertheless, the Czar sometimes exercised power through his delegate in Finland: the General-Governor. It was mainly in the periods of sharpened Russian repression in 1899–1905 and 1908–17 when Russian power was actively used against Finns. During these years the composition of the Justice Department was interfered with due to political reasons that had a clear Russian interest.

Things were radically transformed in 1918, and finally the Form of Government in 1919 changed the outdated structures and ideas. The Supreme Court was established in 1918 as an independent superior court in civil and criminal cases in Finland. At this stage, the members were required to be lawyers and they were given tenure. This basic constitutional status of the Supreme Court has not changed since 1918, even though there have been various reforms and obviously the constitutional context of today differs greatly from that of 1918. The most important single change occurred in 1980 when the Court became genuinely a court of precedential importance; the leave-to-appeal system was adopted in order to do something for the (then) ever increasing case load.

The Situation Today

According to the Constitution Act, 'justice in civil, commercial and criminal matters is in the final instance administered by the Supreme

Court' (CA section 99.1). Being the 'last instance' means simply that the Supreme Court is the last judicial resort in its jurisdiction. The Court's constitutionally special position is revealed in its capacity to supervise the administration of justice in its own field of competence and because it may also submit proposals to the Government in order to initiate legislative action (ie to propose enactment of a new parliament Act or an amendment to an existing Act). Now, it can be stated that the most central judicial function of the KKO is to establish judicial precedents (*ennakkopäätös*) in leading cases, thus ensuring uniformity in the administration of justice by the lower courts. In legal literature, the precedents of the KKO have even been regarded sometimes to have a genuine effect of stare decisis; however, this is probably an exaggeration as these precedents have rather a persuasive force than formal bindingness.[15] The Supreme Court may even annul final decisions of courts on certain specified grounds (chapter 31 of the Code of Judicial Procedure). The KKO also deals with complaints concerning claimed errors in judicial procedure. In certain cases the Court may restore the right of appeal after the expiration of a formal specified period of time.

There are also some other functions that cast more light on the specific constitutional position of the KKO; namely, the Court gives advice to the Republic's President in cases concerning the President's right to grant a pardon. The KKO also gives advice to the Ministry of Justice in cases concerning extradition. So, the KKO is clearly a supreme judicial organ, but it does not fully comply with the separation of powers scheme. One piece of proof of the fusion of powers is that the Court may even provide legal opinions on government bills at different stages of the legislative process. The President of the Republic may also consult the Court concerning bills passed by the Parliament and local provincial Acts adopted by the Åland Legislative Assembly before ratifying them. The Court may also approach the President on its own initiative. To generalise, it has more room for independent manoeuvring than lower courts. Also, in comparison with lower courts, the Supreme Court very seldom holds oral hearings: in this practical sense it resembles courts of cassation.

The President and other members (justices, *oikeusneuvos*) of the KKO are appointed by the President of the Republic. The justices normally

---

[15] A Aarnio, 'Precedent in Finland' in N MacCormick and R Summers (eds), *Interpreting Precedents—A Comparative Study* (Ashgate, Aldershot, 1997) 65–101, 92.

possess earlier experience from different branches of the legal profession, most often in courts, but also in the drafting of legislation, academic positions and as legal practitioners. According to the Act, the Court has a President and at least 15 members.[16] At present the Court consists of 18 members, however there are also other judicial positions in the Court; decisions are made on the basis of the preliminary work and opinion of the referendary (*esittelijä,* literally *'presenter'*). Referendaries, who are fully trained lawyers, prepare the cases and are also legally responsible for the outcome of the cases. From time to time, various proposals have been made suggesting the abolition of the referendary system, but this system is still used today.

Precedent

It has recently been argued that the 'Finnish legal culture is known for its conservative and legalistic attitude towards norm interpretation'.[17] Yet, if we look to the past and perhaps even today, this characterisation is not grossly unfair. Clearly, the Finnish system belongs in a substantive sense to Roman-Germanic law so there is no formal doctrine of binding precedent. However, in practice the situation is not this straightforward. No matter what Montesquieu thought, from the comparative study of judicial power we know that it is not possible to draw a clear distinction between judicial creation and interpretation of norms.[18] This also applies to Finland. In all cases before the Court, a leave to appeal (*valituslupa*) must first be granted before an appeal is allowed concerning a decision of a lower court.[19] However, not all the cases have similar judicial

---

[16]   Act on Supreme Court (Laki korkeimmasta oikeudesta 2005/665).

[17]   M Gräns, 'Duty of Loyal Interpretation' in L Ervo, M Gräns and A Jokela (eds), *Europeanization of Procedural Law and the New Challenges to Fair Trial* (Europa Law Publishing, Groeningen, 2009) 45–86, 61.

[18]   See M Cappelletti, *The Judicial Process in Comparative Perspective* (Clarendon Press, Oxford 1989) 5–7.

[19]   The grounds for leave to appeal are stipulated in chapter 30 section 3.1 of the Code of Judicial Procedure, under which the KKO can only grant leave to appeal on the following grounds: 1) if a decision of the KKO is needed for the application of law in identical or similar cases or for the consistency of case law; 2) if an error in procedure or other error has taken place in the case (ie the law requires that the decision must be overturned; and 3) there are other significant legal reasons for granting the leave to appeal.

weight: only a small amount of judgments are recognised as precedents. The KKO decides on important points of law in cases that are deemed significant for the entire legal order, guiding lower judiciary in future cases. The Supreme Administrative Court does the same, although it does not quite have as clear an equivalent role as a court with power to make precedents.

Precedents are usually created in cases for which the applicable written law does not provide a clear solution for a question of law or in which there is an unexceptionally large space for interpretation. Around 150 such judicial decisions are decided each year. Constitutionally, these cases are the core of case law having the nature of precedents (see chapter 1). The constitutional nature of these judgments concerns constitutional law within two specific meanings: 1) few cases deal directly with constitutional rights, and 2) all of these cases also produce new law (to an extent) which is not stemming directly from the legislative power of the Parliament. All in all, the latter may be regarded as a more relevant feature.

From a legal-linguistic point of view, we find here yet another trace reminding us of the old relation of Swedish and Finnish law: precedent is called generally *'prejudikaatti'* which is a word coming from Sweden to Finland (in Swedish *'prejudikat'*). Furthermore, the meaning of precedent is precisely the same. Precedent is 'a judicial decision on concrete case which becomes authoritative for future cases'.[20] Dissenting opinions are allowed and they are rather frequent; typically, voting takes place in hard cases which frequently become precedents.

Doctrine on sources of law (see chapter one) holds that case law has only a weak binding force, but the actual practice of the lower courts tells another story. From a comparative point of view it must be stressed that these precedents are not binding in the same sense as the precedents are traditionally binding (*stare decisis*) in common law systems. Lower courts may, and frequently do, from time to time depart from earlier decisions made by the KKO. These deviations are normally explained by the considerable change of social circumstances. However, in practice, precedents of the KKO are normally followed in later cases involving a similar point of law. Also the KKO itself sometimes departs from its own precedents—there are no strict formal obstacles for doing this. Nevertheless, such a case must be considered by an enlarged chamber

---

[20] A Peczenik, *Juridikens teori och metod* (Fritzes, Stockholm, 1995) 37.

(11 members) or by a full Court. The precedents are made well known to the legal audience and public since they are published every six months.[21]

Most cases, numbering approximately several thousand per year, are not regarded as precedents. The inner panel of the Court decides which are regarded as precedents and also makes the decisions concerning the publication. Precedents are carefully followed, adhered to and discussed by the legal profession including academic experts.[22] However, Finnish precedents do not form any certain distinctive body of judicial precedents as in common law: precedents in Finland fulfil legislative gaps and provide more detailed information on the content of statutory law but they do not genuinely form new law which would be derived from these precedents. This applies also to the precedents of the Supreme Administrative Court.

Supreme Administrative Court

It is useful to bear in mind that in Finland the legal competences of administrative courts are rather broad comparatively speaking. That is, they are not inferior courts but have an important constitutional role in their judicial capacities. Administrative courts have jurisdiction over appeals from decisions of public organs like local government, municipalities and state government. Also, disputes between administrative bodies or between a private party and public authority may be processed in administrative courts. However, in cases of conflict between a general and administrative court it is the Supreme Court that settles these issues of jurisdictional competence. In general, courts have jurisdiction concerning cases of using the public power if an individual seeks damages or demands criminal responsibility for an act or a decision which has been caused in the use of public power (CA section 118.3).

According to the Constitution Act, the KHO is the court of last resort in administrative cases and also sits in Helsinki. It was established

---

[21] They are also available in a database (FINLEX). Since November 1998 the public has had access to the precedents free of charge (www.finlex.fi).

[22] The leading general law journal in Finland, *The Lawyer* (*Lakimies*) publishes several detailed and often critical learned comments. Also, the legal journal of *Defensor Legis* publishes these kinds of comments. During the last few years especially, cases concerning constitutional rights and constitutional judicial review have gained much coverage.

in 1918 and it had no clear predecessor in the old constitutional system, whereas the Supreme Court may clearly be seen to continue the Swedish and Grand Duchy judicial heritage. When the KHO was engineered, the drafters used many foreign models (mostly combining German, French, and Swedish ideas) according to which the administrative judicial power should be organised separately from the administrative power. During the Swedish and Russian period, the placement of such a function was not understood as a problem but in the independent new republic also the administrative judicial power was deemed to be separated from the executive power under which it had previously been organised. Accordingly, in 1918 when the Act on the Supreme Administrative Court was enacted, it contained a rule (section 5.1), according to which non-legal questions should be directed to the Government.[23] In fact, however, this rule seems to mean virtually nothing because the Court tends to see legal questions in practically all cases. This seems to speak of a certain degree of judicialisation of politics that, in turn, limits the political freedom of movement of political decision-makers and enhances the authority of judicial organs. On the other hand, this judicialisation does not probably reflect much on genuine judicial activism but rather on the quality of legislation becoming more and more open to interpretation.

Today, the Court includes the President and 20 justices (*hallintoneuvos*), as well as a few temporary justices. The Court has also several referendaries and 40 other employees. They are headed by the Secretary General. The Supreme Administrative Court functions in three chambers; the most important cases are decided in plenary sessions. Cases are normally decided by Chambers composed of five judges but in certain special cases (environment, patents) the Chambers also include two expert members having substantive competence in the relevant field.

The basic idea of administrative adjudicating is simple: anyone who is dissatisfied with an administrative decision (*hallintopäätös*) pertaining to his or her rights or obligations may challenge the lawfulness of the decision before an administrative court. The right of appeal in such cases is mainly covered by the provisions of the Administrative Judicial Procedure Act, which is applied by all the administrative courts.[24] In

---

[23] *Laki Korkeimmasta Hallinto-oikeudesta* (74/1918). This rule is also part of the reformed Act from 2006 (section 2.1).

[24] *Hallintolainkäyttölaki* (586/1996). This Act concerns the right of appeal; administrative decision by public authorities may be challenged as provided by this Act.

practice, most of the categories of cases handled by the KHO are not subject to the requirement of leave to appeal, which is clearly different than with the Supreme Court. It is a basic rule that the parties have a right to appeal, and the KHO issues—in the second judicial instance—a decision on merits. It has been possible that the parties to the proceedings are sometimes able to pursue their cases without professional legal help, which facilitates the lodging of appeal and access to legal remedies. However, due to the complex legal nature of many developments, the ability to go to administrative court requires professional legal help as is the case with the KKO.

When refusing leave to appeal, a chamber may be composed of three judges. Cases raising significant issues may be decided by a panel of all the judges of the Chamber, or be subject to the Court's plenary review. Before the examination of the case by a Chamber takes place, the referendary establishes the questions of law and the facts of the case and writes a draft decision. The deliberations and the issue of the decision take place after the referendary has presented written and oral statements in the Chamber's session. This process is basically the same as it is in the KKO. Accordingly, dissenting opinions are possible and do take place.

Special Courts

There are courts which are understood to be special as to their nature, but it does not mean that they would be somehow less judicial than ordinary courts. In fact, the specialisation refers mainly to the kind of specialised field of jurisdiction in which they function judicially. In all other respects, even the special courts are courts run by professional and independent judiciary. Undoubtedly, these courts fall clearly under the judicial branch meant in the Constitution Act.

The Market Court (*Markkinaoikeus*) is a special court hearing cases that have been subjected to its jurisdiction by specific Acts (Act on Competition Restrictions, Public Procurement Act, Act on Certain Proceedings before the Market Court) and other legislation. Judges of this Court are judges who have served on the bench but also judges with certain special economic expertise. The Court may issue injunctions against illegal restrictions of competition and order monetary penalties. It has duties also concerning the supervision of mergers and acquisitions. Further, the Court may overturn public procurement decisions, adjust the procurement process and order different kinds of compensatory payments.[25] It also has a role concerning disputes between the Consumer Ombudsman (*Kuluttajansuoja-asiamies*) and businesses as to whether goods or services have been marketed in an unfair manner. Besides law, this Court also relies on proper business practice generally accepted among those who deal with business on a professional basis.

The Labour Court (*Työtuomioistuin*) has been, from its inception, a special court with narrow jurisdiction covering legal disputes resulting from collective agreements. The Court handles cases that arise from collective agreements or collective civil servants' agreements. By contrast, disputes concerning individual employment relationships (eg disagreements on pay or giving notice) are handled by the general courts. Disputes on individual civil service relationships belong to the jurisdiction of the administrative courts, following the systematic separation between private and public law. However, the significance of this distinction has become less and less relevant during the past years partly because of the case law of the ECtHR.[26] The Labour Court is based on the tripartite principle: judges are nominated after the proposal of the parties in the labour market representing employees, employers and civil servants. The verdict of the Labour Court is final; there is no right to appeal.[27] The tripartite principle has been from time to time a target for critique because of the role of the parties in the labour market.

The Insurance Court (*Vakuutusoikeus*) is a special court for social security, offering legal remedies for those who are unsatisfied with the decisions of social insurance institutions or an unemployment fund.[28] They may appeal the decision first to the Unemployment Appeal Board, and then about the decision of the Board to the Insurance Court. The decisions of the Insurance Court cannot be appealed. The Court has jurisdiction in certain matters of social insurance, such as accident insurance, employment pensions, civil service pensions and national pensions. There has been constantly constitutional debate concerning the position of some part-time members who are nominated by interest groups. This practice has been criticised mainly on a constitutional basis:

---

[25] Act on the Market Court (*Laki markkinaoikeudesta* 1527/2001).

[26] See eg, case *Eskelinen v Finland* (19 April 2007) in which the Court changed its earlier precedent and gave a broader interpretation to article 6.1 of ECHR.

[27] Act on Labour Court (*Laki työtuomioistuimesta* (646/1974).

[28] Act on Insurance Court (*Vakuutusoikeuslaki* 132/2003).

separation of powers and the following independence of a court. On the other hand, these special members bring expert knowledge into the working of the Court.

There has been very little principled constitutional debate over special courts. Rather, problems have been more practical as to their nature. And yet, it has been generally accepted that there is certainly no need to establish new special courts or to expand the jurisdiction of now existing special courts. From a practical point of view it may be noted that sometimes it has been problematic to recruit enough competent lawyers to special courts because within the profession general courts are held in higher esteem. Obviously, the huge amount of case-load in each of the abovementioned special courts is also a factor which may make these courts less inviting for such jurists who are seeking a career within the judiciary: a huge workload with little prospect of advancement in judicial career is sure to lower the interest of prospective young lawyers.

Constitutional Remnant—High Court of Impeachment

The court that is of the most constitutional importance is the High Court of Impeachment (*valtakunnanoikeus*, ie 'court of the realm') which has convened only a few times: 1933, 1953, 1961 and 1993. The last time it convened, in 1993, was when Minister Kauko Juhantalo (Centre) was convicted by the High Court of Impeachment to one year's conditional imprisonment. He was found guilty of demanding illegal advantage in the capacity of minister.

The Court is a special forum for criminal charges against a minister, the Chancellor of Justice or a member of the Supreme Court or Supreme Administrative Court for an offence in office. In this event, the prosecution is taken care of by the Prosecutor-General (*valtakunnansyyttäjä*), the Chancellor of Justice or the Parliamentary Ombudsman. The Court consists of five high professional judges and five parliamentary members. The five parliamentary members of the High Court of Impeachment, who serve for four-year terms, are elected by the Parliament from among its MPs. The term of parliamentary members is the same as the term of the Parliament. If there are no cases, the Court does not convene at all.

The decisions of this high special court cannot be appealed, so, the verdict of the Court is final. The High Court of Impeachment may be formally compared with a sort of constitutional court; however, functionally it is certainly not equivalent to a constitutional court. The fact that it convenes so seldom seriously restricts its practical constitutional significance a great deal. Rather, it is a constitutional curiosity of institutional character with no more than tradition to explain its prolonged existence in today's system. The Court is, from the point of view of court organisation, a kind of anomaly, explained only by constitutional past, ie a constitutional ruin with ingredients from various older constitutional layers. Like some other features in the present Finnish constitutional landscape it tells about mild constitutional conservatism, otherwise it would not be directly regulated in the Constitution Act (section 101) itself.

Appointing and Dismissing Judges

If the independence of judiciary is deemed a crucial part of constitutionalism, then it makes sense to look at how judges are appointed to and dismissed from their positions. In a legal cultural sense, Finland is a civil law system in that lawyers are theoretically educated exclusively by faculties of law in universities.[29] Academic training of lawyers is directed to the profession of judge; that is, training gives a formal base for a judicial career. A master's degree in law (*oikeustieteen maisteri*) is the qualification required of all judges. Most judges do not come from the ranks of practising lawyers, such as solicitors and barristers in the United Kingdom; they rather start their judicial career as junior judicial officials. So, some lawyers choose a very early judicial career after having graduated from a faculty of law. They are normally promoted to higher and more senior positions on the basis of the years in service and also on the basis of their performance and tenure. The French model, according to which judges are recruited by a competitive examination on a technical basis, is not followed.

It has been suggested that the background of judges should be more varied and, thus, the judicial career should be more open. This has been defended by a greater democratic nature of judicial function. However,

---

[29] There are several university institutions teaching and researching law, but only three fully fledged faculties of law (*oikeustieteellinen tiedekunta*) in Finland: Universities of Helsinki, Turku, and Lapland. The master's degree in law is practically similar in all of these faculties; the degree offers an understanding of the whole legal system and allows very little, if any, specialisation. Other departments of law offer more specialised programmes (eg Universities of Eastern Finland and Tampere).

even today the career of a judge seems to be very much a closed career in typical Roman-Germanic fashion. In this, Finnish legal culture belongs clearly to civil law legal culture, although the effect of Roman law was never very strong in Finland if compared with Central Europe: *ius commune* did have an effect in Finland too but indirectly and to a lesser extent than in Central Europe. However, as in all Nordic countries, German legal science of the nineteenth century had a great impact on academic law, including constitutional law.[30] Many times this Germanic connection explains the similarities in legal thinking: systematics of law, basic categories, concepts, doctrines and sometimes even substantive rules in certain similar features. However, in constitutional law the similarities are scarcer than in some other areas of law. Accordingly, all Nordic constitutions have retained a highly national basic nature. However, basic things concerning the formal position of judges appear rather similar, not only in Nordic countries but throughout Western Europe.

According to the Constitution Act (section 102), tenured judges are appointed by the President of the Republic. Is this not a problem form the point of view of separating powers? Clearly, if one underlines the importance of keeping executive power and judicial power apart from each other there appears to be a certain inconsistency here.[31] Be that as it may, it is hard to discern any true significance of party politics here; appointments are made on merit and judges seem to lack any distinctive political affiliation. The appointment procedure is laid down by an Act, according to which there is an independent Judicial Appointments Board. This Board, which consists of professional judges, prepares and makes a reasoned proposal on an appointment to a tenured position in the judiciary. Clearly, this system contains a strong element of judiciary *itself* choosing new judges. This, in turn, seems to be problematic from the point of view of parliamentary centred democracy because the judiciary's accountability is practically limited and its ability to recruit outside the small circles of career judges is minimal indeed.

The Board delivers its proposal to the Government to be presented to the President of the Republic. The constitutional competence of the Board includes, for example, the proposals on an appointment to the president of a court of appeal, senior justice of a court of appeal, justice

---

[30] See D Tamm, 'The Nordic Legal Tradition in European Context' in P Letto-Vanamo (ed), *Nordisk indentitet* (KATTI, Helsinki, 1998) 15–31.

[31] However, this inconsistency is explicitly allowed by the Constitutional Law Committee in its Report (13/1999).

of a court of appeal, chief judge of an administrative court, and administrative court judge. Nevertheless, it must be underlined that both of the supreme courts themselves make a reasoned proposal on an appointment as a justice of the Supreme Court or Supreme Administrative Court. The board is nominated by the Government for five years at a time and it consists of 12 members representing the judiciary, the public prosecution service, the advocacy and the research and teaching of law. Of constitutional importance is the fact that only a Finnish citizen can be appointed to a position in the judiciary. The chief justices of the supreme courts are appointed without any formal preparatory procedure. As stated above, in fact these courts themselves have a significant role in this. The main problem of these appointing procedures is the fact that they are not transparent: how a certain candidate is deemed best remains almost a complete mystery to outsiders.

A Finnish judge sits in office rather securely. A judge may be disqualified from a case if he or she has a close connection with the parties or has a personal interest that is seen to endanger impartiality. A judge cannot be suspended from office very easily because a judgment by a court of law is needed. This reflects the principle of separation of powers and the constitutionally important independency of judiciary. An Act regulates the duty of a judge to resign due to having reached a certain age or after losing the capability to do judicial work. Specific rules concerning a judge's rights and obligations, as well as their other terms of service, must be stipulated in an Act (CA section 103) and not in any lower statute. Even though a technically normal Act, this Act is, as to its nature, clearly constitutional as are all other such Acts dealing with the special status of judges: this legislation defines the actual content and extent of judicial power.

Domestic Courts and the ECJ

The legal cultural relationship of Finnish courts to the ECJ appears somewhat curious. This curiosity is shown clearly when it comes to the idea of interpreting EC law loyally; that is, to follow the duty of interpreting domestic law in the light of EC law. On the one hand, Finnish courts do not seem to like to deal with EC law directly and, thus, only a small portion of the Supreme Court's case law refers to the ECJ's case law. However, there are cases in which priority is given openly and clearly to EC law.[32] On the other hand, however, the legalistic tradition seems to result in very high formal respect towards EC law. The willingness of Finnish courts to regard EC law as hierarchically the highest law appears to be evident in Finnish case law: sometimes domestic sources of law are simply omitted and EC law has a dominant position. In other words, courts tend to cut off national norms from their domestic legal context and look exclusively through EC law. This seems to reflect the openness of Finnish courts toward the ECJ's case law, even though this openness seems to be contradictory to earlier, more nationally oriented judicial mentality.

It has been claimed that the outcome of Finnish judicial mentality, by following the ECJ's case law loyally, has sometimes turned into defiance against the national legislator. The argument is that Finnish courts seem to give more weight to the ECJ's case law than to national legislation. This, however, is not what the duty of loyal interpretation is about. From the point of view of the Constitution, it seems strange that the courts are so eager to ignore the national legal sources and jump hastily to the EC's rules.[33] Denmark has a very different legal mentality in this regard: Danish courts are very willing to display great loyalty toward the Danish parliament in cases in which there is inconsistency between EC law and domestic legislation.[34] All of this hints at how deeply Europeanised the Finnish judicial organs actually are; they go even beyond what the EC law requires and no questions concerning hierarchy of norms or the position of national Constitution are uttered. This, if anything, is a good example of a certain legalistic mentality that was born during the Russian era in the 1800s. The difference is that back then the outside effect was deflected, not embraced.

[32] See case KHO 2002:85 (concerning the method of calculating taxation of cars which are brought to Finland from other EU states).

[33] See M Gräns, 'Duty of Loyal Interpretation' in L Ervo, M Gräns and A Jokela (eds), *Europeanization of Procedural Law and the New Challenges to Fair Trial* (Europa Law Publishing, Groeningen, 2009) 45–86.

[34] See M Wind, 'When Parliament Comes First—The Danish Concept of Democracy Meets the European Union' (2009) 27 *Nordic Journal of Human Rights* 272.

OTHER FORMS OF ENSURING CONSTITUTIONALITY:
OVERSEEING LEGALITY

The Finnish constitutional system relies also on other forms of ensuring constitutionality and legality than just the judiciary. Obviously, if the willingness to abide by constitutional rules would rest solely on the shoulders of the courts, then the system would hardly be following the true spirit of constitutionalism. As it was previously noted, the rule of law principle (though understood in the German *Rechtsstaat* manner) ought to penetrate the whole system of public power. However, some other organs besides the courts have especially certain constitutionally relevant functions that are close to judicial functions, thus, they are dealt with in this chapter. Of these quasi-judicial organs, the most central constitutionally are the Chancellor of Justice and the Ombudsman. Their constitutionally most relevant function is to monitor the implementation of constitutional rights and liberties, human rights included. This special connection to constitutional rights is one of the reasons why an overseer's constitutional position is different from other kinds of supervisors of legality. These two organs have also high constitutional visibility as frontline constitutional institutions.

Both of these organs have a firm and visible position in the Constitution Act and they are highly respected by the public and by other branches of public power. Besides, both of these organs have rather high public visibility, which sometimes gives the false impression concerning their powers and encourages people to make complaints to them, even in such cases in which they have no jurisdiction. The main function of overseeing legality (literally *laillisuusvalvonta*) is to investigate cases of maladministration referred to the overseers by individual complaints. According to Antero Jyränki, this special form of overseeing legality contains all such arrangements that are meant to enhance the principle of *Rechtsstaat* and especially the Finnish basic rule according to which in all public activity 'the law shall be strictly observed'.[35] However, this supervision differs from that of the courts: overseers have no formal power to grant remedy and, yet, their decisions and recommendations are normally both respected and followed by public bodies. Academic public law research and teaching also treats these organs as important sources of information.

---

[35] A Jyränki, *Our New Constitution Act* ['*Uusi perustulakimme*'] (Iura Nova, Turku, 2000) 248.

The Chancellor of Justice

The Chancellor of Justice of the Council of State (*Valtioneuvoston oikeus-kansleri*) has a constitutionally guaranteed formal position as an independent supervisor of legality. The Chancellor is formally appointed by the President of the Republic. It is the Chancellor's duty to monitor the legality of the operations of the Government, other public authorities, and public agencies. In addition, the Chancellor also monitors the activities of the members of the Finnish Bar Association (*Asianajajaliitto*). What makes the Chancellor a somewhat constitutionally puzzling institution is the fact that it is not merely an organ that oversees legality independently like the Ombudsman, the institution's parliamentary counterpart. Instead, the Chancellor is also a sort of 'High Jurist of the Crown' (*kruununjuristi*) because the Chancellor must, if requested, provide information and opinions on legal issues for the President, the Government and the ministries of the Government. Comparative remarks can be made in this context: the Chancellor has plenty of similarities with the Attorney General of various countries (eg the United Kingdom). The closest parallels are the Swedish (*Justitieskansler*) and Estonian (*Òiguskantsler*) Chancellors of Justice.

The Crown-Jurist dimension is clearly reflected in the fact that the Chancellor must be present at the official meetings of the Government and also when matters are presented to the President in presidential meetings of the Government (CA section 111.2). In practice this means that the Chancellor's Office has a dual function of monitoring and advising, which is hard to reconcile with the separation of powers principle. To understand why there is such an organ in Finland can be conceived against the background of Finnish constitutional conservatism, which makes it difficult to make any drastic changes concerning the basic constitutional structure and institutions.

It is possible to argue that the origin of this institution took place in 1713 when Charles XII established a position of high ombudsman (in Swedish '*konungens högsta ombudsman*'). However, the Chancellor institution was actually developed in the latter part of the eighteenth century in a situation in which there was a power struggle for the supreme power between the aristocracy and the Monarch. Historically, the Chancellor of Justice actually originates from Gustavian regulations and governmental practices. In the Gustavian period, the Chancellor was merely the Monarch's tool; the Chancellor was appointed by the Monarch and carried out his duties while always being responsible to the Monarch. During the era of the Grand Duchy, the Chancellor was transformed into a Procurator which was formally the highest supervisor concerning Finnish legislation. In fact the office was immediately subordinate to Russian power and, ultimately, to the Emperor himself. Out of this grew an institution which had the old Gustavian function of the Crown's own lawyer, combined with the Grand Duchy function of overseeing Finnish legality. In 1919 the Chancellor institution was all but new when it was conservatively adopted into the system of 1919 Form of Government.

The Russian-style title of Autonomy (ie Procurator) was changed back to that of Chancellor of Justice (in Swedish *Justitiekansler*), which means that this old Swedish tradition continues its existence in Finland 200 years after Sweden and Finland were separated. In essence, the functions of governmental supervision were combined with advising the high executive organs of the State representing the continuity of strong central power fitted in the republican system in connection with the Government (institutional place) and the President (nomination). Even though there have been many slight changes to this institution, the basic features are still the same: overseeing the legality and simultaneously advising the very same institutions that the Chancellor also monitors.

The Chancellor must submit an annual report concerning the Chancellor's activities and observations on how law has been obeyed and especially on constitutional and human rights. This report is given both to the Parliament and to the Government. In Parliament this report is handled by the Constitutional Law Committee. This reporting practice is also an old one: during the Russian period the Procurator gave the Procurator's Report to the Diet concerning the obeying of law during the period after previous gatherings of the Diet of the Estates.

The Parliamentary Ombudsman

The Finnish machinery of public power is also guarded by the Parliamentary Ombudsman (*Eduskunnan oikeusasiamies*). At first sight it is difficult to distinguish these two high legality-supervisors. To grasp why there are two such similar organs becomes possible only by looking back into constitutional history. To begin with, clearly the Ombudsman is a more recent post than that of the Chancellor of Justice. It might be argued that over 200 years separates these institutions, but this would not be quite correct. Yet, no one can deny that the Ombudsman came much later: it is genuinely a republican institution in Finnish constitutional settings, whereas the Chancellor has roots in monarchical layers.

During the nineteenth century numerous proposals were made in order to found the post of Ombudsman, but these did not lead to the hoped-for results. It was only in the very late phase of drafting the 1919 Form of Government when the provisions regarding the post were incorporated into the Finnish Constitution. In a legal-technical sense, the institution was a constitutional transplant from Sweden where it had been created in 1809. Under the Finnish circumstances this institution was created to become a kind of a counterweight to the Chancellor of Justice: in 1919 the Parliament desired to have a legality-supervising organ that would enjoy the confidence of the Parliament. Undoubtedly, the Ombudsman was originally designed as a kind of a parliamentary-spirited counterweight to the Chancellor of Justice. However, today there are no visible traces of this conflict-embedded origin of the Ombudsman institution; at least, there are no visible tensions between these overseers of legality. On the other hand, the fact that the Chancellor is so closely institutionally connected to the President and the Government makes it is very hard not to suspect certain hidden constitutional tensions between these two overseers of legality.

Nevertheless, the most natural point of comparison is the Chancellor, even though the Chancellor is institutionally located within the executive branch whereas the Ombudsman is located within the legislative power. In fact, however, this means virtually nothing as they are both independent in their functioning as overseers of legality. As we saw, we may say that the idea of the Ombudsman came from Sweden but even more important was the idea that Parliament ought to have its own guardian of law. Accordingly, the Ombudsman is nominated to office by the Parliament. During its first years the Ombudsman had clearly less constitutional prestige than the Chancellor. Today, there are hardly any significant differences concerning the constitutional prestige of these high overseers of legality. Nevertheless, a greater number of individuals would seem to rather turn to the Ombudsman than to the Chancellor. It would appear that in the mental imagery of people, the Ombudsman is connected to the protection of those in weak positions (women, children, institutionalised, minorities, etc).

Generally speaking, the competences of the Ombudsman and the Chancellor to investigate complaints (*kantelu*) are in practice identical.

The duties of these authorities differ only in that the overseeing of the legality of the activities of the Council of State, ie Government in a narrow sense is entrusted mainly to the Chancellor of Justice. Paradoxically, the Chancellor also has important advisory duties while serving the executive power as a top legal adviser. In turn, matters specifically related to conscripts and convicts are within the ambit of the Ombudsman. Even while overseers of legality are guarding the rule of law principle, it is important to distinguish the overseers of legality from the courts of law. In short, overseers are not courts of law and in a narrower sense are not even clearly judicial organs. So, guardians of legality have no jurisdiction to alter the decisions of other authorities on the basis of complaints or to award damages. Their rulings, which are legally administrative decisions, not judgments, are not legally equivalent to court decisions and are not subject to appeal.

The Ombudsman must also report to the Parliament concerning the Ombudsman's work, including observations on the state of the administration of justice and possible shortcomings in legislation. Despite its name, this institution does not oversee the Parliament or its individual members, nor does it take part in any activities of the Parliament. So, the Ombudsman is more a general organ of public legality control than an organ of the Parliament in any meaningful sense.

Other Control Organs

In addition to these constitutionally central overseers of legality, there are certain specialised authorities that have similar duties but in more limited fields. In Finnish constitutional law the concept of 'highest overseeing of legality' (*ylin laillisuusvalvonta*) is strictly confined to the Chancellor of Justice and the Parliamentary Ombudsman, which are regarded as genuinely constitutional organs. Nevertheless, there are yet other overseers who have certain constitutional significance in a sense that their functions are very close to that of the highest overseers of legality. In short, they exercise delegated constitutional authority. These organs include, for example, the Consumer Ombudsman (*Kuluttaja-asiamies*), the Ombudsman for Equality (*Tasa-arvovaltuutettu*), the Data Protection Ombudsman (*Tietosuojavaltuutettu*) and the Ombudsman for Minorities (*Vähemmistövaltuutettu*). They all function very much like the general guardians of legality, but only in respect of certain specialised questions. An independent entity, the Consumer Ombudsman's goals and functions are mandated by legislation, according to which it monitors the safety of the products offered in the market place and consumers' rights to essential information. The Ombudsman of Equality is also an independent authority that functions monitoring compliance with the Act on Equality between Women and Men. It promotes the purpose of the Act by making initiatives, giving advice and counselling.[36]

The Data Protection Ombudsman guides and controls the processing of personal data and it also provides consultation related to personal data questions with a legal nature. The main functions of the Data Protection Ombudsman include influencing compliance with legislation concerning the keeping of registers. This specialised Ombudsman also provides information about the Personal Data Act.[37] The Ombudsman for Minorities is, like other Ombudsmen, an independent authority with a special task. This Ombudsman tries to enhance the status and legal protection of ethnic minorities and foreigners in Finland. It also tries to advance equality, non-discrimination and good ethnic relations.

Of these Ombudsmen authorities, the ones for equality, data protection and minorities have a particularly clear constitutional base on which they fundamentally rely upon; section 6 of the Constitution Act contains an important constitutional rule of equal treatment of everyone (enlisting various discriminatory reasons which are *expressis verbis* prohibited). So, the fundamental authority of these overseers flows from the Constitution and in a more narrow sense indirectly from the Constitution Act: they all seek to guarantee certain dimensions of constitutional rights and human rights in the sense of section 22 of the Constitution Act ('shall guarantee the observance').

THE HIERARCHY OF NORMS AND ITS MAINTENANCE: CONSTITUTIONAL JUDICIAL REVIEW

This section examines the role of the hierarchy of norms and its status in the constitutional system from the point of view of judicial function. The idea of a hierarchy of legal norms is typical for most modern constitutional systems. It has been the hallmark of Continental European constitutional philosophy from the beginning of the twentieth century.

[36] *Tasa-arvolaki* (609/1986) defines and prohibits discrimination based on gender.
[37] *Henkilötietolaki* (523/1999).

Theoretical thinking in a hierarchy of norms relies on the idea of the fundamental unity of a legal system. By far the most famous theorist of this school, Hans Kelsen, formulated this doctrine on the basis of previous work by Adolf Merkl (1890–1970) who thought that law must itself govern its own production; that is, creating formal legal rules is itself also a legal phenomenon. Kelsen suggested that a legal system consists of different steps or layers (*Stufenbau der Rechtsordnung*) so that the validity of each norm may be traced back to a higher one. At the apex of this hierarchical system is the Constitution. Even though this doctrine is today criticised and in many senses also doubted, it still has considerable significance even in today's Europe.[38] Even with its many flaws, it seems to capture something essentially important in today's constitutional thinking. From a national point of view, the position of EU law within domestic hierarchy of norms seems to cause a certain chronic headache for domestic constitutional doctrine: it is difficult to depict domestic and EU systems as genuinely one system but is also equally difficult to try to maintain that they would be truly separate systems from each other. More precisely, constitutionalists would like to have their cake and eat it too.

However, Kelsen's *Stufenbau*-theory is clearly an ideal model that is not fully followed as such in any living constitutional system. This is also the case with Finland. Nonetheless, the central core of this doctrine has had and still has an important role in Finnish constitutional law. As a shadow skeleton, it has both bases in the written Constitution Act and in the general doctrines of Finnish public law. It is part of domestic constitutional mentality. We have already discussed how the hierarchy of norms effects the preparation and passing of new legislation. As we noted, from an institutional point of view, the role of the Constitutional Law Committee is central in this. In the following, the issue on constitutional review of legislation by the courts shall be discussed in greater detail. The underpinning idea is to look at how the judiciary takes part in upholding the constitutional hierarchy of norms. In practice, however, this function of judiciary is exercised jointly with the Constitutional Law Committee and its authoritative statements about the content of the Constitution especially play a decisive role.

---

[38] T Öhlinger, 'Unity of the Legal System or Legal Pluralism: The *Stufenbau* Doctrine in Present-Day Europe' in A Jyränki (ed), *National Constitutions in the Era of Integration* (Kluwer, London, 1999) 163–74.

The Road to Constitutional Judicial Review

The debate over judicial control of constitutionality in Finland has many national features, but it is very much comprehensible for anyone familiar with these questions in other constitutional systems. One specific argument presented before the mid nineteenth century by the classic constitutional figure Alexis de Tocqueville fits surprisingly well in the traditional Finnish constitutional landscape of constitutionality control by saying that 'it is still better to give the power to change people's constitution to men, who however imperfectly, represent the people's will, than to others who represent nobody but themselves'.[39] As Finland's political system has not been a 'quarrelling democracy' but is consensus-oriented, there has not been a true need for a constitutional court to resolve politicised constitutional conflicts.[40] Also, as a unitary state, there is no need to resolve constitutional disputes over competence between federal power and states as in the United States or in Germany.

Even though the Finnish system has regarded the supremacy of constitutional norms to be quite a natural part of the legal system, the question itself has been a highly delicate one in connection with judicial organs. Conceiving of the hierarchical supremacy of constitutional rules enabling the unelected judges to refuse to apply normal parliamentary legislation on the basis of violating the Constitution, has been an especially complex and sensitive question from the days of the late Grand Duchy to the present Eurostate. The practice of judges defying the will of democratically-elected majority law-makers has certainly not been a traditional part of Finnish constitutional morality. This fact itself requires contextual information — once again we find that in order to be able to understand the present system one must look backward.

According to the earlier system, courts and other public authorities had no competence to review the constitutionality of the Acts; instead the control of norms lower than parliamentary Acts was possible. The emphasis on the control was solely located on the preventive and abstract norm-control executed by one special standing committee of the Parliament, the Constitutional Law Committee (see above in chapter three). According to the generally accepted interpretation of section 92

---

[39] A de Tocqueville, *Democracy in America* (Fontana Press, London, 1840/1994) 101.
[40] This has been the role of the constitutional court in Hungary (established in 1990), A Rácz, 'Constitutional Law' in A Harmathy (ed), *Introduction to Hungarian Law* (Kluwer, The Hague/London/Boston, 1998) 23–37, 36–37.

of the 1919 Form of Government, a public authority could not apply a lower regulation (ie decree) that was incompatible with the parliamentary Act or the Constitution Act. In prevailing constitutional literature, an e contrario interpretation was made of this provision, according to which no authority had the right to observe the constitutionality of the parliamentary Act after it had been entered into force.[41] This prohibition also bound courts. In similar fashion the Dutch Constitution Act (article 120) mentions only Acts of the Parliament [when discussing . . .], meaning that regulations with a lower status can be reviewed by the courts.[42]

One of the most important questions of modern constitutionalism was presented by Hans Kelsen in the 1930s: 'Who should be the guardian of Constitution?'[43] Up to this day, the Finnish system has not genuinely followed Kelsen's lead but has persisted in answering the 'Parliament' rather than the 'court'. This, in turn, diminishes the general constitutional role of the judiciary. However, it certainly enhances the democratic and parliamentary features of the system. On the other hand, the role of the judiciary is today stronger than earlier due to the heightened status of constitutional and human rights.

The Judicial Threshold: Requirement of 'Clear Contradiction'

It has been customary to think that 'we the Finns' are somehow separate from the rest of Europe. Perhaps this explains at least partially why some of our national constitutional constructions have persisted so long. Judicial expansion in a legal cultural sense did, however, finally arrive in Finland during the 1990s. Reforms in 2000 brought to the Constitution Act a new section 106, including a provision that enables limited judicial review of the constitutionality of the Acts in the courts and the power to refuse to apply the provision of an Act when the application of the provision of an Act would result in a clear contradiction (*ilmeinen ristiriita*, may also be translated as *'evident conflict'*) with the Constitution Act. From a comparative point of view we can see that after the reform of 2000 the Finnish system has become less suspicious towards constitutional

[41] It is important to note that this was based on constitutional interpretation verified by the scarce constitutional customary law, ie there was no such explicit rule that would have clearly prohibited review of the constitutionality of parliamentary acts (as eg in the Dutch Constitution Act art 120). Thus, interpretation was *e contrario*.
[42] G van der Schyff, 'Constitutional Review by the Judiciary in the Netherlands: A Bridge Too Far?' (2010) 11 *German Law Journal* 275, 278.
[43] H Kelsen, 'Wer soll der Hüter der Verfassung sein?' (1931) 6 *Die Justiz* 576.

judicial review than in the Netherlands: the Dutch Constitution Act (*Grondwet*) clearly forbids this kind of review even today.[44]

Today, courts may thus give priority to the dictates of the Constitution Act on the basis of this written primacy clause. The present control model is a modified transplant from the Swedish system with one significant exception—that the limited review of the constitutionality of the Acts is possible only in the courts, not in other public organs. It must also be noted that the Swedish Form of Government seems to cover, according to the wording, only 'provision in Constitution Act' (*bestämmelse i grundlag*). The more open Finnish expression 'with Constitution Act' (*perustuslain kanssa*) makes it, perhaps, easier to take the coherence of the Constitution into account while practising limited judicial review.

The provision complemented the Finnish preventive and abstract control-model so that the emphasis of the control is still preserved in the advance control done in conjunction with legislative process. As to its formal legal basis, the Finnish model is now mainly based on written provisions (CA sections 74, 106 and 107), constitutional customary law and a doctrine approved by doctrinal study of constitutional law.

In practice, interpretations made by the Committee, which have been mostly linked to questions concerning constitutional protection of property, are highly respected and in legal research the source-of-law-position of opinions of the Constitutional Law Committee is even considered equal to that of a constitutional court. Paralleling the Committee with constitutional court is, perhaps an exaggeration, but it is evident that the status of this unique organ and the traditions and interpretation techniques relating to it are more important that can be deduced from written law. According to the official report of the Committee (PeVM 10/1998), when courts are trying to determine the nature (obvious or not) of collision of an Act's provision and that of the Constitution Act's (section 106), they *must* put special weight on the fact of whether or not the Committee has already reviewed this question preventively. If the Committee has held that a provision is not colliding with the Constitution Act, the courts cannot rule de facto otherwise: they are obliged to follow the Committee. This same basic assumption can also be found from the *travaux* of the Government's bill (1/1998) reasoning concerning section 106 of the Constitution Act.

---

[44] Article 120: 'The constitutionality of Parliamentary Acts and Treaties shall not be reviewed by the Courts' ('De rechter treedt niet in de beoordeling van de grondwettigheid van wetten en verdragen.')

However, from time to time there has been criticism of the Constitutional Law Committee's role and its interpretations. Much of this criticism assumes that the courts would do a better job. Also, it is interesting to note that, in August 2001, the Supreme Court challenged, although indirectly, the supremacy of the Constitutional Law Committee in the area of *a priori* constitutionality control in an Åland legislation-related case. In a book intended for an international audience, it is crucial to underline specifically that the control by the Constitutional Law Committee is, in fact, rather effective and by no means can it be regarded as a façade. In this sense it is a very unique organ even within the global perspective. Importantly, the Committee has not turned into a last resort of political opposition in order to block an Act which it opposes, as is the case with the French *Conseil constitutionnel*. This has increased the usability of the statements by the Constitutional Law Committee.

Compared to other countries, the control of the constitutionality of Finnish law appears to be genuinely different, because it is emphasised as preventive, it has an abstract character, and it is moreover executed through the activity of the Parliament itself. This partly explains, among other things, the institution of the Exceptive Act and the fact that there has been no political desire to thoroughly change a proven and well functioning system. In a Nordic context, attention is drawn to the fact that the Constitutional Law Committee is de facto a quasi-legal organ that uses legal discretion and argumentation in its own interpretation activities (the parliamentary group discipline used in other Committees does not touch the Constitutional Law Committee).

In many respects the Constitutional Law Committee comes relatively close to the French Constitutional Council, even though there are significant differences.[45] Both seem to linger in the twilight zone between legislative and judicial branches. The lack of total and undeniable supremacy and legitimacy may be one of the differences. Also, when compared to Nordic neighbour Norway, the *modus operandi* of the Finnish courts is notably closer to the Swedish one, which includes avoidance of judicial activism. The reason for the relatively weak position of courts in the

---

[45] The composition of *Conseil* is very different. According to art 56 of the French Constitution Act, the nine members are nominated by the President of the Republic (3), Speaker of the National Assembly (3), and Speaker of the Senate (3). Besides, also the former presidents of the Republic may join as life members. The decisions by the *Conseil* have formally binding force (art 62-1 says that decision 'shall be binding on public authorities and on all administrative and judicial authorities').

control of the constitutionality of the Acts might partly be connected to the fact that there, similar to Sweden, is no indisputable Supreme Court, since there are special supreme courts for general matters (ie criminal and civil cases) and matters concerning administrative law, which is not the case in Norway and Denmark.

The strong emphasis on the preventive control in the Finnish system was, nevertheless, somewhat weakened by the Constitution Act of 2000, in addition to which the membership of the European Union and ECHR has increased the pressure for consolidation of the *ex post facto* court-control (constitutional judicial review) in the future. In an EU context, Finland is a rare representative of such a control model, where the control power of the constitutionality of Acts is not in the hands of the courts. Moreover, it can be concluded that there are now some weak signs of growing tendency towards judicial activism (in judicial review) in the Finnish legal culture.[46] Accordingly, the role of the judges is viewed in a more positive light than in the past. In essence, this is the same as the change that took place in France in 1971, although, not through statutory law but by the decision of the *Conseil constitutionnel*.[47] Both of these changes seem to challenge the legislative sovereignty of national parliaments.

However, as the slowly growing case law of the supreme courts seems to indicate, we may expect some kind of slow departure from constitutional judicial restraint. However, it would be a mistake to expect any rapid and drastic changes in the constitutional mentality of high judges. In fact, legal-cultural differences aside, in describing the Finnish judicial mentality we may well cite Lord Nicholls of Birkenhead who says that 'Interpretation of statutes is a matter for the courts; the enactment of statutes, and the amendment of statutes, are matters for Parliament.'[48]

To an outside constitutional lawyer or political scientist it will be interesting to follow how long this traditional feature of the Finnish constitutional system manages to survive in the world of ever-growing judicial power and distrust toward the political decision-making system.

---

[46] This can be seen especially in the case law of supreme courts (landmark cases are: KKO 2004:26 and KHO 2008:25) in which the courts have set aside provision of the Parliament's Act in favour of provision in the Constitution Act.

[47] *Décision n° 71-44 DC du 16 juillet* 1971 (in which Conceil started to regard the old charter of human rights as a legally enforceable part of the constitution).

[48] *S v S* [2002] UKHL 10 at [39] (speaking of the constitutional boundary set by the Human Rights Act 1998).

The change may not take place overnight because judicial review of legislation has been so long regarded as an inappropriate mode of constitutional decision-making. So, even though judicial review has gained popularity among the national jurist-elite, there are many high profile politicians, law professors and judges who would wholeheartedly support Jeremy Waldron's argument against judicial review which states that at the end of the day there are no reasons to assume that rights would be better protected by courts than they would be by democratically elected legislature.[49]

CONCLUSION

The central point in this chapter has been to consider how constitutionalism is upheld by judiciary and other overseers of legality. The primary objective of judicial institutions and other overseers of legality is to secure the rule of law principle. As stated earlier, the Finnish concept of rule of law is close to the German notion of *Rechtsstaat*, which seems to underline the formal understanding of legal security and rule of law. Be that as it may, we may also note that after the reforms of 1995 and 2000 the way the concept of rule of law was conceived has transformed towards being broader and the substantive elements (direct effect of constitutional/human rights) of legal security are now more important than what they used to be. In a more general sense, there has been a movement from formalism toward substantive thinking. The role of the supreme courts has been crucial in the transformation. Yet, it must be kept in mind that even though Finland has no formal stare decisis principle, the important published decisions by the supreme courts carry the weight of de facto precedents. We have witnessed slow steps toward a system of stronger constitutional judicial review, even though the steps have been somewhat half-hearted. Notwithstanding, it is clear that the well known logic of *Marbury v Madison* has not fully penetrated the Finnish Constitution.[50] We may wonder why the slight growth of

[49] J Waldron, 'The Core of the Case against Judicial Review' (2006) 115 *Yale Law Journal* 1346.

[50] *Marbury v Madison* 5 US 1 Cranch 137 (1803) argues that 'if both the law and the Constitution apply to a particular case, so that the Court must either decide that case conformably to the law, disregarding the Constitution, or conformably to the Constitution, disregarding the law, the Court must determine which of these conflicting rules governs the case. This is of the very essence of judicial duty' (at 178).

activity of courts has not produced more tensions in the constitutional system that has such an evidently parliamentary character. The tentative answer is not too hard to find because national high courts do not tend to differ from 'national metanarratives and the interests of hegemonic political forces'.[51]

In guarding the rule of law principle, there are also important elements of a constitutional order other than courts. Obviously, the most effective guard is the constitutional mentality and legal culture in general: no rule, no institution replaces the genuine will to respect the Constitution. As is well known there are many states with formally impeccable constitutional documents, yet some of these states are not imbued with a genuine spirit of constitutionalism: written rules are just like empty shells without practical meaning. Thus, constitutional mentality is of importance: it is hard to impose constitutionalism to a system. Courts cannot create this mentality. Yet, the courts of law are important even though they do not apply constitutional rules on a day-to-day basis. Besides, there are specific institutions to specifically supervise constitutionality and more general legality. These last mentioned organs mainly investigate maladministration within their own fields, but perhaps even more importantly these organs play an active role in enhancing the significance of constitutional rights.

Finnish judges use judicial power independently and supreme courts do create law by precedent. However, Finnish judges may certainly not be properly described as 'oracles of law' as the quintessential English idea of judges sometimes see them as.[52] Also, the idea that judges are merely the *bouche de la loi* does not fit with Finnish realities either. Courts in Finland are certainly more than mouthpieces through which the lawgiver speaks: especially in so-called 'hard cases' law is many times created by precedents and constitutional rights also have a certain impact on the operations of courts. Furthermore, courts also give precise meaning to section 106 of the Constitution Act in their scarce but high-profile judgments concerning this section.

The Committee for Checking of the Constitution did not propose any changes to the Constitution Act concerning judicial review when it left its report in February 2010.[53] Accordingly, the last say in national

---

[51] R Hirschl, *Towards Juristocracy—The Origins and Consequences of the New Constitutionalism* (Harvard University Press, Cambridge Mass, 2004) 214.

[52] See JP Dawson, *The Oracles of Law* (Ann Arbor, Michigan, 1968).

[53] *Perustuslain tarkistamiskomitean mietintö* (KM 9/2010).

constitutional matters rests with the Parliament even in the future. As became clear earlier, Finnish courts do not follow the practice of creating and expanding law by means of interpretation, even though today they are willing to take constitutional rights more into account than previously. Rights in general appear more important than before, even though judicial review as such remains purposefully vague. This is why we turn to discussing rights from the constitutional viewpoint in the following chapter.

FURTHER READING

Aarnio, A, 'Precedent in Finland' in N MacCormick and R Summers (eds), *Interpreting Precedents—A Comparative Study* (Ashgate, Aldershot, 1997) 65–101.

Annual Report of the Ombudsman for Minorities (Helsinki, 2007).

Cameron, I, 'The Influence of European Human Rights Law on National Legislation' in E Hollo (ed), *National Law and Europeanisation* (Suomalainen lakimiesyhdistys, Helsinki, 2009).

Hautamäki, V-P, 'The Question of Constitutional Court: on its Relevance in the Nordic Context' in J Husa, K Nuotio and H Pihlajamäki (eds), *Nordic Law—Between Tradition and Dynamism* (Intersentia, Antwerp-Oxford, 2007) 153–71.

Husa, J, 'Sort-of-Binding: Finnish Precedent as a Source of Law' in E Hondius (ed), *Precedent and the Law* (Bruylant, Brussels, 2007) 267–86.

Jyränki, A, *Valta ja vapaus: valtiosääntöoikeuden yleisiä kysymyksiä* [*Power and Freedom: General Questions of Constitutional Law*] (Talentum, Helsinki, 2003).

[Commission Report 2003:3, developing court system], English summary 548–69.

Ojanen, T, 'From Constitutional Periphery toward the Centre—Transformations of Judicial Review in Finland' (2009) 27 *Nordic Journal of Human Rights* 194–207.

Rautio, I (ed), *Parliamentary Ombudsman of Finland—80 Years* (Eduskunta, Helsinki, 2000).

Rytter, J-E, 'Judicial Review of Legislation—a Sustainable Strategy on the Enforcement of Basic Rights' in M Scheinin (ed), *The Welfare State and Constitutionalism in the Nordic Countries* (Nordic Council of Ministers, Copenhagen, 2001) 137–74.

Saraviita, I, *Finland—Constitutional Law*. International Encyclopedia of Laws (Kluwer, Alphen, 2009).

WEBSITES

All of the following websites also contain information in English.

Courts

www.kho.fi [Supreme Administrative Court].
www.kko.fi [Supreme Court].
www.oikeus.fi/tyotuomioistuin [Labour Court].
www.oikeus.fi/vakuutusoikeus [Insurance Court].
www.oikeus.fi/markkinaoikeus [Market Court].

Overseers of Legality

www.oikeusasiamies.fi [Parliamentary Ombudsman].
www.oikeuskansleri.fi [Chancellor of Justice].
www.kuluttajavirasto.fi [Consumer Protection].
www.tietosuoja.fi [Data Protection].
www.ofm.fi [Ombudsman for Minorities].
www.tasa-arvo.fi [Gender Equality].

Other

www.om.fi [Ministry of Justice].
www.finlex.fi [Legal Database].

7

Fundamental Rights and Their Protection

Introduction – Fundamental Rights: National and International – System of Constitutional Rights and Freedoms – Conclusion

INTRODUCTION

The idea of constitutional rights is old in Finland. From a historical point of view, the lack of feudalism probably explains why personal freedom has traditionally been highly valued in all of the Nordic countries.[1] However, during the Swedish and Russian periods these rights were not constitutional in the modern sense because they dealt with the privileges of the Four Estates. This outdated system was eroded internally in the early twentieth century in two stages. Internal changes took place in the 1906 reform and in 1919 when the Form of Government stepped into force. After World War II, human rights, fundamental rights and/ or constitutional rights were generally deemed a more important part of constitutionalism than was the case before. Many of the atrocities of the War led to a transformation in the global constitutional environment. Finland, too, has experienced its share of this global rights expansion and this has been especially evident within the constitutional sphere. Rights have been the spearhead of new constitutionalism.

In this chapter the discussion concerns the relationship between rights and the Constitution. The chapter will be divided into four main parts which have been selected for examination: national and international elements of rights, fundamental rights as a system (with short outlines

---

[1] Social differences between estates were relatively small and peasants were represented in the Diet as their own Estate, see D Kirby, *Concise History of Finland* (Cambridge University Press, Cambridge 2006) ch 1.

of the main types of rights), general doctrines of fundamental rights and finally applicability of rights.

FUNDAMENTAL RIGHTS: NATIONAL AND INTERNATIONAL

The Finnish Constitution regards rights as legal in nature, meaning that these rights exist under the rules of constitutional law. It has become commonplace in Finnish doctrinal constitutional law of the 2000s to separate two main areas of constitutional law: the institutional part and the fundamental rights part. These areas form the two main substantive corners of Finnish constitutional law. The first one deals with things like the Parliament, President, Government, separation of powers and so on. The second part deals with human rights and constitutional rights and general doctrines concerning them. Whereas the first one has remained somewhat national in character, the latter part has been internationalised to a great extent. In this, Finland is certainly not alone; quite the contrary. It has been noted in the contemporary comparative study of constitutional law that it is difficult to draw a distinction between national constitutional law and more general constitutionalism, especially if we deal with internationally recognised human rights.[2] This is why we might speak of *fundamental rights* covering both areas: fundamental rights consist of constitutional rights and human rights.

There are some terminological difficulties here. Finnish legal language follows basically German and Swedish models here because it separates '*perusoikeus*' (literarily 'basic right') from '*ihmisoikeus*' (literarily '*human right*'): *Grundrecht/grundrättighet* and *Menschenrecht/mänsklig rättighet*. However, in international English-speaking constitutional literature there are many expressions: fundamental right, constitutional right, basic right, etc. In this book 'fundamental right' refers to both rights protected in a constitutional tradition and those protected at international law.

Fundamental rights are located both within the sphere of constitutional and international law. In a broad sense we might say that they are basically rights of human beings. In a classical sense these rights have been directed against the State, the user and owner of public power, and its organs. In this sense fundamental rights are an attempt to restrict the

---

[2] M Tushnet, 'Comparative Constitutional Law' in M Reimann and R Zimmermann (eds), *The Oxford Handbook of Comparative Law* (Oxford University Press, Oxford, 2006) 1225–57, 1228–30.

power of the Hobbesian sovereign: the *Leviathan* with its frightening absolute power over the people.[3] However, some fundamental rights do not only require the State not to do something (negative dimension), they may also require the State to act in certain circumstances (positive dimension). In any case, fundamental rights (based on state constitutions or international treaties) are an important and vital part of the contemporary *Rechtsstaat* thinking. If these rights are conceived from the point of view of sources of law, they are a very high formal source of law in Finland. Their constitutional status is regarded as high both in theory and in practice. It was in 1990 when the Constitutional Law Committee of the Parliament assumed a landmark stance according to which the European Convention on Human Rights (ECHR) (and its Protocols) would be given precedence in a case of norm-conflict with prior national laws.[4] However, the idea originally was to ensure the compatibility beforehand already in the law-drafting phase or at least during the legislative process in the Parliament. This doctrine of allowing precedence to be given to ECHR law has prevailed since and the recent *Uoti*-case[5] (see later in this chapter) has made the role of European human rights even more significant in Finland.

Even though fundamental rights were originally mainly based on constitutional documents, today their foundation is more and more clearly in international conventions. This division between national and international rights is today becoming somewhat illusory. In practice, international human rights and national constitutional rights are *intertwined* in Finland and often it is not easy to separate these two formally separate substantive bodies of law from each other. The constitutional outcome is clear: international and domestic rights mainly limit the sovereignty of the Parliament to use its discretion freely while passing new legislation. Obviously, these rights also set limits to all forms of usage of public power, especially concerning executive and judicial organs. Fundamental rights emanate to all corners of the constitutional system.

---

[3] See Patricia Springborg (ed), *The Cambridge Companion to Hobbes's Leviathan* (New York, Cambridge University Press, 2007) part II.

[4] Statement of Constitutional Committee (2/1990).

[5] See Case KKO 2009:80.

International Ingredients

In the total reform of the Finnish system of constitutional rights, which came into force at the beginning of August 1995, the system of ECHR was incorporated in national constitutional law in a substantive sense, even though no full formal incorporation took place. What was done was to adopt elements from the ECHR within the Finnish system of codified constitutional rights: international norms were rewritten while they were adapted to the Form of Government (1919). In more practical terms, after August 1995, the systems of rights of the ECHR and Finnish Constitution have been very close to each other. In effect, what took place in the reform was complete rewriting of the whole of Chapter II (*Basic Rights and Liberties*) in the 1919 Form of Government. In a more practical sense, the Finnish Constitution seems to have also accepted the European Court of Human Rights' (ECtHR) interpretation, according to which the ECHR is not only an instrument of traditional international law but rather 'a constitutional instrument of European public order'.[6] In comparison to the German Constitution, the Finnish one has been clearly more open to international human rights and especially to the authority of the ECHR.[7]

In addition to the ECHR there are a number of other international human rights conventions to which Finland has acceded, but in comparison to national constitutional rights and those rights stemming from the ECHR, these are of a secondary nature. However, the International Covenant on Civil and Political Rights (ICCPR) is regarded as an important human rights document.[8] In this context the European Social Charter and the International Covenant on Economic, Social and Cultural Rights may also be mentioned, but in practice they are of a secondary nature. The most recent new dimension within the field of fundamental rights is the human rights facet of the European Union. The EU rights dimension is today much more important than what it was in the past: growing out from the case law of the European Court of Justice (ECJ) and finally reaching the status of a separate Charter of Fundamental Rights (2000), though, formally merely 'a solemn proclamation'. This basic rights

---

[6] See *Loizidou v Turkey* ECtHR Judgment 23 March 1995 [75].

[7] See eg, BVerfGE 111, 307 (14 October 2004) concerning the constitutional status of the ECHR within the German system.

[8] In Finnish: *Kansalaisoikeuksia ja poliittisia oikeuksia koskeva kansainvälinen yleissopimus* (in force 1976).

document brought together within the European Union all the rights which were previously scattered to national laws and the ECHR, human rights conventions of the United Nations and the International Labour Organisation. The Treaty of Lisbon has confirmed its legal significance, although there are certain reservations.[9] Despite this, the Constitutional Law Committee has regarded these developments as strengthening the fundamental rights dimension in the European Union in general.[10]

The idea behind the EU Charter was to enhance legal certainty as regards the protection of fundamental rights. This dimension had previously been guaranteed mainly by the case law of the ECJ and article 6 of the EU Treaty. However, in practice the European Union's right dimension and that of the ECHR are closely intertwined. This is simply because all of the EU Member States share a common commitment to the ECHR but the European Union itself has not been a party to the ECHR.[11] In practice there has been some tension between the European Union's basic rights and the ECHR concerning the overlapping constitutional hierarchies, but neither the ECJ nor the ECtHR has been eager to underline conflict: these high courts follow the principle of avoidance of open clashes.[12] After the Lisbon Treaty this potential problem is disappearing.

In turn, the ECtHR did not waste too much time in the 1990s when it started to judge cases against Finland.[13] Generally, from the Finnish point of view, the significance of the ECHR may be underlined since it triggered a major change in Finnish general doctrines on constitutional rights during the 1990s. The change was not restricted to a formal constitutional document, but expanded to judiciary and significantly to academic public law.

---

[9] See The Treaty on European Union [2008] OJ 115/13 article 6, according to which the Charter 'shall not extend in any way the competences of the Union as defined in the Treaties'.

[10] PeVL 13/2008.

[11] See ECJ Opinion 2/94 [1996] ECR I-1759.

[12] In case *Bosphorus Airways v Ireland* (30 June 2005, 45036/98), the ECtHR actually declared that the ECJ human rights protection is equivalent to that of the ECHR.

[13] The first two judgments against Finland were *Hokkanen v Finland* (23 September 1994) and *Kerojärvi v Finland* (19 July 1995).

SYSTEM OF CONSTITUTIONAL RIGHTS AND FREEDOMS

Once again, the relevance of constitutional history is important when trying to understand the Finnish constitutional system, however, in the area of fundamental rights the significance of history seems to be of lesser relevance than elsewhere. During the Swedish and Russian periods there was actually no genuine system of rights in the modern constitutional sense. The privileges of Estates were not really rights in today's constitutional sense: privileges concerned the nobles, the clergy, the bourgeoisie and the peasants as groups, but not so much as individuals. It was only in the beginning of the twentieth century when the modern system started to take shape. The first model was drafted already in 1905, by Leo Mechelin who was a famous statesman, professor and political liberal. However, it was not until 1919 when the present system of rights was born forming a part of the Form of Government; only then was the Swedish system of Estates abandoned. Even though the system was not transplanted from anywhere else it was hardly a domestic invention based solely on national experiences: creative and adaptive indirect transplanting took place.

The rights catalogue of 1919 drew inspiration from the Western European tradition of the 1800s. International models were taken mainly from the Belgian (1831) and Prussian (1850) constitutions, but very likely also from Austria's *Das Staatsgrundgesetz über die allgemeinen Rechte der Staatsbürger* (1867). The system of 1919 Form of Government guaranteed rights in accordance with West-European liberalism oriented standards of the late 1900s and early twentieth century. During the years 1917–19, when the Form of Government and its catalogue of rights were in the making, these rights were probably not meant to fully bind the legislature. Formally, the system remained largely intact during the lifespan of the 1919 Form of Government. In fact, a major change took place only in 1995 when the system of rights was thoroughly revised into its present shape. These revisions marked a paradigm shift into a world more open to fundamental rights as binding rights was evident. Furthermore, rights do not bind only the legislator but all those who use public power. However, what actually took place in 1995?

Constitutional rights in the system in force were moved without changes from the reformed Form of Government into the second chapter of the prevailing Constitution Act. The list of rights is itself not a systematic or in any sense coherent collection; rather, it appears to be a somewhat unsystematic collection of rights listed specifically in sections 6 to 21.[14] It is important to understand that even though constitutional rights have their main constitutional anchorage in the Constitution Act, the short formulations in this Act offer only a partial picture of the system of constitutional rights. In practice, the Government's bill 309 from 1993, preceding the 1995 reform of these rights, is an important constitutional source when it comes to the interpretation of these rights. For the most part, the main responsibility of securing rights resides in the Parliament when it passes new statutory law: it must be sure that it does not infringe fundamental rights when it passes new legislation. It is the function of the Constitutional Law Committee to ensure that legislative proposals that are brought to its consideration are compatible with the Constitution and international human rights (Constitution Act (CA) section 74).

Clearly, the role of the Committee cannot be overlooked in this context. As a basic doctrinal starting point for the system we may refer to the doctrinal landmark Report 25/1994 and a few hundred later Statements by the Committee that in fact offer constitutional guidelines for the interpretation of these rights. During the 2000s the case law by both supreme courts also partially gained new relevance, while giving detailed content to generally formulated codified constitutional rights. Importantly, fundamental rights are spread in the whole legal system through legislative means: Acts and other regulations have tremendous practical significance in numerous areas as, for example, health and medical care, the penal system, social services and the educational system.

One of the most important legal/cultural lessons for anyone looking at the Finnish system of constitutional rights from the outside is to understand that these rights are not merely written black-letter rules, but are mostly regarded as legal principles too.[15] Finnish legal thinking normally separates 'legal rule' (ie written rule) and 'legal principle' (not having a clear base in codified law), but constitutional rights are regarded

---

[14] However, there has been a strong trend in Finnish academic law to regard the system of constitutional rights as a normative and functional unity. In practice, this has meant that each right has been treated as a part of a larger whole: separate rights should be interpreted against the context of the whole Constitution and especially against the system of constitutional rights. This line of thinking has also been clearly visible in the working of the Constitutional Committee.

[15] In Finnish jurisprudence and in legal thinking in general, written legal rules and un-written legal principles have been kept in doctrinal separation, see H Tolonen, 'Rules, Principles and Goals' (1991) 35 *Scandinavian Studies in Law* 269. However, constitutional rights are placing this generally assumed distinction under criticism.

as being both legal rules and more general legal principles even while their base is on the text of the Constitution Act.[16] Given that they are regarded largely as general legal principles, these rights also affect many other areas of law; that is, their scope is not restricted only to constitutional law and strictly legal questions having a pristine constitutional character. As principles they are more able to penetrate into other areas of the legal system. It may be reasonably claimed that from the beginning of the 1990s the whole legal system has been at least partially constitutionalised with the help of constitutional rights. This has changed the atmosphere of legal culture altogether and it has also provided a new vigour to constitutional law in general. Today, certain basic values are closely linked with constitutionally central rights, blurring the distinction between law and politics or public morality. As such, this is no surprise in the world of constitutionalism, indeed, as de Tocqueville has stated, 'The idea of rights is nothing but the conception of virtue applied to the world of politics.'[17]

Accordingly, there has been academic debate concerning the question of whether or not this also means that courts of law should today be seen as political actors. This debate has not produced clear-cut answers or other crystallised ideas even though it has slightly changed the manner in which courts are conceived today. They are no longer seen as purely legal decision-makers. Montesquieu's underestimation of the constitutional input of the courts seems to be slowly vanishing; courts are more than mere mouths of the law. This development has not been welcomed by all: critics include high profile politicians like former Prime Minister Paavo Lipponen, top law professors (eg Aulis Aarnio) and several editors-in-chief of noted Finnish newspapers.

However, there is no systematic or coherent system of constitutional rights in the strict terms of legal philosophy: the list of these rights which the Constitutional Act contains is all but systematic. In constitutional literature and in the practice of the Constitutional Law Committee, a certain classification of rights is, nonetheless, in use although it is not regarded in an overtly dogmatic fashion. However, the classification is certainly helpful for anyone trying to comprehend the system from the outside. Normally the rights are classified as a) personal freedoms and

---

[16] Finnish law here follows Dworkin's ideas, see R Siltala, *A Theory of Precedent* (Hart, Oxford, 2000) 44–46.

[17] A de Tocqueville, *Democracy in America* (Fontana Press, London, 1840/1994) 237–38.

legal security, b) equality rights, c) political rights, d) economic, social and cultural rights, and e) so-called third generation rights which are normally of a collective nature. Let us first examine the rights that concern personal freedoms and legal security.

Personal Freedoms and Legal Security

The Constitution Act (section 7) stipulates that everyone has a right to life, personal liberty and integrity. Within the system of constitutional rights there seems to be a certain inner hierarchy that is visible even if it is not codified.[18] The right to life (*oikeus elämään*) is the most important of all rights; it constitutes a constitutional prerequisite to all other rights. Right to life means specifically that the death penalty is prohibited and that no one can be tortured or otherwise treated in a manner that would violate human dignity. This rule is very close to the German *Grundgesetz*'s article 1 in which human dignity is declared as inviolable and that the respect and protection of human dignity is regarded as a legal duty of all state authority.[19] In a similar vein Finnish rule also binds *all* those who exercise public power.

Constitutional protection of personal integrity and arbitrary deprivation of liberty is prohibited, unless there is a specifically grounded legal reason prescribed by an act. In practice, this means that any kind of penalty that would involve deprivation of liberty can only be imposed by a court of law and only if a specific rule (understood in the narrow sense of the word) in an Act allows this. Moreover, any such action that includes deprivation of liberty may always be submitted for review by a court of law. The Constitution Act also requires that the lawgiver must guarantee these rights of individuals in legislation. This means that no lower decree, public order or other official prescription suffices constitutionally: the obligation to guarantee the rights of individuals is mainly that of the Parliament's.

Other fundamental rights belonging in this group contain the famous *nulla poena sine lege* principle (*rikosoikeudellinen laillisuusperiaate*), which basically says that no one can be found guilty of a criminal offence on the

---

[18] Whether there is an inner hierarchy between constitutional rights is, however, a debated question.

[19] *Grundgesetz* article 1: 'Die Würde des Menschen ist unantastbar. Sie zu achten und zu schützen ist Verpflichtung aller staatlichen Gewalt.'

basis of a deed which was not defined by an Act as legally punishable at the time the deed was committed (CA section 8).[20] Freedom of movement is also an important individual freedom because it allows both Finnish citizens and those foreigners legally residing in Finland to freely move within the country and to choose their place of residence (CA section 9). From a historical point of view, this right is directly opposed to many of the restrictions on an individual's right to move freely that were largely in use during the 1800s and also in the beginning of the twentieth century. This right also includes the right to freely leave the country and, as in other key freedoms, possible limitations to this right may be provided only by an Act. For example, the right of foreigners to enter to and remain in the country is regulated by a separate Act.[21]

The right to privacy, including private life and protection of home, is also guaranteed in the Constitution Act (CA section 10). Freedom of religion and conscience are protected in section 11, providing the right to profess and practice a religion and the right to be a member or to freely decline the membership of a religious community (CA section 11). Despite this religious freedom, both the majority Evangelic Lutheran and the small minority Greek Orthodox churches are officially recognised by the State and their positions are legally ensured and regulated through parliamentary Acts. Both of these churches have legally regulated competence to collect church fees through the national tax collection system. Public schools have religion in their curriculum and the students may choose Evangelic-Lutheran or Orthodox teaching or non-religious teaching. However, education in other religions is also possible at the request of at least three students.

The last fundamental right included in this group is the important protection under law provided by the Constitution Act's section 21, protection under the law and good governance, which was dealt with in the previous chapter.

---

[20] Precisely the same right is also provided by key human rights treaties: article 7 of the ECHR and article 15 of the ICCPR.

[21] Lately, there have been some publicly sharply criticised decisions by the Supreme Administrative Court in which foreigners have been removed to their original countries based on somewhat unclear grounds, see *Korkein hallinto-oikeus* (KHO) 2008:91 (person of Somali origin but with long history in Finland was forcefully removed to Puntland, Somalia).

Equality Rights

Paradigmatically, the main aim of constitutional rights is to offer equal constitutional protection to all individuals. Concerning equality rights, section 6 is the most central constitutional source since it contains many important rights that concern equality. This section also plays a very important role for the Parliament when it is passing statutory law and also to the courts of law, which may directly use these equality rights in their judicial function. Parliament must be sure that the new legislation it passes does not infringe upon equality. The constitutional requirement for equality is reflected in most areas of the legal system: there is a legion of Acts in which this constitutional basic idea is concretised. The most central general concerning the constitutional principle of equality is the Non-Discrimination Act.[22]

The main purpose of this Act is 'to foster and safeguard equality and enhance the protection provided by law to those who have been discriminated against' (section 1). This Act applies basically to various public and private activities, as for example, conditions for access to self-employment or means of livelihood, support for business activities and recruitment conditions covering employment and working conditions, personnel training and promotion. The Act also applies to discrimination based on ethnic origin in the areas of social welfare and healthcare services, and social security benefits.

As to their nature, equality rights are directly enforceable rights (which are called 'subjective rights' in the Finnish doctrine) which in accord, makes them legally rather strong rights because individuals may appeal directly to these rights when dealing with public power. The main rule states that 'Everyone is equal before the law'. From a comparative point of view, we may note that the wording is exactly the same as in German *Grundgesetz*, although there are no direct or historical connections between these two.[23] Yet, the central constitutional idea is very much the same: human beings are equal in their relation to public power which, in turn, is equalled roughly with the law.

Now, even though the wording of this basic rule seems rather narrow it binds all sorts of uses of public power: drafting legislation, governmental power, use of public power by public administration, and use of

---

[22] *Yhdenvertaisuuslaki* (21/2004).
[23] Article 3 (1): 'Alle Menschen sind vor dem Gesetz gleich.'

judicial power by the courts. As such, the deceivingly narrow and legalistic expression 'before the law' (*yhdenvertaisia lain edessä*) has an extremely wide area of scope when dealing with equality rights. Like many equivalent international human rights treaties, this section also lists different kinds of bases that are not constitutionally acceptable reasons to treat persons differently when using public power in any of its possible forms. Basically, the legal core of this right is to prevent Acts and other legislative means from leaving an individual disadvantaged because he/she belongs to a minority. The list of prohibited discrimination grounds consists of gender, age, origin, language, religion, conviction, health, disability or other reasons that concern a person (eg sexual orientation).

The fact that the section specifically mentions 'other reasons' means in practice that the written list of forbidden grounds to treat persons differently does not cover all forbidden bases; instead, it only specifically mentions the most relevant ones without excluding other potentially forbidden bases. It is left for the courts of law, especially to the supreme courts, to decide finally what dimensions the list actually covers. So, case law by supreme courts plays an important role in defining the exact scope and meaning of this right, as do the numerous Acts and lower decrees that further define what this rather loosely expressed right actually means legally. Obviously, the Statements of the Constitutional Law Committee play a significant role here too and they are used routinely when these rights are interpreted.

Women and Children

Next are two equality dimensions that are very typical to the Nordic constitutional tradition and concern the position of children and women. Both are regarded as having a specific connection to equality rights. It is separately stipulated that children must be treated equally and that they must also be able to influence matters that concern them; however, this must take into account their level of development. It is important to note that all the rights stipulated in the Constitution Act concern children as well as adults. There are also other rights connected with children, including section 19 of the Constitution Act, which holds that public authorities must support families and others responsible for providing for children so that they have the opportunity to ensure children's wellbeing and personal development. The Constitution Act also stipulates that the State must provide adequate social and health services, housing, income security, free basic education for children and financial support for families with children.

The most central of the separate Acts regarding children are The Act on Child Custody and the Rights of Access and Child Welfare Act.[24] The main aim of child custody is to guarantee the balanced development and welfare of children in accordance with their individual needs and wishes. The Child Welfare Act requires that municipal social welfare boards and other authorities must follow and develop the conditions in which children and young people grow up and remove and prevent the development of disadvantages within these conditions. The Constitution Act also states that different provisions concerning restrictions which relate to pictorial programmes that are necessary to protect children may be laid down by separate Acts (CA section 12.1). This means in practice that the legislator is allowed to legislate on certain restrictions, at the level of a parliamentary Act, concerning movies, computer-games and equivalent material when seeking to protect children. In a sense, the Constitution Act regards children as being in need of special protection, without these protection measures being necessarily regarded as unconstitutional.

Besides children, equality of the sexes is also separately promoted in the Constitution Act's section 6. In practice the most important constitutional outcome of the idea of equality between sexes is the determination of pay as well as other terms of employment, which are provided in detail by an Act. The key one is the Act on Equality between Women and Men which seeks to prevent discrimination based on gender, to promote equality between women and men, and thus to improve the status of women, particularly in working life.[25] The general tendency towards sexual equality is constitutionally well established in Finland, not only in the area of rights: equal suffrage was instituted in 1906. Yet it was not until 1927 that the the first female Minister was appointed in Finland (Miina Sillanpää). Finally, Finland's first female President was elected in 2000 and first female Prime Minister in 2003. The first female President of the Supreme Court was appointed in 2005 (Pauliine Koskelo). These are all important milestones in gender equality. Parliament normally has some 40 per cent female MPs. Yet, there is still work to do with regard to equality between genders; equal pay especially seems to be hard to achieve by legislative measures only.

---

[24] The Act on Child Custody and Rights of Access (*Laki lapsen huollosta ja tapaamisoikeudesta*, 361/1983) and the Child Welfare Act (*Lastensuojelulaki*, 417/2007).

[25] The short name is the Act on Equality (*Tasa-arvolaki* 609/1986).

Political Rights

The concept of political constitutional rights may face certain criticism: are not all constitutional rights political rights? Obviously, it is rather difficult and perhaps even somewhat arbitrary to proclaim that a certain group of rights would be political. This is because most of the constitutional rights and freedoms contain at least some political dimension that affects an individual's position as a member of the Finnish polity. For instance, freedom of religion most certainly includes political elements, as does freedom of movement. Nevertheless, in the Finnish constitutional tradition the rights that are deemed mostly as political rights are those that secure the direct possibilities of an individual to act freely in a political sense and secure the possibilities to take part in political decision-making. For the constitutional system, these rights are of specific relevance: they make it possible to compete legally over the political power wielded by high public institutions. They express the coherence of the political and legal system.

Freedom of Expression and Assembly

Freedom of expression (CA section 12) is undoubtedly a classical political right. Everyone's right to the freedom of expression (*sananvapaus*) is constitutionally secured and it entails the right to express, spread and receive information, opinions and other communications so that there is no prior prevention. This concept of 'prior prevention' means mostly things like public censorship, by any exercise of public power. This right, like most others, is regulated in a more detailed manner in an Act. In the Finnish system, freedom of expression is connected to the right of access to information which covers, as a main rule, everyone's right of access to public documents and recordings. In different pieces of legislation this right is sometimes limited, but this limitation takes place only after specific constitutional consideration by the lawgiver during the process of law drafting and law passing. Also, the right to freely express opinions and to spread and receive information is significantly influenced by the international human rights treaties (ECHR and ICCPR). As a matter of fact, it is difficult to separate the national constitutional elements from the international human rights elements concerning this right because they are so closely intertwined. For example, a Finnish court may use ECHR rights as a guideline when interpreting a national constitutional right (see later in this chapter).

Another classical political right is freedom of assembly (*kokoontumisvapaus*), which is connected with the freedom of association in the Finnish system. The normative core of this right is everyone's right to arrange meetings and demonstrations and to take part in those without a permit. The concept of 'meeting' is understood in this context very loosely, and accordingly, it consists of various kinds of meetings not depending on whether these meetings are held outside or inside or if they are private or public. The freedom of association includes the important right to be (or not to be) a member of an association and to take part freely in the activities of such an association (eg political party, trade union, etc).[26] Typical to the Finnish system, more detailed rules concerning the exercise of these rights may be given in Acts.

The key Act regulating meetings and freedom of assembly is the Assembly Act, which offers detailed provisions concretising the full constitutional content of everyone's freedom of assembly.[27] The objective of this Act is to guarantee the exercise of the right of free assembly by laying down the necessary provisions concerning the arrangement of public meetings (eg demonstration) and public events (eg amusement, contest). The key requirement of constitutional significance is to arrange meetings and events peacefully and without infringing anyone's legal rights.

From the point of view of constitutional history and continuity, we may note that the freedom of assembly may in fact be deemed as one of the oldest rights in the Finnish system: during the Swedish era this right was understood to be a part of conventional constitutional law. Finns regarded that the old system of rights was transferred to the Autonomic Grand Duchy under Imperial Russia in 1809 (see chapter one). When the Finnish rights doctrine was transforming from Estate-bound thinking towards the modern State, an important step was taken in 1906. Today's freedom of assembly can be seen as a direct historical offspring having many constitutional layers: Swedish era, Russian-period, Form of Government 1919, international law inspired reform of 1995 and the system of today. In this sense, we might claim that this right is the oldest genuine constitutional right in the Finnish constitutional system. In Sweden there still is a Constitutional Act dealing with the freedom of

---

[26] The most central concretising separate Act concerning this specific constitutional right is the Act on Association (*Yhdistyslaki* 503/1989). Regarding political parties, the Party Act (*Puoluelaki* 1/1969) is the central one.

[27] *Kokoontumislaki* (530/1999).

expression separately.[28] Be that historically as it may, it does not seem to have any specific status in the present Finnish system: it is, however, very much a normal part of the fundamental rights system.

Electoral Rights

Electoral rights and participatory rights (CA section 14) are an important part of the system of political rights. These rights are designed to ensure that the people's will is reflected in the work of the Parliament and the Executive. These rights have a constitutional anchor in one of the leading principles of Finnish constitutional law, namely the idea that the power of the State is vested in the People (CA section 2). The actual constitutional substance to this rule takes shape in electoral rights and participatory rights; they state in more detail how this sovereign power is actually channelled to the political system and how power may be obtained through legally regulated political completion. The key Act is the Election Act, which governs the procedures for all important elections: the presidential election, parliamentary elections, municipal elections, and European parliamentary elections.[29] The parliamentary core of electoral rights (*vaalioikeudet*) is the right of the Finnish citizen, who is over the age of 18, to vote in national elections and referendums.

Finnish citizens and foreigners permanently residing in the country (over 18 years of age) have the right to vote in municipal elections and municipal referendums. It is specifically a constitutionally stipulated soft obligation of public authorities to enhance the possibilities of the individual to participate in societal activity. Everyone who has the right to vote has only one vote; that is, there is equal suffrage in all elections which was not the case prior to the Form of Government 1919. In the Estate system, the number of votes was directly connected with the wealth of a person: the rich had more votes than the poor in communal elections. This heritage of Estates has been successfully eradicated from the system of constitutional rights. Yet, it is a fact that a wealthy candidate can afford more extensive election campaigns than a candidate with fewer financial resources. However, there is nothing specifically Finnish in this state of affairs.

Today, everyone who has the right to vote and who is not under legal guardianship may be a candidate in parliamentary elections (CA section

---

[28] *Yttrandefrihetslagen* (SFS 1991:1469).
[29] *Vaalilaki* (Election Act 714/1998).

27). However, if a person holds military office (ie is a professional career soldier), he or she cannot be elected while in active service. There are also a handful of top public positions that preclude an individual being an MP. These include such high posts as the Chancellor of Justice, the Parliamentary Ombudsman and justices of supreme courts. The reasons for these restrictions clearly emanate from the separation of powers arrangement. However, after having left this kind of position this constitutional restraint also ceases to exist; after resignation from military office or from another public office one may serve as an MP without a constitutional problem. In fact, there are normally several former high ranking officers serving as MPs even though their overall number has always remained rather low. High civil servants very seldom, if ever, become MPs even after leaving their posts. Yet, there is a notable exception of former Parliamentary Ombudsman Jacob Söderman who is also a former European Ombudsman: he has also functioned as a minister (1971, 1982), Governor of a Province (1982–89) and MP (1972–82, 2007–11).

Referendums also play a certain role when it comes to participatory rights (*osallistumisoikeudet*). The right to vote in a consultative referendum is clearly a part of everyone's right to participate in societal activity; however, as long as referendums are only consultative in nature, this right remains constitutionally a weaker right than more concrete electoral rights. There are also certain serious constitutional problems with referendums which were dealt with earlier (chapter three).

Economic, Social and Cultural Rights

Historically, economic, social and cultural (ESC) rights represent the second generation of constitutional rights. Importantly, ESC rights are not only regarded as political entities in Finland, but instead these rights actually connect the predominant welfare-ideology and Finnish conception of rule-of-law-state. However, it is a somewhat contested question as to what rights should actually be counted as ESC rights. Doctrinal writing is not unanimous on this. These difficulties also concern very much the Finnish Constitution. This is particularly true in the case of protection of property, which is, age-wise, an older constitutional right than other members of the ESC group. Property right is an ESC right, even though its base is in liberalism rather than welfare ideology so typical to all the Nordic countries and later ESC rights.

Property

The wording of the Constitution Act (section 15) is especially sparse when it concerns protection of property (*omaisuudensuoja*). It is only stated in an almost laconic manner that the property of everyone is protected and that provision concerning expropriation of property must be laid out in an Act. The provision also restricts the constitutionally possible scope of expropriation by stating that this kind of exceptional action is strictly for 'public needs and against full compensation'. Even though this right has deep roots in Finnish constitutional law, it was only actually codified in the Form of Government 1919.[30] In practice, this right has been most often applied by the Constitutional Law Committee and legislature.

Since then, the practice of the Constitutional Law Committee and even the courts of law with respect to the protection of property has been expanding. The doctrine concerning protection of property has gone in a direction that has meant more and more space for group rights and also the weight of environmental rights has been increased. However, the relevant landmark case KKO 2004: 26 decided by the Supreme Court indicates that the protection of property is even today one of the most effective and best protected constitutional rights, and surely amongst the ESC rights it is possibly the strongest.[31] However, as Finnish constitutional practice proves, property rights are certainly not absolute rights even though they have had traditionally a very strong

[30] Here the Belgian model is clear even today; the Belgian Constitution Act article 16 states that 'No person may be deprived of his property (*sa propriété/zijn eigendom*) save in the public interest (*d'utilité publique/ algemenen nutte*), in the cases laid down by law (*par la loi /bij de wet*) and in the manner it prescribes, and provided just compensation is made in advance.'

[31] In this case, environmental authorities had decided on a temporary prohibition concerning alterations to certain premises owned by a housing corporation. The corporation was not allowed to take any measures which would endanger the historical value of the interior of the premises (which had been a pharmacy for a long time). However, the proposal for protection was not accepted. The corporation demanded compensation from the State on the grounds that the temporary prohibition had prevented the corporation from letting out the premises (resulting in a loss of income). In fact, rents from these premises had been the corporation's most important source of income. The lower court rejected the claim as being without legal base. However, the Supreme Court (referring to sections 15 and 106 of the CA) ruled that the corporation had a right to compensation. The majority of the justices based the decision on an evident conflict between section 15 of the Constitution Act and the provision in the ordinary Act.

position in the constitutional system of rights.[32] Before the change in the 1990s, this right was the most reviewed and applied of all the constitutional rights in the practice of the Constitutional Law Committee of the Parliament.

Labour

Originally, the 1919 Form of Government contained an obligation for public power to protect the labour force, and at the beginning of the 1970s this section was even amended so that it also contained an obligation for the State to provide work opportunities for citizens. However, the last mentioned obligation was not a hard constitutional obligation per se but it was understood to carry only a softer principle, according to which the State should enhance possibilities for the citizens to work.[33] Nowadays, the right to work and the freedom to engage in any chosen (legal) commercial activity is guaranteed in section 18 of the Constitution Act. The right to work (*oikeus työhön*) is clearly an ESC right and it covers the right to earn livelihood by freely chosen employment, occupation or commercial activity. Moreover, public power is regarded as having a special responsibility to protect the labour force. Importantly, this constitutional obligation, as so many others, takes its actual concrete shape in the form of Acts and lower decrees which give actual content to this broad right provided by the Constitution Act with very general wording. The constitutional right to work contains one hard constitutional dimension which states that no one can be dismissed from employment without a lawful reason (ie a reason specifically mentioned in an Act). This rule has also been verified by the constitutionally relevant precedents of the Supreme Administrative Court.[34]

By means of legislation, especially, public authorities ought to promote employment and function so that the right of everyone to work is realised as fully as possible. However, this constitutional obligation does not require the public power to employ everyone, rather it sets a general

---

[32] The protection of property seems to have been more far-reaching than in the First Protocol of ECHR article 1 regarding specifically the scope of the concept 'possession'.

[33] This sharply criticised interpretation of the Constitutional Law Committee (Statement 32/1992) deemed this rule to be 'generally programmatic', which meant that it was held in 'more of a political nature' than as a 'clear legal obligation'.

[34] See eg, KHO 2008: 25 in which the Supreme Administrative Court actually ruled a stipulation of Act as being in clear contradiction with the Constitution.

constitutional soft obligation to act in such a manner that would enhance employment and everyone's right to work. Constitutionally, this obligation is vague and it is not regarded as a directly enforceable right. It is also important to take into account that many real-life factors such as number of available positions, required training for specific jobs, experience and occupational skills and official requirements for positions in public service obviously limit the freedom of choice significantly. Clearly, the possibilities for earning a livelihood through commercial activity are also limited by the actual possibilities presented by real business life. Finally, there are some professions that may also require special permits to work (eg doctors, attorneys, translators, etc).

Social Security

The constitutional right to social security (*oikeus sosiaaliturvaan*) is perhaps the most central constitutional ESC right in the Finnish system. This is due to its legal power: it contains subjective right. The constitutional core of this stipulation (CA section 19) is the subjective right of those who cannot obtain the means necessary for a dignified life to receive necessary subsistence and care. However, as the case law proves, this last mentioned right is not absolute as a certain level of activity from people themselves is also required.[35] In other words, this right does not contain a right not to do anything and still expect to be taken care of by the State.

The two most important Acts concerning this constitutional right are the Social Welfare Act and the Act on the Status and Rights of Social Welfare Clients.[36] The Welfare Act stipulates all social services by a commonly applied principle concerning how general social services should be organised. The latter Act specifies the major procedures to be applied in work with social welfare clients and also in matters of data protection. The Social Welfare Clients Act clarifies the meaning and genuine significance of constitutional social rights by demanding social welfare administration to respect client's human dignity, right to self-determination, beliefs and privacy. So, based on the Constitution Act, everyone who is not able to secure the requirements of a decent life has the right to necessary income and care as a last resort. Various means of social and health services are one way to safeguard this constitutional right.

---

[35] See case KHO 2000:16.

[36] *Sosiaalihuoltolaki* (710/1982) and *Laki sosiaalihuollon asiakkaan asemasta ja oikeuksista* (812/2001).

There are plenty of Acts and decrees concerning social welfare in Finland; there are so many pieces of legislation that the area of social law is somewhat difficult to master even by specialist lawyers. In any case, social welfare legislation lays down various separate pieces of legislation dealing with how to organise child and youth care, child day care, care of substance abusers, special care for the mentally disabled, disability services and support, rehabilitative work, informal care support and family care. All these Acts and decrees are derived from the constitutional obligation of the public power to guarantee the right to basic subsistence in all events, especially those concerning unemployment, illness, disability, old age, birth of a child, and loss of a provider. In terms of substance, this voluminous legislation is to its nature constitutional.

Education

The last constitutional rights belonging to the ESC group of rights in the Finnish system are the educational rights stipulated in the Constitution Act (section 16). The core of these rights is the right to basic education free of charge (*maksuton perusopetus*). Detailed provisions on the duty to receive education are laid down by Acts of which the most central is the Act on Basic Education.[37] Basic education is also regulated by the Basic Education Act, by the Basic Education Decree and by the Government Decree on the General National Objectives and Distribution of Lesson Hours in Basic Education.[38] These regulations stipulate on such matters as the core subjects taught to all pupils, and the distribution of teaching hours between various school subjects. Basically, these core subjects which are taught to all pupils are the mother tongue and literature (Finnish or Swedish), the other official language, one foreign language, environmental studies, health education, religion or ethics, history, social studies, mathematics, physics, chemistry, biology, geography, physical education, music, art and crafts, and home economics. In addition, various optional subjects are also taught. These optional subjects may be determined locally by municipal authorities and schools themselves. All these rights are included within the constitutional educational right.

---

[37] *Perusopetuslaki* (628/1998).
[38] *Perusopetusasetus* (852/1998) and *Valtioneuvoston asetus perusopetuslaissa tarkoitetun opetuksen kansallisista tavoitteista ja perusopetuksen tuntijaosta* (1435/2001).

The constitutional obligation of providing basic education is targeted to public authorities. So, in practice, almost all of the schools are public schools and there are only a handful of private schools in Finland. Importantly, the private schools are by no means schools for the elite; rather, most respected schools are in fact normal public schools. Normally under the rule of a leftist Government it has been more difficult to obtain a licence for private schools, whereas under the rule of a rightist Government the policy toward private schools has been more lenient. According to the Basic Education Act (section 4), the local authority shall have an obligation to arrange basic education for children of compulsory school age (seven years) who are residing in its area, and pre-primary education during the year preceding compulsory schooling. Even though the constitutional stipulation imposes an obligation on public power to provide education, it does not actually bind the legislator to follow any certain principle according to which basic education may be organised or bind the legislator to maintain any certain existing educational institution: there are degrees of freedom concerning the practical organisation of basic education, even though the constitutional equality right prevents creating too dispersed a system. So, educational quality should not be too different in different areas of the country.

It must be separately noted that educational rights also offer a certain degree of constitutional protection to the universities. Namely, the freedom of science, the arts and higher education is also constitutionally guaranteed (CA section 16.3). Freedom of science and the arts refers mainly to the general freedom of a researcher to choose the research subject and method. This constitutional freedom also contains the right of academic teachers to teach in such a manner that they themselves regard as most desirable from the point of view of content and method of teaching. Constitutional academic freedom, thus, includes the right of a teacher to maintain personal academic convictions, concepts and so on. In accordance, this constitutional right even includes a student's right to study and obtain information.

It must be noted, however, that the 2000s so far has seen plenty of legislative reforms that have de facto somewhat narrowed the academic right. Narrowing has been done by Acts giving actual content to any such constitutional right that leaves space for interpretation and which is not a subjective right as to its nature. The novel University Act offers more freedom for universities from the Ministry of Education, even though during its passing-stages in the Parliament some constitutional controversial issues were discussed and the original bill was to an extent slightly re-drafted.[39] The bill was changed modestly so that outsiders could not have too much say in the way universities are governed. The sharp critique by deans of all three law faculties and practically all constitutional experts was not given too much weight: the Government was determined to link universities closer to the 'national innovation system' which leaves less room for genuine academic freedom.

Collective Rights

An important feature of so-called third generation rights is the fact that these rights are typically detached from an individual in the sense that their scope of application is not limited to individuals or such rights that may be derived from the sphere of an individual. From a general point of view, collective rights embody the shift from a liberal *Rechtsstaat* towards a substantive *Rechtsstaat* in which rights have a broader scope of application than in the past; today fundamental rights are more clearly connected with the modern constitutional state itself. Now, the right to one's language and culture is clearly a collective right that actually contains several constitutional sub-rights.

Language Rights

The Constitution Act (section 17) stipulates that the official languages of Finland are Finnish and Swedish. This collective constitutional right contains the right of everyone to use Finnish or Swedish before courts and other public authorities, and also the right to receive official documents in that language. Even though the language of the vast majority of citizens is Finnish, Swedish also has a strong constitutional position in the Finnish system. This, again, is one of those central features of the Finnish Constitution that may be understood only against the backdrop of political history. In 1809, when Finland was annexed to Imperial Russia, Swedish remained the only official language and it was only in the beginning of the twentieth century when the language of the majority gained a legally equal position with Swedish.

---

[39]   See Statement of the Constitutional Law Committee 11/2009.

When the 1919 Form of Government was born, the constitutional equality between languages was formally paved. Unlike so many other new states emerging from the aftermath of World War I, Finland did not become a unilingual state but a state with two major ethnic groups enjoying constitutionally equal status. Today, Swedish is the mother tongue of approximately 270,000 people in Finland and about 25,000 people in the Åland Islands. The proportion of Finnish-Swedes (*suomenruotsalaiset*) has decreased since the early nineteenth century when about 15 per cent of the population spoke Swedish as a mother tongue.

Today, the Swedish-speaking Finns amount to some 290,000 people, which is roughly 5.5 per cent of the total population. The majority of these Finns reside in the coastal areas of southern and western Finland. The Åland Islands are a unilingual Swedish self-governing province off the west coast of Finland (see chapter five). Due to being a part of Sweden for more than 600 years, Swedish remained the language of governance throughout the first half of the nineteenth century. In fact, it was not until 1863 that Finnish was recognised as an official language in Finland. The Finnish administration was, in practical terms, partially trilingual, even while Swedish and Finnish had the clear upper hand. After gaining independence, Finnish rapidly became the dominant language. Under the Swedish Crown many ethnic Finns changed their mother tongue and started speaking Swedish. However, it seems that most of them reverted back to Finnish in the late 1800s. From the point of view of numbers the Swedish speakers are a minority, but constitutionally and even more generally legally they are not regarded as a minority. From the point of view of constitutional rights, it is generally regarded that the language right is the most central to the Swedish-speaking group.

The constitutional language right means in practice that members of the Swedish language minority have the right to communicate with the State authorities in Swedish. On the municipal level, this right is legally restricted to municipalities with a certain minimum of speakers of the minority language. Actually, all Finnish municipalities are classified as either monolingual or bilingual. If the proportion of the minority language increases to eight per cent (or more than 3,000 residents), then the municipality is defined as bilingual, but when it falls below six per cent, the municipality becomes instead monolingual. In bilingual municipalities, all civil servants must have at least satisfactory language skills in either Finnish or Swedish (in addition to native speaker skills in the other language). Both languages can be used in all communications with the

civil servants in such a municipality. The central Act which gives content
to this constitutional right is the Language Act which specifies that state
authorities of central administration are always bilingual, whereas their
units of regional and local administration are unilingual if their administrative districts comprise only municipalities with one language.[40]
Linguistic dimension of public administration is debated mostly within
the Swedish-speaking minority. Yet, there are some cases in which the
structure of administration and language rights of the Swedish minority
have been dealt with by courts.[41]

Indigenous People

The indigenous Sámi-people (*saamelaiset*), as well as Roma and other
groups have a constitutional right to maintain and develop their own
language and culture. The Sámi may also use their mother tongue before
public authorities in certain defined regions within Finnish Lapland.
The cultural autonomy of the Sámi is governed by the Sámi Parliament
(*Saamelaiskäräjät*, ie 'the Sámi-moot') which is an elected and representative body.[42] There is a special Act which seeks to ensure that the constitutional right of the Sámi to maintain and develop its own culture and
language is protected.[43]

However, constitutionally the cultural and language rights of the Sámi
are not as strong as the rights of the Swedish-speaking minority. Even
though Finland has been eager to see herself as defender of fundamental rights, there are still constitutional questions that seem to indicate that
the status of the Sámi could be in better accordance with certain international demands of a legal nature concerning the indigenous minorities.
Whereas such Nordic neighbouring countries as Denmark and Norway

---

[40] *Kielilaki* (423/2003). Also the Act on Language Skills (*Kielitaitolaki* 424/2003)
is an important Act in this regard since it stipulates in detail the required language
skills of civil servants.

[41] In case KHO 2008:1 a municipality complained over the decision of the
Government which had altered the borders of two municipalities in the Helsinki
region. The municipality claimed that the Government had breached law, including
the Constitution Act, while doing this. The Court rejected the municipalities' claims.

[42] See K Myntti, 'The Beneficiaires of Autonomy Arrangements—Special
Reference to Indigenous Peoples in General and the Sámi in Finland Particular' in
Suksi (ed), *Autonomy: Applications and Implications* (Kluwer, Dordrecht, 1998) 277–294.

[43] Sámi Language Act (*Saamen kielilaki* 1086/2003). This Act legally binds public
authorities in Northern Finland (three municipalities, State authorities in the North,
and the Provincial Government of Lapland).

both have a ratified Indigenous and Tribal Peoples Convention (C 169) by the International Labour Organisation (ILO), Finland has not. This, alongside the national long-standing debate over the legal ownership of Sámi-lands, indicates that Finland might also need to take a good look in the mirror before it announces making human rights as an 'integral part' of her foreign policy.[44] At the heart of the problem lies the disputed ancient Sámi right of ownership to land and the related rights to practice reindeer herding, fishing and hunting. These rights are unsettled in law and the Finnish Government has not been able to resolve this issue.

Environment

The second genuinely collective constitutional right in the Finnish system is also based on written provision in the Constitution Act (section 20). This right gets impetus from the change of constitutional thinking in general. This right is formulated in the form of a sort of non-precise obligation that gives vague responsibility for the environment to everyone. The written constitutional provision specifically states that nature as well as its biodiversity and the environment are the responsibility of everyone. The national heritage is also included in this area of everyone's general soft-constitutional responsibility. On a more strictly legal basis, the stipulation obliges the public power and its authorities to generally 'endeavour to guarantee' (*on pyrittävä turvaamaan*) the right to a healthy environment for everyone and, furthermore, to endeavour to guarantee for everyone the possibility to influence such public decisions that concern their own living environment.

In comparison with other constitutional rights, the environmental right is somewhat special due to the fact that this stipulation was deemed to underline such environmental values that are not possible to derive from the rights of individuals. Thus, the actual subject of this right is difficult to pinpoint exactly. In this sense, the legal subjects here are in fact the future generations. The latter part of this rule is constitutionally clearer and it is understood to guide all users of public power to act in such a manner that will ensure a healthy environment and also true possibilities for individuals to have their say when environment-related public decisions are made. In practice, the last mentioned democratic

---

[44] Government's Report to the Parliament concerning Human Rights Policy of Finland 2009 (in Finnish) (*Ulkoasiainministeriön julkaisuja* 7/2009, Helsinki, 2009).

dimension normally takes effect when a legislator passes a new Act that concerns the environment (eg construction and real estate). Nevertheless, it must be clearly stated that soft-constitutional right to the environment has not gained a true edge in the case law of supreme courts. Its judicial potential has yet to be realised. Yet, a small number of dissenting opinions in environmental cases before the Supreme Administrative Court may hint that paradigmatic change is on its way. Dissenting judges would have been ready to give more weight to environmental constitutional right, whereas the majority has regarded this right with less normative weight.[45]

There are at least two obvious obstacles for full realisation of this right: its soft nature as a written rule and the fact that protection of the environment depends much on the economic resources available. Nevertheless, this constitutional responsibility for the environment has activated new environmental law thinking with a strong fundamental rights orientation and it has also moved the question concerning the value of nature to be conceived from the point of view of future generations into the constitutional law debate.[46]

General Doctrines of Fundamental Rights

The Finnish Constitution consists of many different elements of which most are codified, some rely on customary type of rules, and some even have a more complex origin. It was pointed out earlier in this book that there are some small but relevant customary law features in the Finnish Constitution. We might even say that constitutional theory and academic constitutional law also had and has even today a certain role here. This role is especially evident in the area of general constitutional doctrines.[47] Constitutional general doctrines (*valtiosääntöoikeuden yleiset opit*) are concepts, principles and theories that concern the organs of the State and their relationships and fundamental rights of individuals. A typical

[45]   In a recent case of Supreme Administrative Court (KHO 2010:6), the paradigm seems to be changing towards giving more legal weight to the environmental right of CA (section 20).

[46]   See also I Saraviita, *Finland*—Constitutional Law: International Encyclopedia of Laws (Kluwer, Alphen, 2009) 284–85.

[47]   See also K Tuori, 'General Doctrines in Public Law' (1983) 27 *Scandinavian Studies in Law* 177.

example of a general constitutional doctrine is the principle of parliamentarism or rule of law principle.

However, within the institutional part of constitutional law, general doctrines possess not quite such an important role as they do in the area of fundamental rights. Simply, when constitutional problems deal with such things like the powers of the President or the relation between the European Union and Finland, there always seems to be free space for constitutional practices and sometimes perhaps even conventions. The fine line between law and politics is not easily, if at all, drawn in the area of constitutional law. However, it seems that the role of general doctrines has been and is more relevant when it comes to rights and especially to the interpretation of them. In this context we need to consider especially two dimensions of general doctrines. The first deals with constitutional friendly interpretation and the second deals with doctrinal constitutional restrictions that are used by the Parliament's Constitutional Law Committee. National doctrinal discussion on the two and even other dimensions of general doctrines is relatively voluminous, but here we must be brief.

Interpretation

The principle of constitutional-friendly-interpretation concerns, as an *interpretative constitutional mandate*, courts of law specifically. Accordingly, this principle is applied after legislation has come formally into force.[48] It is typical for the Finnish legal culture in general to try to avoid conflict situations between constitutional law and ordinary Acts. However, where there is a conflict between the Constitution Act and lower provision, an attempt will normally be made to resolve it by means of constitutional interpretation. The tendency of avoiding open constitutional conflicts between high public institutions is not typical only to Finland. For example, we can also find precisely the very same principle in rather fresh UK constitutional case law.[49] The idea is to interpret ordinary

---

[48] Institutional anchorage in the sense of source of law is to be found from the Government's bill 309/1993, 31 and the Report of Constitutional Committee 25/1994, 4.

[49] In *Jackson v Attorney General* [2005] UKHL 56, Lord Hope of Craighead stated ([125]) that 'In the field of constitutional law the delicate balance between various institutions . . . is maintained to a large degree by the mutual respect which each institution has for the other' (referring to the relationship between the Parliament and judicial power).

legislation and other provisions so as to remove the conflict with the Constitution Act. In addition, if international human rights obligations are concerned, the Constitutional Law Committee has created a principle according to which, when alternative interpretations can be justified, the alternative to be adopted ought to be the one that enhances the realisation of fundamental rights to the fullest. This kind of interpretation is regarded as being either human-rights-friendly (*ihmisoikeusystävällinen*) or constitutional-rights-friendly (*perusoikeustävällinen*).

However, because these two dimensions are normally intertwined, separating these rights is bound to be somewhat artificial as we noted at the beginning of this chapter when stating the difficulty of drawing a clear distinction between these two types of constitutionally relevant rights. Here we can also make a comparative remark. The Finnish doctrine of constitutional-rights-friendly interpretation appears to be a modified legal transplant from Germany. The Finnish version of this doctrine is virtually identical with the one which was assumed by the German Federal Constitutional Court in 1953: if one can end up, within the limits of the Act, with several possible interpretations, then one should choose the interpretation which most conforms to the Constitution.[50] There is some Finnish evidence, not widespread though, in the case law that this principle may sometimes even play a decisive role in judging cases.[51] Moreover, lately the interpretative effect of ESC rights has taken clear steps ahead in case law.[52]

In the Finnish system, most of the constitutional rights are not absolute in the sense that they can be restricted in certain circumstances. In this sense they are not rights having the nature of natural law. Generally speaking, any restriction must be supported by an Act, and may be imposed only to achieve objectives that are acceptable in a democratic society. The acceptability is judged in the light of both national constitutional rights and international human rights, especially those rights that are guaranteed in the ECHR. Of course, some of the codified rights are unconditional in nature, but most allow some space for constitutional interpretation and, thus, room for certain kinds of

---

[50] In Germany this doctrine (*verfassungskonforme Auslegung*) was created in case BVerfGE 2, 266, 282. It has been followed ever since.

[51] See especially cases KHO 1998:79 and 1998:80.

[52] See case KHO 2008:61 (in which ordinary legislation, concerning the rights of disabled people, was interpreted in the light of constitutional rights).

limitations or restrictions.[53] Constitutional balancing does take place between lower legislation (which is hierarchically at a lower level) and the Constitution Act and even more extensively within constitutional law. The actual impact of fundamental rights is best seen in legislative process in which they have a clear and distinctive role.

Restriction of Rights

As stated earlier, the Finnish constitutional system has worked traditionally so that rights have functioned as a certain kind of check concerning the competence of the legislature. Now, after the constitutional rights reform in 1995, this traditional check-function has become widespread. Yet, even today it is the Constitutional Law Committee of the Parliament that has the central role as a key supervisor of constitutionality of Acts. The Committee has actually developed a rather systematic test, though without a written base in statutory law, which a legislative proposal for restriction of constitutional rights must pass in order to be passed as an Act of Parliament at all. This constitutional rights test, which has clearly also drawn inspiration from German constitutional doctrine, has seven different points which are looked into by the Committee.[54] We will discuss them shortly in the following; however, space will only permit us to outline the bare essentials.

The first one requires that possible restriction must be based on an Act of Parliament, not for instance on a lower decree. This requirement has clear connections to direct stipulations of the Constitution Act and especially its second chapter covering constitutional rights. The second one requires that the restriction must be precise and defined in sufficient detail as to its nature. In other words, any such restriction that leaves an unacceptably wide area for interpretation for the users of public power does not fulfil this requirement. According to the third one, the grounds

---

[53] Clearly, such fundamental rights are, eg, the right to life ('no one shall be sentenced to death', ECHR section 7.2), *nulla poena* principle ('no one shall be found guilty', ECHR section 8) and equality ('no one shall . . . be treated', ECHR section 6.2)

[54] The beginning of this doctrine, which has been developed in later cases, may be traced originally to the German Constitutional Court case *Apotheken* from 1958 (BVerfGE 7, 377). In German literature this is generally referred to as *Wesensgehalt*-doctrine which has its codified grounding in German *Grundgesetz* (article 19.2) declaring that the 'essence of the basic right' may not be infringed in any case. See also F Venter, *Constitutional Comparison* (Juta/Kluwer, Lansdowne, 2000) 183–85.

for the restriction must be legitimate when measured against the context of the whole system of fundamental rights; the restriction must be necessary in order to realise an important social interest. In practice this does not equal any general state of crisis but rather to such situations in which it may be generally accepted that the driving force behind the restriction is exceptionally important and there are no real alternatives to choose than to go for the restriction of a certain constitutional right dimension.

The fourth point of this doctrine states that the restriction must adhere to the principle of proportionality (*suhteellisuusperiaate*), which requires the lawgiver to adjust the restriction in proper proportion in light of the legislative goal that it seeks to enhance. The fifth requirement states that the restriction is not allowed if it would enter into the 'core area of the right' (*perusoikeuden ydinalue*); this is the Finnish version of German *Wesensgehalt*. The next point demands that if the restriction is legislated, a due protection under the law must be arranged. In other words, an individual should retain the right to challenge the restriction of a right before the court of law. This right is conceived as fundamentally in connection with the right to protection under law. The final point requires the restriction to comply with the international human rights obligations binding the State. In general, we may claim that the Constitutional Law Committee has applied this test rather strictly, even though from time to time there has been discussion and public critique. In fact, we may regard this test as having the status of customary constitutional law.

Finally, we may also note that the Finnish system also includes one central constitutional obligation imposed on citizens. This may sound strange because in the contemporary world most constitutions concentrate on rights and the idea of constitutional obligations directed toward individuals are much rarer. Nonetheless, the Finnish Constitution Act (section 127.1) obliges every Finnish citizen to participate or assist in national defence. The actual content of this constitutional obligation is defined by a separate Act of Parliament.[55] Also, the obligation to pay taxes has a clear written constitutional base although the provision in the Constitution Act does not state this directly.[56] Clearly, the obligation

[55] Act on National Defence (*Asevelvollisuuslaki* 1438/2007).

[56] CA section 81.1 stipulates that 'the State tax is governed by an Act'. This Act must contain detailed provisions concerning the grounds for tax liability and the amount of the tax.

concerning national defence is restricted to citizens whereas the obligation to pay taxes is not.

Applicability of Fundamental Rights

Since practically all modern constitutions have a similar type of catalogue of rights, it seems justified to ask if there is something typically Finnish concerning these rights. Now, in the Finnish Constitution fundamental rights are understood to express general values of society and state. Fundamental rights link the public morality and legal system together by stressing certain values that are held as central. These values differ from other political or public philosophy-related values because they have been confirmed constitutionally in writing in the form of legally binding rights. The constitutional philosophy which lies behind this system of rights is based on justification according to which these rules must act to benefit individuals in the public sphere and also to an extent in the private sphere. It should also be made clear that for the most part aliens have the same constitutional status as Finnish citizens, even though aliens may be subjected to some legislation specifically targeted towards them.

However, even though there has been discussion concerning the horizontal so-called *Drittwirkung*-effect (the radiating effect of constitutional rights concerning third parties) of fundamental rights, it may be said that de facto the main effect of fundamental rights is still very much vertical.[57] This is probably because in Finland there is no such equivalent super court as the highly respected and powerful *Bundesverfassunsgerichthof* in Germany; the main responsibility of controlling constitutionality of Acts has been and still is with the Parliament's Constitutional Law Committee. Moreover, it may be claimed that the courts of law have been cautious in expanding the legal reach of fundamental rights into an open *Drittwirkung*-direction, even though the academic practice of law has been rather open towards this sort of expanded use of fundamental rights. However, the question concerning the horizontal effect of fundamental rights is an open and still very much debated issue. Traditionally, fundamental rights have protected against the State but according to

---

[57] *Drittwirkung* doctrine clearly originates from the German constitutional law praxis, see Kommers, *The Constitutional Jurisprudence of the Federal Republic of Germany* (Duke University Press, Durham, 1997) 48–49.

some scholars today fundamental rights might even offer protection against 'misuse' of private power.

This debate reflects resisting inertia of earlier layers of constitutional culture against fully-fledged, rights-centred constitutionalism. However, there is more to it. It would be inaccurate to claim that all constitutional actors would think genuinely in a fundamental rights-friendly manner: there are still those individual public servants who have not really grasped the full meaning of fundamental rights and sometimes there are even traces of this old-fashioned attitude among the judiciary too. This is not a remarkable problem even though it tells about a certain internal pluralism of legal culture: rooted cultures of bureaucracy and judiciary cannot be changed within just 10–15 years.

Yet, fundamental rights do bind quite a large area: legislative power, executive power and judicial power are all affected and guided (to an extent) by fundamental rights. It has been stated that 'It is nowadays difficult to find such occasions concerning the use of public power in which the constitutional-rights-aspect would not be somehow present.'[58] The significance of these rights has two kinds of constitutional bases: section 22 of the Constitution Act sets a basic constitutional obligation to protect fundamental rights, and the living constitutional law abides by this basic rule generally rather well. The exact wording stipulates that 'The public authorities shall guarantee the observance of constitutional rights and human rights.' From a comparative point of view, this provision says basically the same as the German *Grundgesetz*'s article 1(3): these rights shall bind the legislature, the executive and judiciary as directly applicable law.

In Finland, nonetheless, the main responsibility for taking care of fundamental rights is the concern of the legislator: it ensures that the new legislation that it enacts does not infringe fundamental rights. While doing this, the Parliament lays the sole responsibility of interpreting the Constitution on its Constitutional Law Committee. In turn, the Committee hears on a regular basis (based on customary constitutional law) public law experts that may sometime seek to enhance their own ideas of constitutional law. The Parliament, thus, is the main target for fundamental rights obligations even though these rights clearly also concern other branches of public power. From the point of view of ESC

---

[58] A Jyränki, *Our New Constitution Act* ['*Uusi perustuslakimme*'] (Iura Nova, Turku, 2000) 45.

rights, the role of the Parliament is crucial: while using its legislative power it must seek to fulfil the ESC-rights obligations laid down in the Constitution Act. So, EU and ECHR dimensions are weaker when ESC rights are dealt with because the national system is more open towards these types of fundamental rights.

It is relevant to understand that private organs may also be bound by fundamental rights in such situations in which public administrative tasks have been delegated to others than public authorities.[59] Some of the recent case law by the supreme courts seems to indicate that while applying section 106 of the Constitution Act, which allows restricted constitutionality control of parliamentary Acts by the courts, there may be some possibility for these high courts to actually expand the legal dimension of fundamental rights also toward horizontal effect. However, this feature remains as yet somewhat vague and still very questionable. Frankly, supreme courts do not appear to fully know themselves how they should apply section 106 of the Constitution Act. It has even been claimed that Finnish supreme courts have started to put aside fundamental-rights-friendly-interpretation and have instead been inclined to interpret the clear controversy requirement too rigidly, thus, actually restraining themselves from using other provisions of the Constitution Act (especially rights provisions).[60] From the point of view of constitutionalism, this is development going backwards: refined instruments of constitutional interpretation are being changed into a blunt dichotomy of constitutional versus clearly unconstitutional.

Scope of Rights

Finally, one important point concerning the scope of application must be made in this context. It concerns the legally relevant question of when fun-

---

[59] It must be added that such a task that would involve the use of significant use of public power may only be delegated to public authorities. Before the reform of 2000, this rule was based on the practice of the Constitutional Law Committee of the Parliament. In 2000, this rule was codified in the Constitution Act (section 124) which provides constitutional criteria for delegating public tasks to private organs. Even so, the role of the Constitutional Law Committee is of importance here because it gives the precise legal content to this constitutional provision in its interpretative function.

[60] J Lavapuro, 'Effects of 'evident conflict' requirement in Section 106 of the Finnish Constitution' [Perustuslain ilmeisyysvaatimuksen vaikutuksista oikeuskäytännössä] (2008) 106 *Lakimies* 582.

damental rights are applicable and when they are not. Namely, an individual person gains fundamental rights protection from the moment of birth and it stops when the individual dies. The scope of fundamental rights is in the main restricted to natural persons that is, ie human beings. However, the fundamental rights protection may also extend to reach legal persons in such cases in which the interests of a legal person may be derived directly from individual persons. This interpretation is made by the Constitutional Law Committee in conjunction with interpreting constitutional property rights. In turn, this means that the State itself, municipalities and other public law legal persons are not situated within the protective scope of fundamental rights. From time to time the municipal sector presents half-hearted initiatives for creation of a constitutional court which could better protect, in their view, the municipalities from the State's interventions. This would also include constitutional rights protection for such public law creatures as municipalities. However, these initiatives have always met a highly unenthusiastic reaction from the State and constitutional experts. In this regard, constitutional mentality has been and still is very much unitary state centred, except in the case of the Åland Islands.

There are also non-national factors that are taken into account. Finnish legislation is many times interpreted by the courts of law in accordance with the ECHR and the accompanying practice of the ECtHR. When legislation originates directly from EU institutions, the human rights dimension is regularly included. So, it is important to conceive different fundamental rights systems as creating a multi-dimensional fundamental rights totality. Nevertheless, there have been some human rights issues in which the national understanding and the ECtHR's understanding have been in collision as, for example, the incompatibility of the Finnish manner to protect children by transfer of guardianship with article 8 of the ECHR shows.[61] In addition, there have been some rare cases in which the Supreme Court has actually refused to use convention-conformity interpretation.[62] The *Uoti*-case, however, may be a sign of a changed attitude (see below). It must be mentioned that there is no such clear stipulation as in the United Kingdom according to which legislation 'must be read and given effect in a way which is compatible with the Convention rights'.[63] Yet, in judicial practice, this kind of interpretative rule is normally assumed to exist. This may be seen, for instance, in the

[61] See eg, ECtHR case *L v Finland* (27 April 2000).
[62] See case KKO 2008:10.
[63] Human Rights Act (1998) section 3(1).

manner how the Supreme Administrative Court transforms and explains (to the lower administrative courts) the actual domestic legal effect of the ECtHR's case law.[64]

Quite recently, even the legislator took into account the weight of the ECtHR's case law. The Trial Compensation Act stipulates that the case law of the ECtHR must be taken into account when delay of a trial is evaluated.[65] Finally, we must consider briefly the case KKO 2009:80, also known as the *Uoti*-case.

The Uoti-*case: Collapsing Domestic Judicial Authority*

The question of the relationship between the ECtHR's case law and domestic supreme adjudication has been partially unclear. Yet, this body of case law is constitutionally important because it deals with the hierarchy of norms. For the most part, both domestic supreme courts have used and referred to the ECtHR's case law while making their various decisions. So, there does not seem to be any deep judicial resistance to the ECtHR's case law. However, there are some indications that the full power of the ECtHR's case law has not been openly admitted in any high profile case. This changed in the recent *Uoti*-case.

This case must be reviewed in light of the wider debate concerning the constitutional relation between the decisions of national supreme courts and case law of the ECtHR. In this case the Supreme Court overturned its recent decision which was taken in Spring 2009 and decided that it had in fact relied on Finnish legislation even though it should have relied on the ECHR article 6 and, importantly, the accompanying case law of the ECtHR. Now, in Finnish legal culture, it is highly unusual that decisions of courts are overturned. Normally decisions are overturned if radically new facts, completely changing the earlier decision, come to light. However, overturning on the basis of 'obviously wrong legal interpretation' is a very rare happening indeed. Yet, in the *Uoti*-case the Supreme Court did precisely this on the basis of re-reading the ECtHR's case law. In bankruptcy proceedings against Mr Uoti, who had not declared all his assets, referred to his right not to incriminate himself. At that time he was also charged with dishonesty by a debtor in a separate criminal case. In the criminal case, the Supreme Court, as a last

---

[64]   See eg, consecutive cases KHO 2007:67 and KHO 2007: 68.

[65]   Act on Compensation of Delayed Trial (*Laki oikeudenkäynnin viivästymisen hyvittämisestä* 362/2009) section 4.3.

instance, said that Uoti had no right to withhold the information on his assets and convicted him of aggravated dishonesty by a debtor (KKO 2009:27). Only some days later, the ECtHR issued its decision in the *Marttinen v Finland* case which concerned debtor's right to silence and the right not to incriminate himself and in which Finland was found to have violated article 6 of the ECHR.[66] Now, with reference to the *Marttinen* case, Uoti requested the reversal of the Supreme Court's judgment in his case claiming that it was 'manifestly based on misapplication of the law'.

In its earlier decision (KKO 2009:27), the Supreme Court had assessed Uoti's right to silence on the basis of the risk he would have faced of being found guilty of dishonesty by a debtor, had he provided the information on his assets. However, now the Supreme Court held (KKO 2009:80) that it could not find sufficient support for this interpretation in the previous case law of the European Court of Human Rights. Actually, in the light of the ECtHR case of *Marttinen*, the right against self-incrimination was interpreted to the effect that if the criminal charge and the information which the debtor is obliged to disclose in the enforcement inquiry and bankruptcy proceedings concern the same facts. The debtor may refuse to disclose the information, irrespective of the significance of the information in assessing the debtor's guilt. So, the Supreme Court found this time that at the time of decision 2009:27, it had not manifestly misinterpreted the right against self-incrimination. However, considering the more recent developments, the interpretation adopted by the Supreme Court was in conflict with the case law of the ECtHR. Uoti had been sentenced to imprisonment and to pay damages, but the judgment had not yet been enforced. In accordance, the consequences of having applied national law in conflict with the ECHR could still be prevented by reversing the earlier judgment. Accordingly, the Supreme Court decided simply to reverse its earlier judgment as far as it was concerning Uoti's conviction for aggravated dishonesty by a debtor and to release him from the liability to pay damages. In short, the Supreme Court changed its position completely.

After this case it seems much clearer and evident that it is not only the written text of the ECHR and its Protocols but also the accompanying case law of the ECtHR which must be given legal weight; a weight greater even than that of the national statutory law. This case is clearly one indicator showing the transformation of Finnish law and the

---

[66] *Marttinen v Finland* (21 April 2009).

heightened importance of fundamental rights. Yet, even this case did not alter the basis of the system: the ECtHR does not seek to replace national courts, even though it seeks to indirectly control them when it comes to the rights of the ECHR.[67] The Supreme Court certainly allowed itself to be controlled by the ECtHR.

New Fundamental Rights Institution

The United Nations has recommended that governments should create specific national institutions for monitoring and guarding international human rights. According to the *Paris Principles*, each country should create an official and publicly funded organ for the promotion of human rights.[68] Further, these national bodies should draw their competency from legislation, preferably from the level of constitutional law. Now, even though international human rights and national constitutional rights today play a central role in Finland, the idea of a novel separate and independent body has been met with little enthusiasm. In this, the quintessentially national conception of constitutionalism can be seen, although not in so strong a form as it takes place in Denmark and Norway.

It has been thought that even though such an institution might be a good idea in general it does not really fit into the Finnish system because this new body would be very difficult to situate regarding its relation to two much older constitutional institutions: the Counsellor of Justice and the Parliamentary Ombudsman. Clearly, the rejection has been legitimised by the poor-legal-transplant argument which basically says that this institute does not really fit into the system. Proponents of this view argue that it would be rather a legal irritant than decent transplant.[69] The general feeling has been that classical national organs for overseeing legality already take care of most these functions. And yet, the Constitutional Law Committee has expressed even twice its support for this new institution.[70] In June 2010, a Working Group of Ministry of Justice proposed a new independent Human Rights Centre to be established.[71]

---

[67] See eg, ECtHR case *Tamminen v Finland* (15 June 2004) [38].

[68] UN General Assembly (UNGA) Res 134 (1993) *The Paris Principles* UN Doc A/RES/48/134.

[69] See G Teubner, 'Legal Irritants: Good Faith in British Law or How Unifying Law Ends Up in New Divergences' (1998) 61 *Modern Law Review* 11.

[70] PeVM 8/2007 and PeVM 4/2009.

[71] The Establishment of National Human Rights Institute (Ministry of Justice 45/2010).

CONCLUSION

The Finnish system of fundamental rights consists of national constitutional elements and international human rights elements that are in practice intertwined. The system of rights, as the whole system itself, consists of many layers. In general we can characterise the system as working well, but it is certainly not without problems. There have been difficulties with such things as limitation of the rights of those who are suspected to have committed crimes (eg animal protection activists), telephone tapping and technical surveillance by the police, right to asylum, and several issues concerning multiculturalism.[72] There is something curious in all this. Finns like to think that they are a sort of a model-student in an imaginary global human rights class of nations, even though sometimes this is not quite the case.

The ECtHR has ruled against Finland in its case law several times.[73] Of all of the Nordic systems, Finland has received the greatest number of cases judged against her.[74] However, if the whole complexity of the fundamental rights system is taken into account, it is very clear that restrictions concerning these rights may not be imposed lightly; mere political, religious, cultural or other beliefs are not regarded as legitimate reasons for such restrictions. Also, the legal status of indigenous and minority peoples is constitutionally secured even though it cannot be denied that constant cultural assimilation obviously takes place. Moreover, it has been noted that the rights of persons with disabilities do not have a very high standing in Finland when it comes to the practicalities of life.[75]

There are also other national concerns. Email surveillance by employers raised a heated constitutional debate during the Autumn of 2008 when several constitutional experts raised their voice in sharp criticism against

---

[72] See eg, J Kortteinen and T Makkonen, 'Some Developments in the Human Rights Situation in Finland During 2003' (2004) 22 *Nordic Journal of Human Rights* 153.

[73] Cases judged against Finland from recent years see, eg, *HAL v Finland* (27 January 2004), *MS v Finland* (22 March 2005), *C v Finland* (9 May 2006) and *Eskelinen v Finland* (16 April 2007).

[74] According to statistics, by the end of 2009 Finland had 103 cases judged against her in the last 15 years. (Denmark had 13, Iceland 6, Norway 20, and Sweden 43—however, all of these were for a longer period of time.)

[75] L Nieminen, 'Human Rights of Persons with Disabilities' (2010) 55 *Scandinavian Studies in Law* 376.

the alleged lenient interpretation by the Parliament's Constitutional Law Committee. The Committee was accused of letting its rights protection guard drop markedly too low because of huge economic interests presented especially by the Finnish telecom giant Nokia.[76] In turn, there has been very little, if any, critique of fundamental rights in Finland, even though some think that these constitutionally relevant rights may leave aside individual responsibilities and other morally valuable goals which are not protected and codified as fundamental rights.

From a comparative point of view it is useful to underline the existence of a surprisingly great, yet surreptitious, German doctrinal influence on Finnish constitutional law: it seems that many ingredients have their original background in German public law of the post World War II era. Historically, this is not a genuine surprise because Finnish public law has adopted ideas, theories and methods from Germany from the 1800s onwards starting from the German conceptual legal science (*Begriffjurisprudenz*) and more recently from the German *Rechtsstaat* theories.[77] However, it must be said that during the 1990s and 2000s German ideas have not been directly transplanted but rather they have been tailored to fit with the assistance of academic public law. In particular, some of the ideas of Robert Alexy have gained a strong foothold in the intellectual fabric of academic practice of doctrinal constitutional law.[78] In a positive light, there is a clear underlying legal-cultural connection that has not ceased to exist. In a critical tone, we may note the fact that Germany and Finland have very different constitutional histories and landscapes which, in turn, ought to make one treat such transplants with due suspicion. This does not mean to say that German ideas would be unfitting for the Finnish system, but rather that transplanting law from other systems is always a risky business and contains a risk of failure.

Also, from a comparative point of view, perhaps the most central observation is the generally heightened profile of fundamental rights altogether. Constitutional safeguards are obviously important but do not suffice if the legal culture does not follow. Rights in general play a much more visible role in the Finnish constitutional discourse of today even though the genuine legal-normative significance is not as high as

---

[76] Statement of the Constitutional Law Committee (29/2008).

[77] From a historical point of view, see Klami, 'A History of Finnish Legal Science' in *Oikeustiede-Jurisprudentia* XIX (Suomalainen lakimiesyhdistys, Helsinki, 1986) 218–20, 232–35.

[78] See R Alexy, *Theorie der Grundrechte* (Suhrkamp, Frankfurt am Main, 1986).

it may appear. However, it is crucial to conceive that rights discourse is remarkably more relevant than what it was before the mid 1990s. It seems evident that this tells about the transformation of Finnish constitutional mentality: democratic will-formation channelled through the Parliament should not anymore easily violate fundamental rights which have been positively enacted as constitutional rights and which are supported and complemented by international human rights. Possibly, this development belongs to the larger phenomenon of 'no apparent transition scenario' by which Ran Hirschl means such systems which have undergone constitutional reforms strengthening judicial review without any apparent great changes concerning political or economic regimes.[79] Yet, changes do take place as we will see in the following chapter.

FURTHER READING

Arajärvi, P, 'Nordic Welfare and the Right to Education and Culture' in M Scheinin (ed), *The Welfare State and Constitutionalism in Nordic Countries* (Nordic Council of Ministers, Copenhagen, 2001) 349–80.

Hidén, M, 'Constitutional Rights in the Legislative Process' (1973) 17 *Scandinavian Studies in Law* 97–125.

Husa, J, 'Nordic Constitutionalism and European Human Rights— Mixing Oil and Water?' (2010) 55 *Scandinavian Studies in Law* 101–24.

Nieminen, L, 'Impulse auf der finnischen Verfassungstradition für den europäischen Grundrechtsschutze' in P Tettinger and K Stern K (eds), *Kölner Gemeinschaftskommentar zur Europäischen Grundrecht-Charta* (CH Beck, München, 2006) 1–9.

Ojanen, O, 'The European Arrest Warrant in Finland: Taking Fundamental and Human Rights Seriously' in E Guild (ed), *Constitutional Challenges in the European Arrest Warrant* (Wolf, Nijmegen, 2006) 89–101.

Ojanen, T, 'EU Law and the Response of the Constitutional Law Committee' (2007) 52 *Scandinavian Studies in Law* 203–26.

Saraviita, I, *Finland—Constitutional Law: International Encyclopedia of Laws* (Kluwer, Alphen, 2009).

Scheinin, M, 'Constitutional Law and Human Rights' in J Pöyhönen (ed), *An Introduction to Finnish Law* (Kauppakaari, Helsinki, 2002) 31–57.

---

[79] R Hirschl, *Towards Juristocracy—The Origins and Consequences of the New Constitutionalism* (Harvard University Press, Cambridge Mass, 2004) 8.

Scheinin, M, 'Minorities, Human Rights and the Welfare State: the 1995 Fundamental Rights Reform in Finland' in K Pohjolainen (ed), *Constitutionalism in Finland: Reality and Perspectives* (Finnish Society of Constitutional Law, Helsinki, 1995) 30–37.

WEBSITES

All the following websites also contain information in English.

www.finlex.fi [Legal Database].
www.ihmisoikeusliitto.fi [The Finnish League for Human Rights].
www.kios.fi [The Finnish NGO Foundation for Human Rights].
http://web.abo.fi/instut/imr/ [Institute for Human Rights, Åbo Akademi University].
www.ykliitto.fi [The UN Association of Finland].
www.folktinget.fi [The Swedish Assembly of Finland].

8

Changing the Constitution

————————

**Loose or Rigid Constitutionalism – Formal and Informal Changes
– Controversy: the Role of Exceptive Acts – Conclusion**

Constitutional law deals closely with politics, but it is also very much
an area of legal system located within the legal sphere. In Finland, as in
most systems, it is the core of public law. But is it somehow different
from other areas of law? There are as many answers to this question
as there are critiques against any such answer. In Finland, many would
say that constitutional law is different from other areas of law because
it is in direct contact with political life and involved in a constant battle
over political power. However, this is so evident that most often this
fact is not separately stressed. But, if the constitutional law of modern,
stable and democratic countries is compared with other areas of law, yet
another observation is easy to make: other areas of public law change
normally much more rapidly. Such countries as the United States (1789,
1791) and Norway (1814) and, to some extent, France and Belgium,
have 'old constitutions', although with numerous later modifications.
The Constitutional Act of Finland came into force in 2000 but this was
a formality if one looks past the mere surface of positive law.

The Finnish Constitution contains certain rules and ideas which can
be traced back to eighteenth century, some even further. Does this tell of
conservatism or reluctance to change? This is not a simple question. It is
crucial to understand that constitutions change; they are not expressions
of eternal natural law. Constitutions and their accompanying regimes
rise and fall—the collapse of socialist law surely demonstrates this. Yet,
constitutional systems tend to change somewhat slower than other areas
of law, but they do change; one way or another. This is accepted by the

Finnish constitutional mentality too, at least from the 1960s onwards. In this chapter there will be only space to consider certain core aspects relating to changing and change of the Constitution. The following will be devoted to a discussion concerning the nature of amending the Constitution, the tension between formal and informal changing, the significance of constitutional practice or customary law, and finally the controversial role of exceptive Acts. These Acts are yet again a trace from the earlier layers of Finnish constitutional history; like an iceberg much of the Constitution remains under the surface.

LOOSE OR RIGID CONSTITUTIONALISM

One of the central questions within constitutional law in general is the question of how it can be changed. For those who stress the importance of a legal-positivistic codified constitutional document, this question is a simple one if a state in question has a written constitutional document: one needs simply to look at what the constitutional document stipulates about its amendment. However, for countries like the United Kingdom, New Zealand or Israel, the legal-positivistic approach does not work at all or, at best, only partially. Moreover, the legal-positivistic manner for conceiving constitutions and constitutional law is not adequate if we are interested in how written/codified constitutions actually work and function as a part of the larger political system, that is, what living constitutions are like.[1]

It would not really make much sense to a non-national and non-doctrinal constitutional analysis to uphold as valid constitutional law mere written provisions. Surely, constitutions do not live in isolation from the political sphere and society in general but their life is a kind of *double life* between politics and law.[2] This idea has been very clearly understood in Finnish constitutional law from the nineteenth century, even though today's development toward a stronger fundamental rights culture and more vibrant judicial constitutional review is now slowly changing the traditional undertone of Finnish constitutional law. Yet, the basic underlying constitutional mentality has not changed funda-

[1] See P Berger, 'White Fire: Structural Indeterminacy, Constitutional Design, and the Constitution Behind the Text' (2008) 3 *Journal of Comparative Law* 249.
[2] Georg Jellinek regarded this as the basic 'dual nature of state' (*doppelnatur des Staates*), *Allgemeine Staatslehre* (Häring, Berlin, 1905) 329 *ff*.

mentally, even though rights are today in a more central position than in the past. Constant debate about the role and competences of the President seems to prove that constitutional mentality does not always follow closely codified constitutional rules.

Importantly, constitutions are only partly legal entities; they also contain the core design of a state concerning the division of power, structure of the state itself and rights of an individual in his or her relations with public power. These core solutions are part of the public philosophy or constitutional morality of a state even though they also have a legal-constitutional role. This deals with such questions that Germans once called *Verfassungslehre,* Constitutional Theory, which combines political theory (*Staatslehre*) and constitutional law (*Staatsrechtslehre*).[3] However, we do not need to dwell in German theory too much even though we would accept some of its basic assumptions. Namely, constitutions contain both legal and political material acting in interaction with the surrounding society and political system.

From a political point of view constitutions may be seen as formal power maps but also as living entities that will succeed only if the rules and institutions of a constitution accord at least reasonably well with social interest and values that are dominant in a polity. So, if a constitution fails flagrantly to reflect dominant public philosophy within a society we may assume that this kind of constitution's prospect for stable and successful operation is rather slim.[4] Revolutions are a manifest example of situations in which the formal constitution and the real constitution are in so grave opposition that the system can no longer hold itself together. Nevertheless, after each revolution the new power normally seeks to erect a new constitutional order. All this makes it easy to understand that each constitution must also change so that it will evolve with the transformation of political society of which the constitution is an integral part. Written rules of amending are of importance but there is more to it. We have also incremental tiny steps taken in the practical constitutional life of a state.

---

[3] A paradigmatic, yet also infamous, example of this approach is Carl Schmitt, *Verfassungslehre* (Duncker & Humblot, Berlin, 1928/1983).

[4] See R Hague, M Harrop and S Breslin, *Comparative Government and Politics* (MacMillan, Houndmills, 1994) 262–67.

Changes Taking Place

Even when constitutions look similar as to their formal surface there are differences concerning how the living constitutions actually function. Even identical norms may lead into completely different constitutional practices: the President's power concerning foreign policy was de facto different before and after World War II, even though the written stipulation remained the same. From a broad comparative point of view we may distinguish flexible and rigid constitutions. Normally, we regard such constitutional Acts that do not require a special legislative process to amend them as being flexible. It is commonplace to hold that the US Constitution is very rigid, whereas the UK Constitution is very flexible. But, this is only a partial truth and it hides as much as it reveals. In reality things are much more blurred and Kelsenian purity is missing.

On the other hand, those constitutional acts that require a special process for amending, changing or repealing them are regarded as rigid. Against this background we may say that the Finnish Constitution has been and is even today as to its basic nature a rigid constitution. To change it significantly, one needs to change the formal text too. However, as has been noted, this manner of classifying constitutions has certain innate problems and, accordingly, KC Wheare proposed that we should not give too much weight to formal criteria but rather see 'whether they are in practice, through the force of a variety of circumstances, easily and often altered or not'.[5] If formalism is put aside, then, the Finnish situation appears in a different light. Indeed, knowing only the written rules laid down in the Constitution Act would not help very much if one needs to grasp the essence of a constitution. And yet, it is beyond any rational doubt that enacted law is the first and foremost source of the Constitution in Finland. However, there is no genuine contradiction here because written and unwritten elements coincide and are interdependent.

Now, if we give more weight to practical criteria, then, the Finnish Constitution may not be regarded as a genuinely rigid constitution. Indeed, the Finnish Constitution has been described by largely accepted characterisation according to which it is a 'rigidly loose' (*jäykän joustava*) constitution.[6] Indeed, it is not difficult to see that even such a constitu-

---

[5] K Wheare, *Modern Constitutions* (Oxford University Press, Oxford, 1980) 15–18, quote at 17.

[6] The expression 'rigidly loose' is from Paavo Kastari's book *Legal Basis of Our Form of Government* ['*Valtiojärjestyksemme oikeudelliset perusteet*'] (WSOY, Porvoo, 1969) 86.

tion or such parts of those that are formally designed to be completely un-amendable do change in various ways as the German *Grundgesetz* of 1949 proves: especially the interpretations of *Bundesverfassungsgerichthof* have de facto changed the German Constitution.[7] There is no equivalent Finnish institution and yet the constitutional experience points towards the same direction: written rules—as important as they may be—are hardly ever an accurate description of constitutional reality. The constitutional function of all these kinds of rigidities (adapted in positive law) is basically simple: to prevent hasty changes to the constitution and in this manner also to provide a stable basis for the organisation and use of public power. So, constitutions are *per definitionem* conservative legal-political creatures. Finland may be one of the Nordic-style welfare states with reform-seeking policy, but its constitutional law appears rather conservative with respect to its ability to change.

To be clear, it is not argued here that the Finnish system is fundamentally different from the requirements of its written constitutional rules. Nor it is argued that Finland is politically a conservative state. Instead, it is claimed that there are certain nuances that cannot be described in a reliable manner just by using categories of constitutional and unconstitutional or legal constitution and political constitution. There is something in between, something which we may call constitutional culture or, if we change the angle, constitutional mentality. In accord, there are numerous ways in which the Finnish Constitution changes and how it is changed. And, there are numerous ways to deploy constitutional-culture rooted inertia against such changes. Next we will consider the ways to change the Constitution in Finland although we may claim already at this stage that most of the different ways to change the constitution are familiar to other systems except one peculiar rarity, the exceptive Act, which makes the Finnish system highly interesting from a comparative point of view.

---

[7] According to the *Grundgesetz*, articles 1 and 20 may not be changed under any circumstances. However, it is not difficult to see that article 20, which states the Republic of Germany to be a democratic and social state whose power emanates from the people and of which forms of state power are bound to constitutional order, law and justice, has changed under the process of European integration.

FORMAL VERSUS INFORMAL CHANGES OF CONSTITUTION

It makes perfect sense to distinguish such constitutions as the Constitution of United Kingdom or New Zealand from constitutions such as the Constitution of the United States of America or Germany, if we look only at the formal criteria when it comes to the ease of changing them. However, as stated above, this is just one part of the picture. Indeed, a convention may stand on more firm constitutional ground than codified black-letter rule in a constitutional document. Moreover, the lesson we learned from socialist constitutional documents taught us that sometimes the written rules have hardly anything to do with the constitutional realities. There are systems with written constitutions without constitutionalism. So, it made hardly much sense to decide how constitutional rights actually functioned in the former Soviet Union merely judging on the basis of a written constitutional document. Accordingly, as was noted above, formal criteria do not suffice for the purposes of realist constitutional studies. The fact that it is possible to change the constitutions of the United Kingdom or New Zealand by a simple majority vote, whereas in the United States or Germany a much more complex procedure is needed, is all but decisive. Similarly, the Finnish Constitution may also be changed in multiple ways which are only partially formal. The difficulty lies in the fact that these different ways of change are not easily discerned from each other: there are interdependences which make it difficult to draw a clear picture.

Significantly, changes also take place in informal manners that have to do with constitutional practice and that reveal the importance of conceiving the Finnish Constitution as a living constitution. A prime example of a major transformation with only minimal textual changes to the constitutional document itself is the impact of the European Union: change has been truly fundamental but if one reads the Constitution Act (which stepped into force five years *after* the accession to the European Union) only, this is almost impossible to grasp. Only now, 15 years later, there are serious plans to change this. So, it is of importance to know not only the text but also constitutional practices or, in other words, the living constitution. Informal ways to change the Constitution in Finland may be seen as consisting of practices and respected doctrines and even constitutional conventions as well as constitutional interpretation. The nature of the unique Finnish constitutional feature of exceptive Acts will become more fully apparent as the discussion proceeds.

Procedure for Formal Constitutional Amendment

To begin with, as Professor Emeritus Antero Jyränki states, 'In Finland enacting constitutional Acts is not regarded as a different function of a State than enacting normal Acts'.[8] This explains why the Finnish system does not use any extra-parliamentary methods (for example referendums) in amending the Constitution Act, methods that are in use, for example, in France and Denmark. Formal change of the Constitution Act is clearly the domain of the Parliament which importantly holds the central power of *Kompetenz-kompetenz* in this regard. Of course, even in the Finnish system we may theoretically divide the dual role of the Constitution Act in this matter since these rules are simultaneously rules which do not only bind the legislator (as using a simple majority) but they also bind the constituent authority (French *pouvoir constituant*) from creating or amending the Constitution Act itself.[9] However, this distinction has been very much blurred in constitutional practice even though several learned writers have upheld this distinction in the constitutional literature.[10]

As discussed earlier, a simple majority of parliamentary votes is required to approve or reject ordinaryActs. However, a somewhat more complicated formal procedure must be meticulously followed if a bill regards the Constitution Act. Every bill that deals with enacting, amending or repealing the Constitution Act or enacting limited derogation of the Constitution Act must be dealt with through more specific procedure prescribed by the Constitution Act itself (section 73). This kind of bill must first be approved by a simple majority of votes on its second reading in the Parliament. After this, there must be a period of abeyance (*lepäämään jättäminen*) until after the next general parliamentary election. The rationale behind this is connected with the idea of sovereignty of the people and the accompanying understanding of democracy: by means of this abeyance voters may also have a say concerning the amendment of the Constitution Act. However, constitutional issues hardly ever transform into an important part of pre-election, real-life

---

[8] A Jyränki, *Power and Freedom* ['*Valta ja vapaus*'] (Talentum, Helsinki, 2003) 235.
[9] See A Ross, *On Law and Justice* (University of California Press, Berkeley, 1958) 80–81.
[10] This distinction was first presented by Abbé Sieyès in 1789 in his famous pamphlet '*Qu'est-ce que le tiers-état?*' and it has been used in constitutional literature ever since.

political debate. Yet there are signs that this might be the case in the upcoming parliamentary elections (2011).

In the next phase, after the election, the newly elected Parliament continues discussion of the bill. In practice, those who oppose the bill keep opposing it and those favouring the bill keep supporting it: the genuine effect of general parliamentary elections tends not to alter the basic situation. Those citizens casting their votes do not tend to place too much weight on constitutional questions unless they touch on disputes of general interest, such as the powers of the President of the Republic. Accordingly, the deep-reaching reform of the system that took place in 1995 hardly aroused any general interest from the public, whereas even a tiny planned change concerning the President is sure to arouse great public interest. In any event, after the first stage, the new Parliament must then approve the bill by a two-thirds majority of votes cast in order for it to become accepted. This is the normal manner in which the Constitution Act may be changed and it has always been followed to the finest detail. This method of formally changing the Constitution Act is thought to be the paradigmatic manner to make changes to Finnish written constitutional rules. Nevertheless, there is also a second manner for changing the Constitution Act more urgently (Constitution Act section 73.1). Here, the system appears to differ from most other systems by combining a speeded up process with a sharply heightened demand for legitimacy.

Expedited Procedure

The more urgent manner for change requires exceptionally strong backing from MPs. This urgent amending requires a majority of five-sixths by a single Parliament without general elections in between the two stages. Even after the urgent declaring (*kiireelliseksi julistaminen*) has taken place, two-thirds of the representatives have to support the amendment in order to make the urgent bill accepted. In practice, of course, if the bill has first acquired a five-sixths majority it is no problem to gain a more modest two-thirds majority. This means that voting takes place in two stages: 1) if the matter is regarded to be urgent (five-sixths majority), and 2) if this urgent bill is going to be accepted (two-thirds majority).

In practice, this urgent method nearly always faces an insurmountable obstacle because no conceivable government coalition ever holds five-sixths of the majority in the Parliament. Even though there have been broad and politically diverse coalitions a five-sixths majority seems very much unattainable, at least under normal circumstances. Yet it is thought that during a national emergency this sort of unnaturally large majority would be possible to attain.

Significance of Practice

The legal-constitutional effect of the Constitution may be seen most clearly in the actions of key branches of the State: the Parliament, the President, the Council of State and the high courts of law. In practice, the centre of constitutional interpretation has been the Parliament for decades and the Constitution Act of 2000 sought not to change this state of affairs. It is the Parliament itself that carries out most of the interpretation when it applies the constitutional rules that bind it; even though this is most evident when the Constitutional Law Committee of the Parliament uses its special prerogative and obligation to give authoritative interpretations concerning constitutional questions and disputes which take place before the Act comes formally into force. However, it is not only the Parliament that plays a role in this. Other high branches of public power also have their role when it comes to giving actual content to constitutional rules, principles and doctrines in the course of political and judicial life. This kind of commonplace course of constitutional life is obviously much more subtle than with the Committee, yet it cannot be denied that it takes place.

Actually, we can see that Finnish constitutional culture has partially leaned toward practice or customary constitutional law and pseudo conventions for a long time: during the long period of autonomy under Russia, Finns were not only defending the naked text of the Form of Government of 1772 but also, and sometimes much more importantly, the constitutional customs and conventions based on earlier Swedish tradition. Importantly, the symbolic function of old Swedish constitutional heritage was perhaps even more important than detailed constitutional technicalities. In fact, both the Finnish political practice and academic doctrine were doing their best in order to try to strengthen the Finnish-Swedish elements when it came to constitutional issues. There was a constant constitutional-political tug-of-war going on. As a result, it became commonplace to clutch onto old traditions and to regard as suspect all reforms of constitutional significance. This underlined and encouraged a conservative mentality when it came to constitutional affairs.

Even though the Finnish system is basically a written one and includes one central Act which has nationally the highest position within the hierarchy of legal norms, we may safely claim that the role of constitutional practice has also been important and still plays a relevant role as part of the Finnish Constitution. Historic experiences have had a great impact: formalism is the normal *modus operandi* but dire practical needs may override it from time to time. Even though it might make sense to describe Finnish legal culture as legalistic, this description does not capture the full reality of constitutional law. And yet there have always been open questions and legal-positivism inspired doctrinal rejection when it comes to constitutional customs and conventions. The deep German jurisprudential grip over the minds and hearts of doctrinal writers has been surprisingly firm. However, the manner of how customs and conventions have been regarded has to do with the question concerning the attitude toward constitutional interpretation in general, not only among public law professors exercising influence indirectly through the Constitutional Law Committee in their capacity as outside experts.

Changing Through Interpretation

Basically, there are three typical manners by which to change constitution: formally changing or adding codified written norms, or interpreting either written provisions or by means of constitutional customary law. The Finnish system has actually had a twofold approach in this regard. Interpretative changes to the Constitution may take place in three basic forms: *contra* Constitution Act, *intra* Constitution Act, or *praeter* Constitution Act. In practice, interpretations are hardly ever clearly against the Constitution Act's wording, by far most interpretations are *praeter*; in effect, they fulfil less than perfectly the text of the Constitution Act.[11] Obviously, this fulfilling takes place within the freedom of interpretation that written norms and followed practices allow. In any case, the significance of constitutional interpretation (*valtiosääntöoikeudellinen tulkinta*) has been recognised and perhaps even acknowledged in Finnish

---

[11] See A Jyränki, *Power and Freedom* [*'Valta ja vapaus'*] (Talentum, Helsinki, 2003) 244–45.

constitutional culture for decades. It has been sort of a *communis opinio* or at least *opinio doctorum* that 'The Constitution may be developed besides by the constitutionally stipulated procedure for amendment but also by constitutional interpretation', as Professor Emeritus Mikael Hidén stated more than 25 years ago.[12] Importantly, this interpretation has not been primarily undertaken by the courts of law but by executive and legislative branches. Key constitutional players have themselves redefined the actual meaning of constitutional provisions.

On the one hand, formal textual changes have always been clearly stressed by the official constitutional *Weltanschauung*. However, it has always been an undeniable fact that constitutional norms have also changed through gradual interpretation. Undoubtedly, the main actor has been and is even today the Constitutional Law Committee of the Parliament. It holds a nexus-position. Nevertheless, high state organs such as the President, the Council of State and, especially during the 2000s, both of the supreme courts, also played their interpretative constitutional role.

Today, courts have a more visible role in the area of human rights and constitutional rights. This has to do with the fact that Finnish constitutional culture does not tend to allow a custom to genuinely grow into an actual customary constitutional rule. Before this takes place, an established practice is rather enacted and amended into the constitutional document itself: written rules tend to follow one step behind the practice and not the other way around. This gives a certain sense of an organically developing Constitution. For example, some of the changes concerning the position of the President and the relation between the President and the Council of State and the Parliament were already in use during the office of President Martti Ahtisaari, that is, before the Constitution Act of 2000 formally stepped into force. Moreover, some of the customs were already created during Koivisto's 12 years in office, such as the idea of the President staying out of active domestic policymaking. Some also date the idea according to which the President cannot overturn the will of the Government if the Government Coalition is completely united to the Kekkonen period. Typically, the written text follows the practice which evolves by taking constantly tiny steps which are not considered as illegitimate by other key constitutional players.

---

[12] M Hidén, 'Tulkinnan muuttaminen valtiosäännön kehittämiskeinona' ['Interpretation as a Means of Constitutional Change'] (1983) 25 *Politiikka* 377, 377.

We may safely claim that the role of interpretation has always been somehow a bit touchy in the Finnish constitutional culture. In this sense, there has been a certain prevailing mentality of legalism, but only to an extent. Officially, the national form of constitutionalism has followed rather a literal legal-positivistic approach to constitutional questions. Typically, it has been generally thought that there is at least one crucial principled problem with changing the Constitution without formally changing the text of a constitutional document—the lack of legitimacy. Accordingly, it has been widely regarded as a problem that changing through interpretation lacks *democratic legitimacy* whereas changing the text in a formal prescribed manner requires a two-thirds majority in the Parliament which, in turn, has strong direct democratic legitimacy gained through free general elections.

The deeply rooted idea of democratic justification of the Constitution also explains at least partly why the power to change the Constitution has been kept so tightly in the hands of a democratically chosen legislator and the Constitution-giver itself rather than be given to the courts of law. For historical reasons, Finns have always seemed to share with Montesquieu a distrust concerning the constitutional role of judiciary. As such, even in this regard, it is not a surprise that the Constitutional Law Committee of the Parliament has always stressed the principled importance of its own interpretations in regards to other possible competing sources such as the President, the Council of State and courts of law. While doing so, the Constitutional Law Committee has for decades leaned on the support of outside constitutional experts while struggling successfully to keep a hold of its own interpretative power. A further twist on this is the fact that the Committee also regards itself as being able to change its earlier interpretations.[13] So, its self-image is surprisingly that of a quasi constitutional court. Interpretations by the Committee have not been rigid, even though certain basic lines have normally been preserved. Paradoxically, there has been legal criticism against the Committee because it is so slow-moving and perhaps even too loyal to its earlier statements. One cannot help but sense a certain paradox when some law professors criticise the Committee for not being political enough.

---

[13] See the Report of the Constitutional Committee 17/1989 in which 'the requirements of societal change' were taken into account while earlier interpretation was changed.

Only very recently has this 'mental pact' between the Committee and academic public law started to show signs of friction and inborn tensions: there are those experts who are listened to but not followed and then there are some who are completely shut out of the work of the Constitutional Law Committee.

Academic constitutional law has always regarded the birth of customary constitutional law with the greatest of suspicion. And yet, there is much evidence that in fact established practices by State organs and steady lines of interpretation by the Constitutional Committee have indeed created a body of unwritten constitutional law fulfilling the gaps of constitutional documents. No realistic account of the constitutional system can leave this out. In other words, it is possible that on several occasions long-time practices have indeed turned into a kind of customary constitutional law, even if the legislator has not transformed these practices into written constitutional provisions. The most central of these customs is the binding force of the statements of the Constitutional Law Committee. However, the unease lies in the quintessential difficulty of discerning a non-binding established practice from a binding one. There is some form of case law which seems to have practically an undisputed role, though. This case law, however, is not domestic and it does not concern other constitutional branches of power but, rather, rights.

In this respect, the constitutional significance of the European Convention on Human Rights (ECHR) and the European Union must be addressed. One must recognise the role of two powerful non-domestic courts. In terms of European human rights it is the European Court of Human Rights (ECtHR) in Strasbourg which has the last say on what the ECHR really means. And, in terms of EC law, it is the Luxembourg-based European Court of Justice (ECJ) that interprets what EU law really requires Member States to do in order to fulfil the legal requirements of EU obligations. So, the European case law may also effect domestic constitutions; in this sense European human rights and European integration law may also change the Finnish Constitution. Even though the judgments of the ECJ and ECtHR have undoubtedly a de facto binding force, these judgments certainly do not cover all areas of national constitutional law.

The most important single development on the domestic scene is the fact that during the 2000s the national supreme courts have slowly awakened and taken steps in the field of giving content to rules concerning constitutional rights. As courts do this they change the precise content of fundamental rights; that is, they play a de facto role in changing the Constitution.

Customs and Conventions

It has already been stated in the first chapter that there are no genuine constitutional conventions in the sense of English constitutional law in Finland, even though some practices do seem to be rather similar to genuine constitutional conventions. Accordingly, it is probably more accurate to speak of 'constitutional customary law' (*valtiosääntöinen tapaoikeus*) instead. This seems to imply a lesser degree of bindingness. Finnish academic practice of doctrinal constitutional law has regarded the very idea of binding constitutional customary law with suspicion, at least since gaining independence. Under Russian rule this was different since Swedish constitutional documents were defended by any peaceful means necessary. In the constitutional field customs are mainly long-standing habits of key bodies of the State; practice-based established patterns of constitutionally relevant behaviour of high state institutions. The customary constitutional rules arise from usage and yet they are adhered to because political expedience and public constitutional morality demand that these rules should be observed. Not even the total reform of 2000 altered this and, thus, we may claim that 'it is still possible that certain unwritten constitutional practices and even legal norms are still in force', as says Professor Emeritus Ilkka Saraviita.[14]

Now, even though there are constitutional customs it must be underlined that for the most part the Finnish Constitution is a written-law based constitution and customs do not play such a significant role as they have in UK constitutional law. In addition, case law of domestic supreme courts does not play a similar role as it does in the United States or Germany. Enacted constitutional law is the predominant source of the Constitution of Finland. By and large, this is an accurate description. However, it would not be correct to claim that the living Finnish Constitution would have been wholly reduced to a legal-positivistic codified constitution only. Moreover, the customs are not 'laws' in the sense of enacted law and yet in some cases even the courts of law respect and abide them: no written formal rule gives supreme standing to the statements of the Constitutional Law Committee, yet this takes place. In the

[14] I Saraviita, *Finland—Constitutional Law*. International Encyclopedia of Laws (Kluwer, Alphen, 2009) 65.

words of Alf Ross we may speak of a 'conviction that the behaviour demanded by custom is also a legal duty'.[15] Let us consider four examples here:

1. The Speaker of the Parliament and Prime Minister ought to be from different political parties even though there is no such written rule. It has been customary that both of these high positions should not be fulfilled by persons coming from the same political party. The legitimacy of this custom has two bases. On the one hand, this is seen to enhance the parliamentary features of the system. It supports and complements codified constitutional rules. On the other hand, it is thought that the Speaker also has an important public position which means that by spreading the share of these kinds of constitutional-symbolic positions the outcome is more democratically legitimate. Clearly, this rule has a certain symbolic dimension in it because the Speaker's possibilities to use his or her own political discretions are quite limited. Yet, this position gives high public visibility.

2. The President of the Republic ought to give up formal connections with his or her political party after being elected as President. When Koivisto was elected as President (1982), he followed a custom that seeks to underline the independent position of the President of the Republic so that this institution would not have any formal connections to political parties. Clearly, this speaks its own language and tells much about the deep sentiments of how the institution of President is conceived even today. Yet, this does not prevent critics from regarding many of the actions by the President as being politically designed. There is merit in this critique since it is hard not to regard the actions of the President as always political as to their nature. Obviously, this custom also has a strong symbolic dimension underlining the independent and 'un-political' character of the presidency. Sitting Presidents themselves have underlined the importance of this custom and its constitutional significance, even though during the office of President Halonen this lost some of its earlier significance.

3. The third example concerns the position of the judicial branch of power. The important decisions rendered by the supreme courts and reported in yearbooks legally bind lower courts when they judge in later similar cases. As discussed in chapter one, Finland's legal system does not officially recognise the binding power of precedents.

---

[15] Ross (n 9) 93.

However, it would be constitutional hypocrisy to claim that there is no principle of precedent in Finland. The persuasive authority of these cases is undisputed and evident. Yet, there are no legal or constitutional rules that would formally bind the lower courts to follow supreme courts and yet this is precisely what they do. Clearly, this can be seen as a strong and well-founded customary constitutional rule applied by the judiciary. In contrast with the two earlier mentioned customs, this customary rule has low symbolic significance; instead its practical significance may be regarded as being remarkable for the whole legal system. In practice, the yearbook cases (*vuosikirjatapaus*) of the Supreme Court and Supreme Administrative Court are closely followed and almost always also abided by the lower courts. The weight given to the ECJ and ECtHR judgments enhance the actual constitutional relevance of precedents as a source of law even further.

4. The most central of these customary rules concerns constitutionality control of parliamentary Acts and it has deep roots in the period of autonomy. This is connected with the peculiar system of guarding the constitutionality of parliamentary legislation. The statements of the Constitutional Law Committee are legally binding on a) the Parliament concerning the right procedure for enactment, and b) the courts of law while deciding over the 'clear controversy' under section 106 of the Constitution Act.

Parliament has always followed, though not always very happily, the statements of the Committee and it is also regarded in the Ministries who are drafting the laws that the Committee is the constitutionally authoritative interpreter of the Constitution. This is not questioned. Law-drafting civil servants must be aware of the statements of the Committee if they are to fulfil their duties properly.

Courts, on their part, have also recognised unwaveringly the superior constitutional source-of-law power of the statements of the Committee in their case law. This recognition has been markedly visible after the total reform of 2000. Yet, there is no such written constitutional rule that would obligate the courts of law to follow the Committee in the manner that they are doing. *Travaux* and judicial culture are the two main factors that explain this constitutionally relevant judicial behaviour. There is a conviction that this behaviour which custom demands (in Ross's sense) is also a legal-constitutional duty.

It has been largely accepted that customary constitutional law becomes possible only under certain specific circumstances that require stability and longevity of the practice. Moreover, this kind of practice should be implicitly recognised as a constitutional rule by the constitutional actors themselves who must think that this sort of rule genuinely contains constitutional obligation.[16] The above list is not exhaustive but it offers a clear indication of certain customary dimensions of an otherwise mainly codified constitutional system. Obviously, one may notice that these customs are all, in a sense, special cases, but this is not the point here. Rather, the fact that there are binding non-written customs is of importance; such customs may even change the Constitution.

CONTROVERSY: THE ROLE OF EXCEPTIVE ACTS

What actually marks the Finnish system as being different when compared to other Nordic constitutions and other constitutional systems is undoubtedly the institution of 'exceptive Act' (*poikkeuslaki*), which enables enactment and application of Acts contradictory to the Constitution Act without changing the text of the Constitution Act itself. Throughout the twentieth century, the exceptive Act was the true hallmark of the Finnish Constitution even though it was hidden from those looking at the system from the outside; no textual changes were made to the constitutional documents and yet the Constitution was many times de facto changed by exceptive enactments. As a constitutional invention 'exceptive Act' is an interesting one as it combines direct and non-direct ways to change the Constitution: as if it would make it possible to have one's cake and eat it too at the same time. The curiosity is that Parliament knowingly passes an Act which is explicitly contrary to supreme law. However, does not constitutional common sense prevent this? Should it not be quite impossible in constitutionalism?

Birth and the Original Doctrine

Now, the peculiar constitutional consequence of an exceptive Act is partial displacement of the content of the written constitutional document,

---

[16] Ross (n 9) spoke of the binding force of law that was 'experienced in the moral consciousnesses (58) and is derived from 'social facts' (40).

without changing the text meanwhile. This doctrine is rather close to the infamous German doctrine of exceptive laws used by the Weimar Republic before the Third Reich, but again the only rational explanation stems from Finnish constitutional history. To be sure, this was not a legal transplant from Germany. Importantly, the whole doctrine of exceptive Act was crafted not to undermine the Constitution but rather to simultaneously respect it and to create needed flexibility. To achieve this, the crucial precondition was and is that the decision concerning the exceptional Act is made in the same qualified order of enactment, as change to the Constitution Act (or its predecessor constitutional documents) would have to be done. This, if anything in the constitutional field, is a Finnish constitutional specialty, of which the origins date back to the 1870s. Paradigmatically, though not for the first time, this took place when the bill for the new Act concerning military service (*Asevelvollisuuslaki*) was handled in 1878; many of the provisions in the bill were in contradiction with the 1789 Privileges of Estates. The problem was crystal-clear: How to have one's cake (ie Swedish constitutional documents) and eat it too (ie to pass legislation contrary to constitutional rules)?

In essence, the basic idea of the institution of the exceptive Act (which is hierarchically at the same level as ordinary legislation) is that its substantive constitutionality is considered acceptable by the Constitutional Committee of the Parliament, *if and only if* the parliamentary Act, which causes an exception to the Constitution, is legislated in the same order of enactment as a change of the Constitution Act would have to be passed. The core is the substantive constitutional legitimacy which is gained at the cost of constitutional formality. This invention arose out of practical constitutional need; it was not crafted by any constitutional theorist. This doctrine was invented in the political pressures of the late 1800s because on the one hand Finland was in desperate need of new legislation and on the other hand Finns were completely reluctant to touch the Form of Government of 1772, Deed of Assurance and Security of 1789 and the Privileges of the Estates, fearing that if the Constitution would be opened then the Russian side would be able to change it later according to its will. Unfortunately, most of the needed new legislation seemed to be in contradiction with the Swedish-origin constitutional heritage. The puzzle was how to get around this.

So, Finns wanted to keep in mind, in their sincere view, the constitutional commitment (from the Finnish point of view) from the First Grand Duke of Finland, the Russian Czar at that time. In Porvoo 1809

Alexander I had reconfirmed the religion, the fundamental laws, the rights and privileges according to the Constitution of Finland. This was the quintessential constitutional starting point for the Finns even though the Russians were not always that convinced.[17] This base was protected by all possible means and, importantly, highly legalistic arguments deriving force from Swedish constitutional heritage were put into use. Courts had no role in this peaceful constitutional resistance and creativity: this probably partially explains much of the modest later role of the judiciary.

Accordingly, Finns had to create a mechanism that would gain the required domestic constitutional legitimacy and yet flexibility so that the Finnish Constitution would be secured against unwanted Russian influence. The irony in the history may be seen in the fact that this doctrine is still a working part of the Finnish Constitution almost 100 years after Finland gained independency. Moreover, this doctrine itself explains why it is precisely the Constitutional Law Committee which is in so central a position as a user of the core-constitutional-control-power: someone not elected by the Russians (as judges in courts of law) was preferred to take care of this crucial constitutional function of constitutionality-control of new legislation.

From a comparative point of view, Finnish doctrine may be seen partially parallel with the Canadian 'notwithstanding clause' (or 'la clause dérogatoire') which allows the Federal Parliament or Provincial legislature to go around judicial review by temporarily overriding the Canadian Charter of Rights and Freedoms.[18] However, the Finnish approach is more demanding since it requires same majority which is required for constitutional amendments.

Critique of Exceptive Acts

It should not come as a surprise that the system of exceptive Acts was criticised during the 1900s by various actors: a legion of senior politicians and constitutional experts alike. Yet, constitutional history does not fully explain the situation of today. The most severe problem that this doctrine caused was the fact that in the 1980s it became more and

---

[17] See HT Klami, 'A History of Finnish Legal Science' in *Oikeustiede-Jurisprudentia* XIX (Suomalainen lakimiesyhdistys, Helsinki, 1986) 212–13.

[18] See S Grover, 'Democracy and the Canadian Notwithstanding Clause: Are They Compatible?' (2005) 9 *International Journal of Human Rights* 479.

more difficult to grasp the totality of the Constitution because there were hundreds of exceptive Acts in force due to the interpretations of the Constitutional Law Committee: mostly when a constitutional problem was detected or even seriously suspected the Committee recommended virtually automatically using the same legislative procedure that would have to be used while changing any of the constitutional documents themselves. Only rarely bills were not legislated because of constitutional counter-arguments. The Constitution started to look like a garment made of shreds and patches with no real coherence. This problem was recognised generally during the 1990s; the constitutional atmosphere was transforming. As a result, today the Constitutional Law Committee always prefers to demand changes to a bill rather than choosing the procedure of exceptive legislation.

Even though Finnish legal culture has taken its share from German legal culture it has never been so overtly system-oriented; and yet this incoherent nature of the Constitution was no longer tolerated. Nevertheless, it was only during the mid 1990s when this old doctrine started receiving more and more suspicion: could it be anymore part of the legitimate Constitution at all? How could it have a legitimate existence in the modern constitutional law of a state abiding the rule of law and wanting to uphold constitutionalism? And yet, even the 2000 total reform did not abolish the institution of exceptive Acts. Instead, there are now certain substantive limits concerning what exceptive Acts can be legislated (section 73.1: *limited exception*). Once again the conservative feature surfaced: why change it if it is working? And who cares if it does not fit into any learned constitutional theory? So, instead of abolishing it, it was tailored to fit within the changing constitutional frames.

Modified Doctrine of 2000: Limited Exception

During the preparation of the constitutional rights reform (1995), it was planned that exceptive Acts should be abandoned concerning the sphere of rights.[19] This, however, did not take place. The present Constitution Act contains the option to enact exceptive Acts, which have been one of the distinctive features of Finnish constitutional law and clearly one the key factors behind its durability. Simply, exceptive

[19] *Perusoikeuskomitean mietintö* 1992:3 [*Report of Ac Hoc Committee on Fundamental Rights*] 144 ff.

Acts have allowed flexibility for a system which has been in many senses rather rigid and formally inflexible. Yet, despite the decision to retain the option of exceptive Acts, the present scope of their use shall be restricted to allowing only limited exceptions (*rajattu poikkeus*) to the Constitution. Frankly, the reform of 2000 was in this regard a half-hearted one.

According to the *travaux préparatoires* of the Constitution Act, exceptive Acts should not be capable of deviating from the central provisions of the Constitution Act. When this possibility was kept in the system, against many sorts of criticisms especially by the majority of constitutional experts, the idea was to limit its use and to take a clear step away from using it in a routine way. Today, the option of exceptive Acts should be used sparingly and in very exceptional cases where there are particularly pressing reasons. The current constitutional practice regards the use of exceptive Acts as something that should be and is in most cases avoided. In practice, the only area of legitimate usage is the field of EU matters and international matters which are regarded as the main scope-area of exceptive Acts today.

Crucially, the accession to the European Union (although five years before 2000) was also accepted by using an exceptive Act with the blessing of the Constitutional Law Committee.[20] This EU-related interpretive line has continued ever since. Again, we may see the irony of history: in the 1800s exceptive Acts were created because of Russia and today in the 2000s they are enacted because of the European Union. Now, both are external factors with which the national constitutional system has been forced, more or less, to comply: there has been constant constitutional dialogue between internal and external pressures. The method of exceptive Act has been used, and sparingly still is, as a constitutional device deployed in order to weld together the national Constitution and serious outside constitutional pressures.

However, as the practice has shown, Finnish constitutional law has not yet purged itself from internal-base usage of this doctrine that has been so long a vital part of it. The grip of the deeply rooted constitutional culture was best shown in 2006 when the President of the Republic was able to expand its constitutional power at the expense of the Council of State and by relying on the exceptive Act method. The episode of 2006 was all the more strange when it is taken into account that the Parliament did this willingly and with the support of the powerful Constitutional

---

[20] Statement of Constitutional Law Committee 14/1994.

Law Committee which had lowered its constitutional guard in this case
to a surprisingly low level.[21] Simply, the constitutional culture embedded presidentialism once again took the upper hand. The Government
Coalition, meaning the Council of State, did not dare to confront the
popular President (in the area of foreign policy) and withdrew from its
original intention to amend the Constitution Act itself; rather the Council
of State willingly made way to Finnish presidentialism and paved this way
by enacting an exceptive Act.

Finally, it may be noted that the Constitutional Law Committee has
struggled to create a new general doctrine concerning constitutionally
justified usage of exceptive Acts under the present Constitution Act.
According to this idea, one should always try to avoid enacting an Act of
constitutional exceptions. This has been coined as a 'principle of avoiding exceptive Acts' (*poikkeuslakien välttämisen periaate*).[22] From a merely
quantitative point of view, the avoidance strategy has been a genuine
constitutional success, though. However, the interpretative practice of
the Committee itself has been all but clear on this. Steps taken by it
appear slightly hesitant: in most cases it has been avoiding as far as possible the use of exceptive Acts but there are a couple of examples that
seem to confront this. So, today it is rather difficult to say whether or
not the principle of avoiding exceptive Acts really is a part of the living
Finnish Constitution: in fundamental rights-related issues it seems to
be working but in institutional issues this doctrine looks more poorly
established.

CONCLUSION

The discussion in this chapter has brought to the surface elements that
are at least partially, if not in clear contradiction, pulling in different
directions. The Finnish Constitution is simultaneously loose and rigid
carrying, thus, inborn tension between the black-letter rules of constitutional law and socio-political reality. It is of importance to note that
while the text of the constitutional document may stay unchanged,
practices, applications and interpretations may and do change. Further,
these changes may also have constitutional relevance. Should one read
the written constitutional rules only, one would not really conceive the

---

[21] See Statement of Constitutional Law Committee 6/2006.
[22] See Statements of Constitutional Law Committee 59/2001 and 34/2004

reality of a living Constitution. Against this background the nearly enigmatic expression 'rigidly-loose' makes sense. Nevertheless, enacting formal constitutional Acts is more difficult than enacting normal Acts—this is not merely an obsolete written rule but also something that takes place in constitutional reality. Yet, constitutional practice also has clear relevance especially concerning functions of the Parliament, the President, and the Council of State. In any case the key role in changing the Constitution de facto or/and de jure resides in the Constitutional Committee of Parliament. Moreover, there is room even for certain customs and lesser conventions too, as well as some amount for precedents having certain constitutional relevance.

What has been, and at least partially still remains, a certain stylistic hallmark of the Finnish system is the role of exceptive Acts. These constitutionally peculiar enactments enable the obeying of and at the same time the ability to go around the constitutional requirements of changing the constitutional document by means of legislating. Even though today's doctrine is modified and includes an idea according to which these Acts should be avoided and should be used only in a limited sense, the practice is still lingering. Despite justified critique, this doctrine has actually facilitated the majority of policy-making by transforming the inherent constitutional inertia into being more manageable.

Somewhat surprisingly, when Finns were almost ready to banish this old practice, international obligations and especially EU membership injected new life into exceptive enactment. The reason for this appears clear: it was chosen rather to keep this constitutional curiosity than to accept international obligations in an openly monistic manner. So, the true reason was not the desire to keep this old practice but rather to keep it in order to protect the Constitution from a monistic approach to international law and make, thus, sure that the system remained at least formally within a dualistic approach. This was the fundamental choice of the Parliament: even though Finland is an obedient member of the European Union it was not ready to change her traditional approach to non-national legal obligations. This is the situation of today too: the European Union's influence is reflected mainly through practice and not through codified constitutional provisions. This state of affairs is not especially constitutionally transparent or legitimate; the void between reality and text may simply be too great. This is precisely why some changes are to be expected in this regard.

FURTHER READING

Anckar, D, 'Evading Constitutional Inertia: Exception Laws in Finland' (1988) 11 *Scandinavian Political Studies* 195–210.

Jyränki, A, Lakien laki ['*Law of the Law's*] (Lakimiesliiton kustannus, Helsinki, 1989).

Jyränki, A, 'Constitutional Definition of Rights and Freedoms' in *The New Constitutional Law* (International Association of Constitutional Law, Paris/aix-en-Provence, Fribourg, 1991) 3–25.

Kirby, D, *A Concise History of Finland* (Cambridge University Press, Cambridge, 2006).

Ojanen, T, 'The Impact of EU Membership on Finnish Constitutional Law' (2004) 10 *European Public Law* 531–564.

Saraviita, I, *Finland—Constitutional Law*: International Encyclopedia of Laws (Kluwer, Alphen, 2009).

9

Challenges and Future Directions

$\longrightarrow\!\!\!\!\diamond\!\!\!\leftarrow$

Constitutional Luck? – Present State and Controversies – Conclusion: Future Prospects

This concluding chapter pays attention specifically to the present state and controversies, reform-proposals and future prospects of Finland's Constitution. Themes covered here are also themes which seem to generally reflect the present constitutional atmosphere. The underlying idea is not to draw any specific or doctrinal conclusions based on the discussions in earlier chapters, but rather to further discuss generally about key contemporary challenges and possible future directions. However, it must be stated that some of the parts which risk predicting the future in the following text are not based on such solid ground as in the earlier chapters; certain elements of speculation cannot be fully avoided.

CONSTITUTIONAL LUCK?

Constitutions and especially written constitutional Acts are constantly facing certain unavoidable paradoxical tensions. The Finnish one is certainly no exception to this. On the one hand, constitutional law tries to freeze the official power structure and, in this sense, all constitutional law is conservative in nature. This means that constitutional institutions and customs that have evolved over a long period of time are likely to be preserved (Latin *conservare* means literally to 'preserve'). In other words, constitutions are patched up to preserve existing state conditions and constitutional arrangements so that only gradual change takes place instead of abrupt revolutionary change. Yet, the very idea of modern constitutionalism was born precisely because of the great revolutions of the late 1700s. Now, is this not a paradox; revolutionary conservatism dressed up in constitutional clothing.

On the other hand, all constitutional law is destined to change no matter what the constitutional Acts themselves say. One needs only to take a look at the American Constitution to grasp this. Pure constitutional *Fortuna* is often needed and much less seems to depend on the constitution itself. Even though constitutions are attempts to gain normative mastery over politics, the reality cannot be ruled out: constitutions are many times determined to a large extent by factors beyond the control of constitution-givers and other constitutional key players. Examples are easy to find. For Finland it was sheer luck that Gustavus III's Form of Government was so ruler-friendly that the Russian Czar could accept it in 1809. Also, without freedom from Sweden, Finland would not have developed into a state. It appears to have been pure luck that brought Finland out of the turmoil of 1918 as a republic that had the formal dimensions of a democratic state. It is likely that it was only luck that saved the country from an extreme right coup in 1930 so that parliamentarism and respect for law muddled through as triumphant.

After the collapse of the Soviet Union, Finnish constitutional rights got their chance to be fully reformed in the wake of joining the European Convention on Human Rights (ECHR) in 1990, facilitated politically by the fall of the great eastern superpower, although the change was in the air even before its collapse. It was a touch of luck that when the Constitution Act of 2000 was drafted and prepared the President was relatively weak so the reform was able to take place. Obviously, this list could be continued. However, even these rudimentary examples seem to tell about the nature of Finnish constitutionalism. In short, it is not just a question—not at least in Finland—of black-letter positivistic constitutional law; some things can be controlled by means of provision while others cannot. As de Tocqueville has pointed out, 'A lawgiver is like a man steering his route over the sea. He, too, can control the ship that bears him, but he cannot change its structure, create winds, or prevent the ocean stirring beneath him.'[1]

And yet, if the ship (ie the constitution) is too weak to stand the rough sea, the possibilities of survival are slim. Even the best of the ships may sink if the storm is too strong. The same is true of constitutions: it does not matter how legally polished and utterly impeccable the codified con-

---

[1] A de Tocqueville, *Democracy in America* (Fontana Press, London, 1840/1994) 163.

stitutional document is if the practice simply does not pay attention to it or if constitutional culture is in a disastrous state then no Constitution Act, good or bad, will maintain it. One will conceive, mutatis mutandis, as to why the British system has survived so long without a written formal constitutional key document or why the US Constitution works even today. What really matters is the living constitution combining provisions, customs, practices and doctrines, not only the legal-technicalities of the constitution. The Finnish system with many layers and evolutionary phases seems to be a living example of this; normative texts are important but the accompanying constitutional culture is the genuine fundament. The will to respect the Constitution is what truly animates the system: we may speak of a *culture of constitutionalism*. This Finnish constitutional culture has evolved over the last 60 years in a relatively peaceful environment: there have not been divisive constitutional issues concerning such themes as race relations, the death penalty or abortion, which have all been dealt with in a rather consensual manner.

In this book the significance of constitutional history, certain amounts of constitutional conservatism, and a kind of pragmatism have all been underlined as quintessential dimensions of the Finnish version of constitutionalism. Finnish legalism has been balanced by the high regard for traditional constitutional order: the 'Specific feature in Finnish thinking has been the persistent principled grip of legal continuity even when facing great changes of State order'.[2] Besides, the strangely colliding internal elements seem to be a crucial part of Finland's constitutional mentality: a parliamentary system with a rather strong President, rigid but loose Constitution, fundamental rights oriented but without true constitutional judicial review, jurisprudentially Germanic but practice-wise more Nordic, written law-oriented but also partially abiding customary rules, etc. However, this set of tensions within a constitutional order is not really anything new under the sun. In Ancient Rome, the Constitution of the late Republic was not evaluated by asking whether it makes sense, but rather by asking whether it works. Romans were, too, very reluctant to change anything and in fact their constitutional system was full of illogicalities brought in by several hundred years of practice. Only when something turned out to be completely inefficient or grossly unjustified, was the Constitution slightly reformed.

---

[2] A Jyränki, *Law of the Laws* ['*Lakien laki*'] (Lakimiesliiton kustannus, Helsinki, 1989) 540.

Constitutional Conservatism?

Some of this may come as a surprise to those who regard the Nordic systems as reformative, modern, and certainly not conservative. And yet, the history-based constitutional conservatism is clearly a part of Nordic constitutional mentality. Finland is no exception to this: Finns are normally reluctant to change their Constitution too much. If something is changed it normally means just codifying such semi-customs that have already been silently accepted in constitutional practice. Normally, formal amendments come one step behind the constitutional practice. This is the standard *modus operandi*. Only in 1995 when the constitutional rights were completely reformed was a big leap taken instead of the normal tiny steps. Also, joining the European Union was a kind of a covert constitutional revolution even though nobody truly grasped this in the mid 1990s. So, we may add to the above list of internal collisions yet one more crucial collision: inward-looking but international. Even the Constitution Act itself reflects this: section 1.3 says that Finland participates in international cooperation, whereas section 94.1 says that international obligations 'shall not endanger the democratic foundations of the Constitution'.

These confrontations are, however, not purely coincidental. In most of the cases we may see the gap between the political and legal elite, and the ordinary citizens who would rather have a strong President than more parliamentarism, or who would rather have a purely national Constitution instead of a Europeanised one. Again, as it is well known, the gap between the elite (patricians) and ordinary citizens (plebs) was very much also the problem with the governance of ancient Rome.[3] Notwithstanding, Finnish executive power is due to historical reasons very much concentrated; in Rome there was no such concentration of powers in the era of the Republic.

Finland may be regarded as a successful state in the sense of how wealthy it is, how politically stable it is, and how its inhabitants are generally doing in their daily lives as rights-enjoying individuals. So, in this sense the constitutional system may also be described as working well. However, as always there are inner problems, tensions and controversies that concern not only daily political and social problems but also the state of constitutional arrangements. However, nothing drastic seems to be in the making

---

[3] See A Lintott, *The Constitution of Roman Republic* (Clarendon Press, Oxford, 1999) 191–212.

even though some controversies do exist. Some individual happenings may appear insignificant but are, in effect, tremendously revealing. For example, a great number of Finns didn't accept the participation in the European Monetary Union in 1999 and the following Euro banknotes becoming the only legal tender in 2002. Giving up the national currency, *markka*, is just one of the sensitive spots which reveals the barrier between the rulers and the ruled, ie elite and ordinary citizens.

More importantly, the ever-growing significance of the European Union and the very idea of the European Union's own constitution are apparently accepted by political and legal elite as well. Yet, any opinion poll will immediately reveal how dramatically unpopular such an idea is among the public; it seems to threaten the national Constitution and finally the existence of the State itself. None of this seems to worry the political and legal elite. In this respect there is a cliff between the patricians and the plebs: to claim otherwise would mean closing one's eyes to reality. However, we may ask, how is this different from other EU Member States? Yet, the deep constitutional problem of legitimacy remains: if the Constitution is truly a product of the political will of the people (as a result of popular sovereignty), then how should the obvious tension between the elite and the people be resolved in constitutional terms? It is very likely that these tensions are going to be the questions troubling constitutional legitimacy: they will not cease to exist and will continue to haunt the Finnish system in the years to come. It has become increasingly difficult to explain the Constitution to the members of the Finnish polity.

PRESENT STATE AND CONTROVERSIES

It was stated earlier that Finnish constitutional law has a certain crucial doctrinal influence from the modern German doctrine of the late 1900s. This is true when it comes to fundamental rights and general doctrines, but not when it comes to EU-related issues. The much debated *Lisbon* decision of *Bundesverfassungsgerichthof* in June 2009 stated basically that the national judiciary and legislator ought to keep a close eye on the powers conferred to the European Union and make sure that the European Union really stays within those conferred powers.[4] This debate seems

---

[4] Judgment of the Bundesverfassungsgericht, Second Senate of 30 June 2009 in joint cases 2 BvE 2/08, 2BvE 5/08, 2 BvR 1010/08, 2BvR 1022/08, 2 BvR 1259/08 and 2 BvR 182/09 (Lisbon Treaty).

to have completely bypassed Finland: the constitutional debate has not been critical towards the European Union. Yet, a concrete proposal has been made to amend the membership openly in the text of the Constitution Act. Also, some other rather modest proposals for reform have been made.

Proposals for Reform

Generally speaking, debates concerning the reform of the Constitution are normally divided into the following three areas:

1. The position of the President and the Government and relationships between different branches of power.
2. The constant developing of fundamental rights.
3. Adaptation to international developments, especially to European integration.

However, the actual reform work has deviated from these questions at least partially. Fundamental rights do not seem to stir much high profile constitutional debate. On the other hand, institutions and EU-related questions seem to be able to stir the interest of the public even though they are also seen as important constitutional dimensions by the experts.

The Ministry of Justice has followed the working of the Constitution Act since 2000. It published its first Report in 2001 concerning the follow-up of constitutional law (*Uuden perustuslain seurantaraportti I*). Several reports and accounts which have concerned themes considered as important for the future of the Finnish Constitution were published during the 2000s. Covered areas have dealt with the national referendum and its role in the future, parliamentary control of the Finnish Security Police (*Suojelupoliisi*), and the institution of the President in a larger comparative European perspective. After these stages, in 2008 the Memorandum of Working Group for the Reform of Constitution (*Perustuslaki 2008 työryhmä*) was published. The Working Group dealt broadly with several issues but there were only two major questions that were selected as being valid for explicit further work. These themes were selected by a group headed by the Minister of Justice, Tuija Brax (Green League). Themes concern the national referendum and popular initiative and the leadership system of foreign policy. These were the main questions which the Parliamentary ad hoc Committee for the Checking of the Constitution, led by Chancellor and Honorary Minister Christopher Taxell, dealt with.

The Committee's first deadline was 30 November 2009 but it failed to deliver its Report and received an extension of a few weeks. However, the work of this Committee was hampered due to the Lisbon Treaty coming into force on 1 December. It was generally assumed by the Government Coalition and constitutional experts that this would have ended the President's active role with the European Council becoming the official EU institution and thus moving much of the old foreign policy-based competence of the Finnish President into the hands of the Government Coalition. Even though the European Council will continue its work being composed of the heads of the state, the Finnish Constitutional Act regards virtually all these questions now as being EU matters; that is, internal matters which are not in the power-scope of the President. However, President Halonen has fought vigorously against this constitutionally rather obvious matter of fact.

Halonen's actions made the work for reforming the Constitution more charged and, specifically, injected political energy into the left-wing parties defending the powers of the socialist President. The Government Coalition hoped to present its proposal for amending the Constitution Act in the spring of 2010. However, both the Social Democrats and Left Alliance opposed even a small transfer of powers to the Prime Minister. This means in practice that only tiny changes were attainable: the consensus-requirement prevented all that exceeded minimum level. The Chairman Taxell was forced to seek a joint compromise when and if the proposition of his Committee has any chances to pass the Parliament. In February 2010, the partially dissenting report of the Committee came out proposing some minor amendments to the Constitution Act to take place in 2012 (ie when the next President steps into office). Let us consider first the institutional questions and then the question concerning the national referendum and popular initiative.

Executive Institutions and their Relationships—'Battle of the Plates' Saga

To begin with, it is easy to say that no new constitutional institutions are being engineered. So, whatever happens in the field of institutional constitutional law takes place within the frames that already exist. In other words, tiny reforms will deal mainly with the relationships between the key branches of governmental power. As the judicial branch is not seen as problematic, it is also not seen as being in need of reform. It is rather the relations between other organs that have been looked into. The actual problem concerns the division of authority between the President and the Prime Minister. The underlying problem from 1995 has been the so-called 'Battle of the Plates'. Throughout the years there has been constant issue over how many plates ought to be reserved for the Finnish top-leaders at EU summits. The reason for this curious debate arises from the Constitution and specifically from the recently enacted Treaty of Lisbon. This problem has its deep roots in the presidential past and growing parliamentary features of the system: who should the Finnish representative be in EU summits? Presidents Ahtisaari and Halonen both clinched onto their power to lead foreign policy, however today the Treaty of Lisbon has made most of the EU politics domestic as to their nature: it is not regarded as a part of foreign policy anymore. This means enhancement of the Government Coalition's and Prime Minister's power. Crucially, though, major political parties have different views on this.

Taxell's Committee had to request first an extension to Christmas and then a second extension to the end of January 2010 because it was unable to reach the required consensus among the three biggest parties. After the Treaty of Lisbon came into force the situation escalated in the beginning of December 2009; Jacob Söderman, prominent Social Democrat MP and known expert of constitutional law, suggested that the Social Democrats should walk out from the Taxell Committee because of the Government's position concerning Finnish representation in future EU summits. Yet, the Government's decision was in line with the Finnish Constitution. At the bottom of this is the growing fear of the political left that the right wing Government Coalition is going to hand over the leadership of foreign policy to the European Union. This, in turn, is allegedly going to be blocked by the President with real constitutional powers.

Now, we do not need to take a stance in this debate. However, it is quite impossible not to predict that the political situation in 2009–2010 did not favour but small technical changes to the Constitution Act. This once again shows how resistant the Finnish Constitution is to any hasty changes. The Committee's most remarkable idea for reform would place the Prime Minister more clearly at the head of EU policy in the domestic field, thus separating the President more explicitly from EU matters than what the present formulations of the Constitution Act say. Also the Committee's idea to take away the President's power to nominate the

Office Chiefs of the Ministries would be taken away.[5] Of these two the previously mentioned is much debated and its future looks all but certain: it may well turn out to be the key political issue of the election in 2011. So, anything exceeding small steps will not take place. The system will retain its character as a parliamentary system with a President. From the comparative point of view, the Finnish system does not come close to the Irish one, which has a more powerful parliament restricting the role of the president. To continue comparison, the Polish and French systems clearly have a stronger presidency than that of Finland.

Popular Initiative

The Finnish system is clearly a parliamentary system, which means that the use of constitutional power is exercised mainly by the Parliament and the Government Coalition can act only if it has the support of the parliamentary majority. However, the rise of fundamental rights is a crucial sign that the sovereignty of the majority seems to be slowly eroding or at least transforming. Referendums and the growing pressure toward popular initiatives seem to indicate that there are also other kinds of challenges to a parliamentary type of democracy. Basically, the initiative and popular referendum could permit citizens to set the political agenda by placing statute law and even constitutional amendments on the ballot or by vetoing actions taken by the legislative body. Also in Finland, from time to time, the idea of popular initiatives comes to the surface. Those who support it say that the possibility of citizens to use direct democratic power, when voters could go to the ballot if sufficient valid petition signatures would be gathered, would also enhance democracy and, thus, the legitimacy of the political system.

However, this idea is constantly confronted by those who regard the idea of direct democracy with suspicion. Among the political elite and constitutional experts, as well as among political scientists, the idea of growing elements of a direct democracy is confronted with disillusioned reluctance. As all the biggest political parties seek to defend the parliamentary type democracy, it is unlikely that strong elements of direct democracy will be an important part of the Finnish constitutional system in the near future. However, in the long run it is very likely that these elements are also going to be taken into the system. Yet, this

---

[5] *Perustuslain tarkistamiskomitean mietintö* (*Komiteanmietintö* 2010: 9).

will take place only in a manner that ensures that these elements form a mere supplement to representative democracy. The problem is that direct democracy enjoys popularity among the general public. This is easy to understand; representative democracy looks slow and inefficient because it is by nature required to make compromises. As an attempt to answer these demands, the Committee for Checking of the Constitution proposed in February 2010 that popular initiative (50000 signatures) for passing an Act would become a possibility. However, such a referendum would still only be consultative in nature.

CONCLUSION: FUTURE PROSPECTS

The Finnish Constitution has several layers and a surprisingly long history, even though the main constitutional document is only 10 years old. The Finnish system strongly resembles other Nordic systems with certain exceptions of which the President is the most clearly visible. We can also describe the Finnish system as working rather well and it seems to abide by the general idea of constitutionalism. Yet, there is something going on under the surface. It seems that the constitutional structures have not followed the change of the time: the difference between public power and the people seems to be growing. Internationalisation and Europeanisation may be inevitable but they are also a challenge to the system and the inborn constitutional mentality because much of Finnish constitutionalism has been deeply embedded in national history and in national circumstances. Constitutional pluralism may be unavoidable but it is hard to explain and justify to Finnish voters. But what will happen in the future? We may once again look to ancient Rome in seeking a parallel.

Ancient Roman Quintus Horatius Flaccus asked 'Quid leges sine moribus vanae proficiunt?'[6] Horatius, as he is known in English, pointed out that what use is there of laws if they are not upheld by the actual custom of the Roman people? However, what on earth does this tell about the present realities of the Finnish system? Actually, it tells a, surprisingly, good deal. This idea of Horatius does not actually threaten modern constitutionalism but it underlines the idea that the constitution of a polity should not be construed as being in opposition to the general norms or constitutional morality of that polity. In this sense, constitu-

---

[6] *Carmina* III, 24, 35–36.

tional mentality is an important part of political ethics. It is not merely a question of law in any narrow sense. This is connected also to the question concerning fundamental rights which seems to give more weight to individuals than to parliamentary channelled democratic will-formation: we have not seen all of the ramifications yet. The transformation which the change of the fundamental rights paradigm has brought about has not yet fully penetrated Finnish constitutional culture.

The thorniest question of today and most likely for the near future is the challenge to combine human rights, expanding judicial power, parliamentary system and an ever evolving European Union. In more general terms, the enigma is how to combine domestic and non-national constitutional elements; the challenge is to find a functional balance between national normative constitutional requirements and non-national factual developments like Europeanisation and globalisation. However, Finland is clearly not alone with these problems. To conclude, for a Finnish constitutional doctrine this enigma is oddly familiar and brings about the irony of history: Finns have already struggled with these problems in the 1800s and early 1900s. Constitutional déjà vu perhaps?

Index